Gardening
in Shade

Also by Jane Taylor

Collecting Garden Plants
Fragrant Gardens
Gardening for Fragrance
Kew Gardening Guides: Climbing Plants
The Milder Garden
The Romantic English Garden

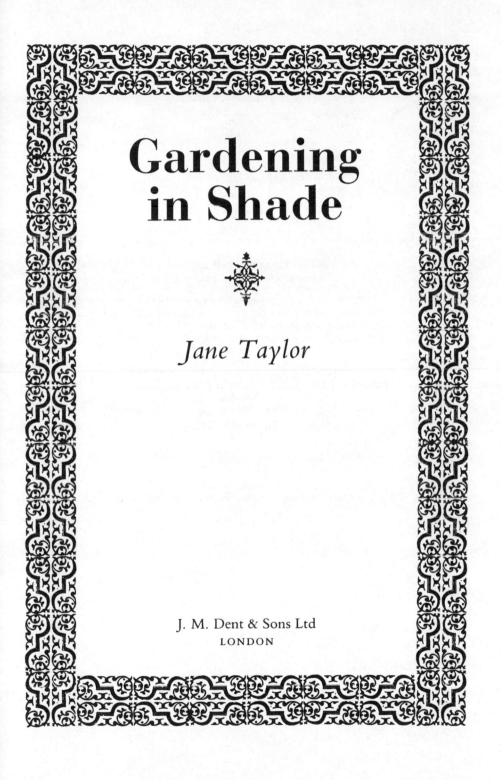

Gardening in Shade

Jane Taylor

J. M. Dent & Sons Ltd
LONDON

First published 1991
Copyright © Jane Taylor 1991

Typeset by Deltatype Ltd, Ellesmere Port
Printed in Great Britain by Butler & Tanner Ltd, Frome &
London
for J. M. Dent & Sons Ltd
91 Clapham High Street
London SW4 7TA

British Library Cataloguing in Publication Data
Taylor, Jane
Gardening in shade.
1. Great Britain. Gardens. Shade – tolerant plants
I. Title
635.954

ISBN 0–460–86020–8

Contents

Foreword

This book could not have been written without years of trial and many errors, in gardens where all the types of shade I shall describe each presented their different challenge and opportunity. Many people have helped me, with ideas, with plants, with encouragement, and I thank them all. Some of them, reading their names in the preface to my previous book, *The Milder Garden*, expressed surprise that I should mention them at all. I think this shows how generous are gardeners towards each other, and how little they expect in return. That their plants should be loved and grown by as many people as possible is their chief concern, a concern now formalized in the conservation movement.

Here I want to thank also Malcolm Gerratt, of Dent, who has encouraged me ever since I was almost thrust upon him as the author of *Collecting Garden Plants*, and allowed me to indulge in the luxury of recalling in words thousands, literally, of the plants I have grown over the years. I thank also Jane Blackett, whose enthusiasm for this book, and skill in straightening out some of my more infelicitous sentences, made her the ideal editor. Graham Thomas read the entire manuscript, and made many welcome suggestions for improvement, as well as helping to clarify certain taxonomic questions.

Preface

When I mentioned to a knowledgeable gardening friend that I was planning a book on shade, he exclaimed, 'How wonderful! All those dark green leaves.' As he mumbled botanical names, I gathered that his mind's eye held pictures of luxuriant foliage, from the humble ivy to glossy *Pseudopanax* via polypodies and the maligned aspidistra. At the time, we were standing beside a nurseryman's display of 'deads', dried grasses and *Sedum* 'Autumn Joy' and teasels, all dusted with artificial frosting in a discomfiting evocation of the weather ahead. The imagined leaves cheered us both, and I felt that winter might not be so bad after all.

Gardeners are no different from other people. Like everyone else, they tend to want what they have not got. If your garden is open on all sides to the sun and wind, you may long for a shady corner to grow trilliums or *Lapageria rosea*. If, on the other hand, you have a small garden dominated by large and greedy trees, you may legitimately wish for a corner to grow belladonna lilies, or rock roses, or sunflowers. The dense and rooty shade of a horse chestnut or a beech is uncongenial to the conventional border, bedding and roses style of gardening. But before I come to the problems of shade, I shall look at the opportunities, considering the plants which cause gardeners to put up screens of netting or overhead laths to make a cool corner while waiting for their shrubs to grow, or to risk their backs wielding a pick on the concrete path at the foot of a shaded wall so as to make another bed for hellebores or camellias or *Pseudowintera colorata*.

Shade as an opportunity, then, starts with creating shade to find congenial homes for the plants you have chosen. Sooner or later in the life of your garden will come the moment when you find you have some proper shade, warm and sheltered or cool and woodsy. Imperceptibly those small trees you planted have turned into a little copse, and you can play with woodland gardening. If your soil is acid you can grow rhododendrons and camellias and their companion plants. But perhaps your taste does not run to the frankly artificial rhododendron woodland; maybe you prefer to respect the *genius loci*, and add with discretion to the native flora of wood anemones and primroses, *Daphne laureola* and wood spurge and ferns.

It is true that unless you inherit or acquire a piece of ready-made woodland you may never be faced with making the choice between the exotic and the native. Your life may be such that you never stay long in one place, will never see your trees grow big enough to cast the longed-for dappled shade. But the sunless side of a shrub, or even of a rock, may be shady enough for a small and treasured plant; or the walls of your house may cast a shadow within which you can create a patch of coolth.

The most exciting kind of shade is warm and sheltered. Here you can indulge in all manner of good things: South American gesneriads, *Begonia grandis*, lapis-berried dianellas and much else. Many foliage plants will reach their greatest beauty in these conditions, and if your soil is acid you can add the delectably fragrant, lily-flowered rhododendrons of the 'Fragrantissimum' type or those, like *R. dalhousieae*, which have flowers moulded as if from wax.

After dry and rooty shade, where the best response may be the minimalist one of encouraging mosses to grow, the most difficult to cope with is cold and windy shade, where cutting winds threaten growth that has lacked the benign, ripening rays of the sun. If you will settle for herbaceous plants, safely below ground during winter, planting such an area will be easier than if you want the solidity, and wind-shelter, of evergreen shrubs to take you through the cold months. But with yews, *Euonymus fortunei*, the hardy hybrid rhododendrons (on acid soils only), *Mahonia aquifolium*, and even that standby of landscapers, *Lonicera pileata*, you can weave a tapestry of foliage among deciduous shrubs such as the coloured-stemmed dogwoods and *Kerria japonica* that are cheerful throughout the seasons.

Perhaps you have a chiefly shady garden, and wish nonetheless to grow the bright flowers that inhabit herbaceous borders. Happily, a surprisingly large number of flowering perennials, among them some of the most beautiful, will do well in light shade. And to contrast with them there is an abundance of lovely leaves in lime-yellow and cream variegations; even some grey-leaved plants will do in dappled shade – though I was gently castigated by my good friend Christopher Lloyd for suggesting some of them in an article a few years ago. Whether or not you agree with me on this, it is undeniably true that the amount of shade (or sun) a given species of plant will stand depends upon what part of the world you garden in. In England, even in the south, *Ceratostigma plumbaginoides* is emphatically a plant for a sunny spot; it flowers too late in the season, in these high latitudes, to perform at all unless you give it all the light it can get. But in our Swiss garden, it grows and flowers abundantly in the dry, dark shade of conifers, and we use it as a standby for the most awkward corners, rather as people rely on *Euphorbia amygdaloides* var. *robbiae* or *Pachysandra terminalis* in other countries.

Few people would construct a rock garden in the shade. But you may inherit one, or find that the once-sunny site where the rocks were set is now in the shadow of a hedge or tree. Rather than lamenting your rock roses, seize the opportunity to grow haberleas and ramondas, the choicer primroses, or (soil permitting) autumn-flowering gentians and all the enchanting species of *Gaultheria* with their fruits of turquoise or crimson or white. The plants of the shady rock garden merge into those of the woodland understorey; in cool, leafy crevices you could assemble a collection of the named forms of *Anemone nemorosa* or of the smaller trilliums, for example.

Thus far I have considered the plants that will grow in shade, with only a passing glance at the source of the shade itself. The shadows cast by trees are another delight in a garden with shade. The dancing, dappled shadows of open-canopied trees where the sun's rays shaft through, the long shadows across the lawn of a single stately tree as the sun sinks towards evening, the escape from the glare of the midday summer sun – these are joys not to be disdained even in a climate such as Britain's where for more than half the year one must battle with cold, wind and rain or fight to keep one's spirits high under lowering grey skies.

The living shade of trees is qualitatively different from the shadows cast by buildings. Generally, the shade of trees is that of an overhead canopy, albeit extended beyond the canopy by the angle of the sun. That of a building may be wholly oblique, with the sky above the shaded area open to the light if not the sun. If the sun strikes for part of the day, we have what can be called part shade, a different thing altogether from the light shade of thin-canopied or sparsely planted trees. The time of day when the sun's rays reach the planting area may affect the choice of plants: a wall which receives the afternoon and evening sun affords more protection to tender plants than one which is sunny in the morning and shadowed from noon, for by nightfall much of the stored warmth of the morning sun will already be lost.

Planting in shade, then, calls for observation. The amount of light that reaches a shady area may be little, or ample; the shadows that fall will move as the day progresses from sunrise to sunset; the shadowed area may be cool, or sheltered, or windy; the benefits of dappled shade may be partly outweighed by the roots of the trees that cast it; the seasons bring their own variations in light intensity. You need to develop a sensitivity to these nuances; and when you do, you will never again wish for a garden without shade.

London
November 1990

I

Creating Shade

IF I were ever to start a garden from a bare site fully exposed to the sun, the first thing I would do would be to create some shade. In common with many of my gardening friends, I love leaves, and almost all but silver-leaved foliage plants are at their best in varying degrees of shade, from flickering dappled shade, obliquely cast, to the cool shadow of a tree canopy. Then again, I prefer pastel shades to the 'riot of colour' which is often as banal as the phrase so commonly used to describe it. And as pastel shades are second only to white in reflecting all available light, they reach their full value in shade, whereas they might be only pallid and wan in the glare of the day. This is not to say that I dislike strong colours; I simply prefer not to overdo them, favouring, on the whole, soft harmonies rather than shrieking contrasts.

The ideal garden shade in which to enjoy these gentle colours is the varied play of light and shadow that comes from an overhead canopy of trees, for, as well as giving grateful shade, trees are beautiful in themselves. Deeper pools of shadow will fall where evergreens or a densely foliaged tree or shrub block the source of light, or on the sunless side of walls and banks. None of this can happen instantly, no matter how much you invest in extra-heavy standard trees or large specimen shrubs. While waiting for trees and shrubs to grow, you can make instant shade by artificial means, erecting screens of proprietary shading material or wattle hurdles, or building the more permanent structure of a lath house, with roof and walls formed of strips of wood nailed at intervals to the uprights and crossbeams.

Indeed, given space, I would always want to have at the least a small area of permanent artificial shade where choice, shade-loving seedlings and cuttings, and newly-acquired plants, can stand out without risk of scorching. The same structures can act as windbreakers also; it may be a simple matter of setting the screening material in an L-shape instead of a single panel, so as to afford protection from the prevailing wind as well as the midday sun.

A lath house which is unashamedly a working area should be treated – and sited – as such; but laths can also be used to bring patterned shade to part of a sitting area that would otherwise become too hot in summer, and here you would grow plants that at all times look decorative, or bring in temporary imports, in containers, from the working lath house. The chapters that follow will describe plenty of plants to choose from. By contrast, screens to provide shade for individual plants can be only temporary structures. They add nothing to the visual effect of the garden, and your aim should be to replace them with the permanent shade of shrubs or boulders or, ultimately, the canopy of trees, as quickly as possible.

Take care, though, not to go for quick-growing shrubs simply for the sake of making some shade. Some fast-growing shrubs are coarse, scarcely worth their garden space; others are valuable as quick fillers but soon need removing as they become leggy, or simply die on you. A judicious combination of fillers and permanencies, slower but longer-lived shrubs and trees that you will still appreciate ten or twenty years on, will serve you better than an unbalanced collection of ephemerals, however useful these may be in the early years.

Once you begin to look at your site with its potential for shade in mind, you may find all manner of possibilities that did not at first present themselves, and that can be exploited while your trees are growing. Perhaps a bed can be contrived in the shadow of the house. So long as you bear in mind the risks of damp invading the structure of your house, and construct your planting areas accordingly (keeping the soil below the level of the damp course, if the bed is to run right to the house wall), you may find that you can remove with pick and shovel the sort of concrete path builders seem inordinately fond of, so as to replace it, and its foundations, with a leafy, open mixture congenial to all but lime-haters. With a little more effort you may even be able to make it acceptable to calcifuge plants, but there is always the risk of your nice ericaceous mix being contaminated. The surrounding soil is certain to be full of residual lime from the rubble and concrete of the path.

If in your area there is natural stone, you may be able to acquire some boulders large enough to make shade for a few little plants. But large rocks are difficult to handle, and often look inappropriate unless on a sloping site. A more suitable way of using stone, for many gardens, is the frankly artificial raised bed, which can be angled to present one side almost fully to the sun so that the other will be cool and shaded. You can also use – if you can get them – old railway sleepers, but these do not lend themselves so well as stone to having small plants tucked in the vertical surfaces. Given a supply of suitable stones, flattish and not too large to handle comfortably, and a sufficiency of soil mixture to fill the raised bed as you go, one of the most satisfying activities in the garden is to construct the bed and plant its retaining walls as you go. You can settle rock pinks and so forth on the sunny side and the hardy European gesneriads, *Haberlea* and *Ramonda*, on the other, small ferns and *Geranium dalmaticum* and even *Bergenia stracheyi*, with little primroses at the foot of the wall. But I must not pre-empt my own intentions to write more fully about plants for shady rock gardens later in this book.

A garden that lends itself to island beds gives you plenty of scope for creating shade. Orient your beds from east to west, and plant a spine of shrubs as tall as the width of the bed allows. To the south (or to the north, if you are reading this in Australia or New Zealand) all will be in the sun; but on the other side of the shrubs, there will be cool shade. Do not underestimate the amount of space you will want for your shade-loving plants, by assuming that you will want to grow more on the sunny side; once you get started, you are likely to find more and more plants for the cooler side of the bed, and the only way to fit them all in may be to extend it outwards. For remember, your shade-casting backbone of shrubs will be a virtual permanency, and should be planned as such, for the last thing you want is to find after some years, with your shady bed filled with lovely leaves and elegant flowers, that the shrubs are in the wrong place.

The best hope for most gardeners faced with a shadeless site, then, is initially to exploit the shelter of every shrub as it grows. It does not much matter if many of the shrubs are deciduous, for – in high latitudes, at least – the hours of daylight are few in winter, and the light intensity so low that even shade-loving plants are unlikely to be discommoded by finding themselves in the open. Shelter from frost and wind is another matter, of course; fortunately there are plenty of hardy plants preferring coolth and shade.

Shade-providing Trees

This is not to say that you can forget about planting trees. However anxious you may be to get on with making virtually instant shade, do try to plant a tree or two – or more, if your garden is large enough – so that

Gardening in Shade

the overhead canopy of dappled shade will be preparing itself for you while you make do in the early years. Generally, the best long-term results come from planting reasonably small specimens ('small' may mean anything from a 30cm/12in seedling to a young standard tree), but if you are prepared to invest in extra-heavy standards – supposing you can obtain them in the varieties you want – you can seemingly gain time. It may be an illusory gain, though, for larger specimens need much more aftercare, especially in the matter of staking, and often the check they experience on transplanting means that they do not make very much growth for some time; smaller specimens may, meanwhile, overtake them.

It is also most important, if you seek to create a miniature woodland, to build up the organic content of the soil as quickly as you can, both by incorporating as much well-rotted compost or manure at planting time as you can spare, and by frequent top dressings thereafter. It is no longer environmentally acceptable to use peat whenever you can contrive a suitable substitute, so severely damaged are the peat bogs from which this irreplaceable natural resource has been dug to satisfy the needs of rapacious gardeners. What is especially alarming is that this has happened so quickly; read any gardening book of a hundred, or even perhaps of fifty years ago, and you will scarcely encounter the word 'peat'. Our forefathers used leaf mould, bracken mould, stable or farmyard manure, garden compost; all of which nourish the soil in a way that peat cannot, as well as rapidly increasing its organic content. Suppliers are answering the demand with new composts based upon coconut fibre, which have given excellent results so far. Ground bark is also available as a sterile top dressing; coarser bark chips can be used to surface paths among trees.

From my own experience I know how quickly it is possible to make a leafy, friable soil from unpropitious ground; for I made a garden, once, on coal-mine waste which consisted only of stone, shale and coal dust. By diligently adding all the humus I could obtain, within three or four years I had a 15cm/6in layer of topsoil loose enough to plant in with a trowel; the original subsoil, having been broken up when the garden was first planted with its major components, was thereafter left well alone and covered each year with another layer of humus as top dressing. The only caveat is that in your zeal to top dress, you must not allow the mulch to accumulate around the base of your trees and induce collar rot; where there was any danger of this, I used to make a barrier of stones a few inches out from the trunk, or fit a corset of wire netting, to stop the mulch from drifting.

Many of the small ornamental trees that are suitable for today's smaller gardens grow quite reasonably quickly, especially if given this kind of encouragement, so that a rowan or a crab or a silver barked birch, a maple or *Prunus sargentii*, tall enough to walk beneath and plant beneath, need not be a dream of the distant future only. One of the prettiest garden pictures I ever saw was a planting of *Euphorbia wallichii*, Mr Bowles's golden grass, and *Geranium lambertii* with nodding, white, crimson-veined, cupped flowers, under a youngish *Robinia pseudoacacia* 'Frisia'. This rather over-planted tree was redeemed from banality by the green and gold and white planting beneath, all dappled with the shadow of its elegant foliage. Little bulbs – especially half-height daffodils such as 'Dove Wings' and the brighter 'Tête à Tête' – flower there in spring. In another context I see 'Frisia' almost daily in a brilliant planting – brilliant both in the sense of inspired and because of the vivid colouring that impacts upon the retina with the insistence of sunlight – in London's Park Lane. Here, beneath plane trees, 'Frisia' is joined by the equally bright foliaged *Catalpa bignonioides* 'Aurea', of which the leaves, in contrast, are immense and heart-shaped. The inspiration, in this planting, was to set it where no one is ever likely to see it for more than a few moments, so that it never risks losing its immediacy. A newer introduction of this colouring is *Betula pendula* 'Golden Cloud', a silver birch with reddish young shoots and clear yellow foliage, needing dappled shade and good living to do its best.

Another picture that I hold in my mind's eye is a soft-coloured group beneath a common rowan, *Sorbus aucuparia*. The tree was planted as a seedling, and quickly grew large enough to give shade to *Brunnera macrophylla*, *Dicentra spectabilis*, the silver-leaved *Lamium maculatum* 'Beacon Silver', *Geranium macrorrhizum* 'Ingwersen's Variety', lily of the valley and Spanish bluebells. If I were planning a similar group from scratch, I would choose a different rowan: *Sorbus cashmiriana*, perhaps, with its madder-crimson spring growths, soft pink flowers in May, and opaque-white, marble-sized fruits that hang on the branches long into winter. Or it might be *S. hupehensis*, white-flowered, but distinguished by glaucous-tinted foliage that would echo the blue leaf tones of *Dicentra* 'Langtrees', or the similar 'Pearl Drops', which has white flowers tipped with pink, smaller than those of the common bleeding heart, *D. spectabilis*, on more enthusiastically spreading clumps. Some forms of *Sorbus hupehensis* have white fruits, smaller than those of *S. cashmiriana*; others, distinguished as var. *obtusa*, bear clusters of pink berries.

A smaller, more spreading tree than *S. hupehensis*, *S. vilmorinii* has exceptionally pretty, dainty foliage turning to crimson and purple in autumn, among which the generous clusters of small fruits open crimson and fade through the winter to white faintly flushed with rose. Indeed, one could go on and on about rowans. There is scarcely a bad plant among them, and some especially good seedlings have been named: 'November Pink', 'Pearly King' (a *S. vilmorinii* hybrid), and 'Kirsten Pink' among them; while less familiar species with pink or white fruits include *S. prattii*, *S. koehneana* and *S. poteriifolia* of gardens.

Many of the scarlet- or yellow-fruited rowans are fine for giving shade, too. The common rowan itself, *Sorbus aucuparia*, has variants with yellow fruits or with coral and terracotta bark – 'Beissneri', which has lacy foliage as well. 'Apricot Lady' is a selection or hybrid named for the colour of its fruits, which ripen among brightly tinted autumn leaves. Probably the most famous of the yellow-berried rowans is 'Joseph Rock', a splendid thing with amber fruits and sombrely rich autumn foliage of crimson, plum and purple flaring here and there into vermilion. They grow in any reasonable soil, acid or alkaline, but their wildling looks seem to me to call for nothing too domesticated at their feet. You could set your chosen rowan in a plinth of evergreen foliage of skimmias, *Helleborus foetidus* and sarcococcas, with *Narcissus cyclamineus* hybrids tucked among them. 'Little Witch' and the long-trumpeted 'Peeping Tom' have something of the ears-back-in-the-wind look of the parent, and its cheery yellow colouring, but at twice or thrice the size; 'Dove Wings', 'Jenny', 'Charity May' and 'Jack Snipe' are paler.

The whitebeams are in the same genus as the rowans, yet are of very different appearance, with undivided, often bold leaves, grey or silvery-white beneath. They are especially valuable on chalk soils, where the largest-leaved forms can rival the big-leaved rhododendrons or magnolias that are denied to chalk gardeners. The young, unfurling leaves of whitebeams, indeed, look almost like the chalice-shaped blooms of a magnolia. Easiest is the common European whitebeam, *Sorbus aria*, which comes in various forms such as extra-bold 'Majestica' and the exquisite 'Lutescens' with young foliage textured like cream plush on both surfaces. The Himalayan *S. cuspidata* needs shelter to protect the huge leaves from being snapped off by wind, so is less suitable as a shade tree unless in very enclosed gardens. Tougher than this is *S. thibetica* 'John Mitchell', with almost circular leaves, white beneath.

THE FLOWERING TREES OF SPRING

The pinkest trees in spring are the Japanese cherries. If I were making a garden in a street where there were plenty to be seen, I should probably leave them alone, though I might plant a white 'Tai Haku' or primrose-cream 'Ukon' to leaven so much candy– and sugar-pink. ('Tai Haku', indeed, is beautiful as a shade-provider for deciduous azaleas, with pale narcissi, Welsh poppies, and forget-me-nots.) Nor are they the most suitable trees for a small space; they are a touch too greedy at the root, a bit too heavily leafy all summer, and not quite generous enough in their autumn colours. Instead, I would consider a species such as *Prunus sargentii*, or one of the smaller hybrid cherries such as 'Okame'. Sargent's cherry has coppery young growths among which the single flowers, opening quite early in spring, modestly display their rosy tones. In a garden I made, I set this cherry in a spread of *Geranium macrorrhizum album*, which bears its white flowers in pink calyces in late spring, with *Iris foetidissima* 'Variegata' set against the paddles of *Bergenia crassifolia*. The bergenia bears its mauve-pink flowers at much the same time as the cherry, and its leaves turn blood-red in the winter where the sun touches them, making a cheery winter picture with the white-striped leaves of the iris. The geranium, too, often turns to crimson in winter, while the cherry is second to none in its fiery autumn tints.

The pretty hybrid 'Accolade' has Sargent's cherry as one parent; it is a small, spreading tree covered in hanging clusters of semi-double, bright pink flowers in early spring. Another offspring of *Prunus sargentii* is 'Kursar', its small flowers richly coloured among the bronze young leaves. 'Okame' is a small tree with carmine-pink flowers at much the same season as Sargent's cherry; it, too, flares brightly in the fall. Cherries with flowers of this colour need careful handling; they clash painfully with the hard yellow of the forsythia most commonly seen, 'Spectabilis', but are soothed by white, the blues of grape hyacinths or a quiet background of blue-grey conifers.

The winter cherry, *Prunus subhirtella* 'Autumnalis', is a very graceful little tree, wide-crowned yet not densely leafy, so it makes useful shade; it comes in white or blush-pink and flowers in any open weather during winter. Also in the genus are almonds and apricots and peaches, all with double garden varieties. Of quite different value as garden trees are the two species with fine bark, *P. serrula* and the uncommon *P. maackii*. The first has stems like polished mahogany, and willow-like leaves, the second displays bark that flakes and peels to reveal a shining, golden-brown surface. Neither is much to look at in flower: but how long does cherry blossom last, anyway?

Less aggressively pink and flouncy than the popular Japanese cherries, the crabs are pretty spring trees several of which contribute again in autumn with fruits, or leaves that die in vivid colours, or both. They are tolerant of a wide range of soils from heavy clay to chalk, though less

happy on thin, acid sands. The crabs, too, flower late enough to escape
spring frosts. Unless you have a great fondness for lumps of dark brown
foliage in the landscape, give the purple crabs a miss; they are hard to fit
comfortably into any planting scheme and there is a good deal of purple in
their flowers, too, which jars among the predominantly fresh colours of
spring. The exception is 'Almey', which is no more than bronze-flushed
in summer leaf, and has flowers of an unusually pure red for the genus,
followed by bright orange, red-cheeked fruits. The Japanese *Malus
floribunda* is wildly popular, and indeed in its short season exceedingly
pretty, its branches bowed with the weight of crimson buds opening to
pink and paling through blush to white in a varied play of colour. The
crabs bred for fruit – those astringent little apples that make such excellent
jelly – are very like orchard apple trees in blossom, and often deliciously
fragrant.

Almost as tough and easy – you see them in every London street where
there are gardens, and in many suburban areas too – are the cultivars of
Magnolia × *soulangeana*. In winter their clean, bold branches are tipped
with fat, furry buds promising the great white or pink or vinous globes of
spring; their emerging foliage is strikingly pale even among the tender
greens of spring; and with judicious pruning you can keep them
uncluttered enough to show the branch structure even in full summer
leaf. There are dozens of varieties: 'Brozzonii' is a fine late flowering
white with the faintest flush of carmine at the base, while 'Lennei', later
still, has flowers like huge, purple tulips and a flopping habit that makes it
more of a great bush than a tree. This makes it fine as a canopy over spring
bulbs, but not so good if you want to keep the interest going all year.
'Picture', of similar colouring, is more upright and tree-like. Beneath
white magnolias a spread of *Omphalodes cappadocica* or of grape hyacinths
will lie like fallen sky in spring. Small ferns, *Cyclamen hederifolium*, and
Primula 'Wanda' could be tucked in beneath the magnolia's lower
branches.

As well as these easy-going magnolias, there are many highly desirable
species also worth trying if your soil is of the ideal moist, leafy yet well-
drained texture that suits the genus. One of the most beautiful is *Magnolia
salicifolia*, a slim, twiggy tree with small but abundant, pure white flowers
powerfully scented like orange blossom. Its small leaves cast a light,
dappled shade, making it a good companion for rhododendrons and
camellias. The Loebneri hybrids are similarly little leafy, and have the
huge advantage of tolerating chalk; 'Merrill' has semi-double, starry,
white flowers, and 'Leonard Messel', a more open tree, has many-
petalled flowers of creamy-white suffused with lilac-pink. The summer-

flowering magnolias, *M. sieboldii* and its kin, tend to shrubbiness, but can be pruned to shapely little trees. The most distinct is *M. wilsonii*, a rather upright tree with narrow, pointed leaves; it is more lime tolerant than *M. sieboldii* but less so than its offspring *M.* × *highdownensis*, of which the other parent is *M. sinensis*. All have fragrant, nodding, white flowers with a central boss of crimson stamens.

Suitable for just about any soil are the dainty *Amelanchier canadensis* and its kin, *A. lamarckii* and *A. laevis*. A froth of starry, white blossom in spring, they offer some of the brightest tints of autumn. They tend to make small, often multi-stemmed trees, and – lacking the hint of mauve-pink of the magnolias – can safely be paired with the sharper colours of spring: yellow and lime, and coral and scarlet. A group that worked well in one garden I knew had the amelanchier set among semi-prostrate *Chaenomeles speciosa* 'Simonii', which has blood-red flowers followed by large, aromatic quinces, and *Euphorbia polychroma*, with the declamatory yellow daisies of doronicums and Mr Bowles's golden grass, *Milium effusum* 'Aureum'. If you have the taste for them, orange and red daffodils would fit well in this group. Equally successful is the combination of amelanchier with pink and white azaleas and a white-stemmed birch, white or palest cream narcissi, arching Solomon's seal or the cream fuzz of *Smilacina racemosa,* and ferns.

LEAF AND BARK

Few maples are much to look at in flower – one of manageable size that is good in spring is *Acer negundo violaceum*, a form of the box elder, which is more often seen in one of its variegated manifestations. The Italian maple, *A. opalus*, is a medium-sized tree which bears conspicuous, sharp yellow flowers on bare stems in early spring; it casts a rather heavy shade when mature. But very many maples are elegant in leaf, graceful or striking in branch structure, vivid in autumn, and small enough to be worthy trees in their own right and to provide shade in gardens of modest size. The snake-barks add marbled or striated branches to maintain interest through winter; from among the many that are known you could choose *A. capillipes*, with greenish, white-striped bark, coral-red on the young stems, or *A. rufinerve*, green and white with a white bloom on young shoots and bright crimson and yellow autumn colour. 'Silver Vein' is a fine selection with beautifully marbled bark. The trunk and branches of *A. griseum* are shaggy with peeling, mahogany and tan bark, the trifoliate leaves are glaucous beneath and turn to vivid crimson in autumn. Needing light shade itself to avoid sun-scorch, *A. japonicum aureum* is a delightful tree, slow-growing but worth the wait, with fan-shaped leaves of soft lime-yellow. Virtually all maples colour brilliantly in autumn; one that is notably reliable in this respect is *A. tartaricum ginnala*, with three-lobed leaves and a half shrubby, half tree-like mode of growth. All these maples fit well into informal plantings with other shrubs and trees, *Pieris* and azaleas and *Enkianthus*, while in more gardened settings they can be joined by hostas and epimediums, wood anemones and ferns.

A birch may make a good shade tree, though you have to watch its greedy surface roots. The silver birch of Europe, *Betula pendula*, is one of the daintiest in foliage, its little leaves falling like golden coins in autumn; but for bark it is surpassed by *B. utilis jacquemontii*, which has wondrously milk-white stems. *B. ermanii* is almost as good in creamy-apricot, especially if you can obtain the form 'Grayswood Ghost' which is pale-ivory barked. The paperbark, *B. papyrifera*, can be good or indifferent: at its best, it is very white and peeling, with larger leaves than the European birch. *B. albo-sinensis septentrionalis* is very desirable in its best forms, with apricot, peeling trunk and stems. Azaleas, again, make pretty companions in acid soil; where the soil is limy, spread a carpet of *Anemone apennina*, sweet violets, primroses and snowdrops instead.

Trees in the legume family are often good as shade providers, for they tend to nourish, rather than rob, the soil in which they grow. As well as the golden robinia already mentioned, you could choose one of the honey locusts, forms of *Gleditsia triacanthos*. The type is very thorny, but 'Ruby Lace' and 'Sunburst' are unarmed. The second is like a more refined *Robinia* 'Frisia' with daintier foliage, unfurling yellow and ripening to green through the summer, so that it makes a less blatant statement in the landscape than the unrelenting gold of 'Frisia'. 'Ruby Lace' has red new leaves aging to olive green, so that again it is more adaptable to the landscape than the heavy purples of crabs or the egregious *Prunus cerasifera* 'Pissardii'. Laburnums, of course, need no introduction; some people avoid them on account of their poisonous seeds, but a well-grown laburnum in bloom is a splendid sight, and the hybrid 'Vossii', with extra-long trails of golden rain, produces fewer seeds. In the famous laburnum tunnel at Barnsley House, the underplanting is of variegated hostas and *Allium aflatunense*, its mauve globes coinciding with the canary tassels of the laburnum. As well as creating friendly shade, incidentally, laburnums also flower with unchecked abundance under the shade of taller trees, as evidenced in many London squares where the laburnum's golden chains hang beneath close planted planes, and in the green half-light seem all the lovelier.

The Judas tree, *Cercis siliquastrum*, is related, but quite different in foliage, for the leaves are heart-shaped. Bright magenta pea-flowers burgeon from the bare stems, the branches and even the trunk in spring; there is an exquisite white form, and an uncommon variety with thundery-purple flowers named 'Bodnant' from the garden where it arose. The North American redbud, *C. canadensis*, has brighter green leaves, and flowers less freely in a maritime climate, but is very fine where its wood is well ripened by summer sun; it has a form called 'Forest Pansy' with burgundy-flushed leaves which seems wholly desirable as a youngster, but I reserve judgment until I see a mature tree, for it might earn opprobrium as do the purple crabs and plum for their heaviness in the summer scene. Perhaps its spare, branching structure will be its salvation. All the Judas trees cast a light, dappled shade.

SPRING INTO SUMMER

Also from North America, *Cornus florida* and its forms do best in areas of summer sun, while the Asiatic *C. kousa* and its Chinese variant will thrive in cooler, more temperate zones. The showy part of the floral structure, in both species, is the broad bracts surrounding the flower itself; *C. florida* is white, with excursions into clear pink of various intensities and selections with broader, bolder bracts, while *C. kousa* comes chiefly in white, and makes an elegant spreading tree of tiered habit. Both have magnificent, fiery autumn colours, most vivid when they are grown in full sun. The pink forms of *C. florida* look well with coral-pink Mollis azaleas, creamy narcissi and green heucheras, but fight with mauve-pinks. The Pacific dogwood, *C. nuttallii*, is beautiful but temperamental; its hybrid, 'Eddie's White Wonder', is a splendid thing. 'Norman Hadden', a fine hybrid dogwood with creamy bracts aging to blush, is *C. kousa* crossed with the rather tender, evergreen *C. capitata*, itself a delightful umbrella-shaped tree for milder gardens.

All the snowdrop and snowbell trees, *Halesia* and *Styrax* and *Pterostyrax*, are enchanting shade-providers, often of elegant habit with arching, spreading branches. The most tree-like of the halesias is *H. monticola*, which has white bells, or pink flushed with rose in var. *vestita*; the flowers are followed by winged fruits. *Styrax japonica* and its kin have similar flowers but the fruits are little velvet-coated globes. Thriving in leafy, acid, moist soil, the snowbells assort with woodlanders such as will be described in later chapters, and with shrubs of the woodland edge. Similar conditions suit the stuartias, camellia relatives which form small trees bearing their creamy flowers in summer; rich autumn colour follows, and in winter the marbled bark is beautiful. Cool roots are

preferred also by *Oxydendrum arboreum*, the sorrel tree, an elegant thing
with vivid autumn tints after the drooping sprays of milk-white lily-of-
the-valley flowers have faded. It is the ideal companion for small
ericaceous shrubs and other acid-lovers.

The hoherias are white-flowered also, but will grow in ordinary
garden soil, provided it is not thin and dry, in reasonably sheltered
gardens. The two deciduous species are the hardiest; both have leaves
shaped a little like those of a poplar, elegantly pointed at the tip, but
unlike any poplar they bear generous clusters of translucent, honey-
scented, white flowers in summer. In bloom they look like a most
refined, late-flowering cherry. Of the two, *Hoheria glabrata* is the first to
flower, at midsummer; it has two further seasons of effect in spring,
when the young foliage unfurls in a mixture of clotted cream and
silvery-green, and again in autumn, when the dying leaves change to
tones of honey, straw-yellow and lemon-white. A fortnight after *H.
glabrata* begins to flower, the first blossoms of *H. lyallii* open; they are
held among smaller, powder grey, downy leaves. It is rather more tree-
like than the multi-stemmed *H. glabrata* and tolerates drier conditions.
Another small, spreading, shrubby tree with white flowers in summer,
rather later than these hoherias, is *Eucryphia glutinosa*; a lover of moist,
acid, woodsy soils, it can form a pretty companion for woodland plants
that demand similar conditions. The cup-shaped flowers are filled with a
fuzz of stamens, and the pinnate leaves turn to brilliant shades of crimson
and flame before falling in autumn.

Where there exists shade in the garden, it is more often from
ornamental trees that have been planted as much for their own appeal as
for their shade-making canopy. Most of these trees form a lowish
canopy, and some have branches that sweep almost to the ground, or are
multi-stemmed and bushy. Yet it is easier to garden beneath a high
canopy. Not all forest trees are suitable either in scale or by the nature of
the shade they cast and their root systems. Sycamore, horse chestnut and
beech all cast so dense a shade that little will grow beneath them; the first
two also have hostile leaves that fall to lie like a clammy poultice on
anything you do manage to establish beneath their branches. Pines shed
their needles to make a dense mat that chokes most plants beneath their
canopy. The deciduous conifers, *Taxodium distichum* and *Metasequoia
glyptostroboides*, look as though they should be more friendly, for their
frond-like, grass-green leaves are soft to the touch; yet, after turning to
fox-red and apricot in autumn, they fall to make a covering more
reminiscent of a frayed coir doormat than of the melting leaf mould that
woodland plants desire. By all means plant them for their beauty, and

underplant them when young; but be prepared to move the underlings, or see them stifled, as the tree matures.

Many gardeners would claim that the single best genus of forest trees for shade is *Quercus*, the oaks. An established oak canopy would be the supreme gift for any gardener; the soil beneath is usually somewhat, but not excessively, acid, leafy and moisture-retaining. The fallen leaves of deciduous oaks, too, make a friendly blanket. However, reality impels me to recognize that ready-made oak woods, however small in area, are a privilege denied to most of us. This is not to say, though, that you cannot plant your own oak or oaks, which will earn the gratitude of future generations of gardeners and will give you a good deal of pleasure in the growing. As for which species to choose in a large genus, all I can do is describe those that I have grown, which are very few.

The scarlet oak, *Q. coccinea*, has bold, deeply lobed leaves which turn in autumn to intense scarlet; ultimately a large tree, it is striking even in youth. The pin oak, *Q. palustris*, is similar, with a more elegant habit, the branches gracefully arching; the leaves are more deeply cut and rather smaller, but are no less vivid in the fall. By comparison the red oak, *Q. rubra*, is a coarse, large, fast-growing and densely leafy tree which has matt-surfaced, not glossy, leaves, turning to varied shades of fox-red and tan in autumn. The chestnut-leaved oak, *Q. castaneifolia*, and the Turkey oak, *Q. cerris*, are large and rather grand trees, fast-growing and unsuited to smaller gardens. The Hungarian oak, *Q. frainetto*, is another rapid grower; it and the Turkey oak are happy on chalk soils. The common or English oak is, of course, *Q. robur*; the rugged outline of a mature tree needs no description, and the unfurling leaves in spring are deliciously fresh in acid-yellow. The durmast oak, *Q. petraea*, replaces it in wetter districts in the west of England. Quite different in leaf is *Q. phellos*, the willow oak, a quick-growing, tall tree with slender, fresh green leaves turning to tawny-gold or mahogany in autumn. Avoid at all costs, as a shade tree that is, the holm oak or ilex, *Q. ilex*; admirable as a shelter tree in large, exposed coastal gardens, it is a bad neighbour, robbing the soil and shedding quantities of hard, unrottable leaves and scurf in early summer.

II

Cool Shade

Some of the most beautiful of spring and early summer flowers are at their best in cool, humus-rich soil that does not dry out, in dappled or part shade. Although they are often described as woodlanders, it is seldom necessary, on a small scale at least, to think in terms of true woodland for these plants: a bed of suitably enriched soil on the sunless side of the wall or house may do just as well, or a border shaded by an old fruit tree . . . the possibilities have already been rehearsed. What is important, apart from a suitable soil, is shelter from drying winds.

I want here to consider mainly the smaller perennials and bulbs that do best in these conditions; shrubs are likely to be mentioned only incidentally, unless it be the smaller shrubs that do not fit comfortably in any other chapter. Since my main purpose is not simply to make lists of plants but to suggest how they may be used to best advantage to make our gardens beautiful, it may be that in describing a certain species I will suggest appropriate companions that could as well be shrubby as not.

For example, hellebores – which I shall discuss at greater length in Chapter x – assort well with shrubs; the plum and maroon kinds with *Corylopsis pauciflora* or the larger *C. sinensis* 'Spring Purple' in which the young foliage echoes the hellebores' deep colouring, or the paler sorts – creamy whites, unmarked or richly freckled or shaded with green – with *Daphne mezereum* or *Rhododendron* 'Tessa'. In light shade the purple form of *Euphorbia amygdaloides* will retain its rich leaf colouring and add spires of acid-green in spring.

The freshness of spring – the sharp pale yellow, unfolding leaves of oak, the pale spears of *Hemerocallis fulva*, the first clear lemon foliage of *Hosta fortunei aurea* – is enhanced by the colours of many bulbs, such as narcissi in white and yellow, or scillas and grape hyacinths in blue. The lilac-pink of erythroniums or the mauves and purples of crocuses belong in a different setting, with greens of blue and grey tone, with perhaps the pink of almond and cherry blossom beyond.

Spring – the Peak Season

Spring is heralded, in many gardens, by snowdrops and winter aconites. Arbitrarily, I have decided not to describe snowdrops until a later chapter, with the hellebores; you will find them between pages 205 and 208. The aconites, species of *Eranthis* not of *Aconitum*, are often fickle; *E. hyemalis*, the common winter aconite, grows and seeds abundantly for some people and obdurately refuses to establish in the gardens of others. I grew up in a garden where it formed sheets of yellow beneath an ancient medlar; and later, in my own garden on completely different soil, I found that it spread just as freely. But just as the common snowdrop is beautiful in a mass but, individually, surpassed by named cultivars, so the aconite has a superior rival in 'Guinea Gold', which falls in the Tubergenii group. One parent is the common *E. hyemalis*; the other, *E. cilicica*, is now considered to fall within *E. hyemalis*; it has larger flowers with less lemon in their yellow colouring, borne later in the year on bronzed stems. 'Guinea Gold' comes early and has large, bright flowers on long stems; it does not come true from seed. The common aconites and snowdrops can be dug as they are just shouldering through the soil and brought indoors to enjoy in comfort; as they go over, pop them back in the garden and they will come to no harm.

The lesser celandine, *Ranunculus ficaria*, is far more aggressive than even the most willing aconite; though as it dies down very soon after flowering, and its sheeny lemon stars are cheering in the dark days, most people will tolerate it among shrubs if not in beds of choice small plants. Its selected forms, however, are charming and not invasive; pretty things to collect and admire at close quarters. One of the best of the single-flowered forms is 'Brazen Hussy', in which the usual bright flowers are set off by dark, almost black foliage. *Cupreus* has flowers of burnished copper, and *citrinus* of pale lemon, while *albus* is a frail-seeming white with rather squinny petals – 'Salmon's White' is a finer, ivory selection with large, broad petals around a pale lemon boss. 'Primrose' is a large-flowered form with creamy-yellow petals. Then there are various doubles: *flore pleno*, citron with green heart; 'Picton's Double' with clear yellow flowers well filled with a dense pompom of petals; a double cream form in which the dusky reverse of the petals touches up the neat little rosettes; and 'E. A. Bowles' in shiny lemon, loosely double. 'Collarette' has a tight-packed centre and a prim little lemon frill. Of late the celandines have become a cult, and new names crop up regularly; these few are those I have grown myself.

By contrast, *Hacquetia epipactis* has only one manifestation. It is, unexpectedly, in Umbelliferae; but nothing ever looked so unlike a cowparsley. The buds appear at the soil surface very early in the year and, almost before they are through, begin to open, so the little acid-yellow flowers in their green ruff appear stemless at first; the stems gradually lengthen to 10cm/4in or so over the emerging clump of divided leaves. For so small a plant it has very stout, deeply delving roots which do not take kindly to disturbance; better to increase it from seed.

The species of *Adonis*, which also prefer to be left alone, grow rather taller and start to flower a little later. The native European species, *A.vernalis*, is as handsome as any, with wide, burnished-yellow flowers, coppery on the reverse, on 15cm/6in stems set with very finely cut foliage. The Far Eastern *A. amurensis* is rather taller, and greener on the reverse; it varies from the typical yellow to pink or cream. 'Fukujukai' is a fine selection with sharp yellow, glistening petals, and there is a double form with a green central boss. Then there is *A. brevistyla*, which has pure white flowers with blue shading on the reverse, and golden stamens.

WOOD ANEMONES

White, pink and blue – lavender-blue, that is – are the chief colours of *Anemone nemorosa*, which like the lesser celandine has produced many extremely collectable variants. The type is white, with a faint suffusion of pink on the reverse; a walk through any copse in which the wood anemone grows wild will reveal forms with pinker petals. Some have been named and vegetatively propagated by division of the fast-increasing roots: 'Rosea', white on first opening but blushing with age, and 'Lismore Pink' which is uniformly pale pink. 'Pentre Pink' is said to have the later flowers wholly deep pink, deepening to red as they die.

But it is the blues, and the variants in pure white or with doubled petals, that most appeal. The largest in flower of the whites is 'Leeds' Variety', twice normal size, with only the faintest flush of mauve-pink on the reverse. 'Wilkes' White' is smaller and flushes with age like apple blossom; 'Wilkes' Giant' remains pure white. 'Hilda' is especially pretty with rather small, many-petalled flowers. The doubles include 'Bracteata Plena', a very old selection with many narrow petals, the outer often green-tinged; 'Alba Plena' with a central double boss and regular outer petals; and 'Vestal', similarly constructed but quite distinct when the two are set side by side. In the curious form called 'Virescens' the flower is developed into an elegant, wide rosette of airy formality, composed of divided, chartreuse-green leaflets.

The deepest blue is 'Royal Blue', not a very apt name for its speedwell-blue with paler reverse; 'Robinsoniana' is paler lavender-blue within and silky fawn on the reverse, and 'Allenii' has large, single flowers of dusty lavender with rosy reverse. 'Lismore Blue' is the counterpart of 'Lismore Pink', and has the same dark stems and mahogany petioles; the petals are clear lavender-blue, greyer on the reverse. Much the same grey-blue tints are on the reverse of the cerulean 'Blue Bonnet'. 'Bowles's Purple' lives up to its name until the flower opens, when its soft blue-lavender colouring is revealed. Nearer to true blue is 'Blue Beauty', with large, cupped flowers on strong stalks, of sky-blue within and cream on the reverse. Then there is 'Hannah Gubbay', with lacquer-red buds opening to a small, purple flower that ages towards deep blue, on almost leafless stems.

Not unlike the wood anemones, except for its colour, *A. ranunculoides* is slightly smaller in stature but just as accommodating, running about in leafy soil in the shady conditions that emulate its native deciduous woodland in northern Italy. The flowers are bright buttercup-yellow; there is a double form, and a hybrid with *A. nemorosa* which comes under a variety of names such as *A.* × *intermedia* and *A.* × *seemannii*, but is – I believe – rightly called *A.* × *lipsiensis*. As you might expect, the blend of white and yellow results in a primrose-yellow child, very pretty and quite easy in cool, leafy soil.

PRIMROSES AND VIOLETS

Quite arbitrarily, I shall return to anemones later, for it is time to suggest some of the little companion plants for the wood anemone and its allies. Some of the named forms of primrose do very well: forms of *Primula vulgaris* itself and those with the blood of *P. juliae* also. The double primroses are too precious, too finicky in most gardens, to risk with even such unassertive spreaders as the anemones, but a few of the singles are more accommodating, or you can simply raise seedlings (though not, I implore you, of the immense-flowered vulgarities that are sold in street markets and garden centres, with bilious eyes and ferocious colouring) and pick the ones you want to keep. This saves much of the fussing around with regular division and replanting in fresh soil that addicts of the old named primroses are condemned to. Here, then, I will name only some that I have found quite obliging, saving the tricky treasures for a later chapter.

In the leafy, enriched soil that all primroses like, with some shade, I have never had any difficulty with the Garryarde primrose 'Guinevere'. Its bronzed leaves and muted lilac-pink flowers assort well with the white, pink-flushed forms of the wood anemone; and 'Guinevere' seems willing to produce pretty, self-sown offspring which inherit its leaf colouring but veer towards palest Dresden yellow, cream, white or French grey in flower tone. *P. vulgaris* var. *sibthorpii* is a pale mauve-flowered form of the wild primrose, and 'Groeneken's Glory' is brighter rosy-lilac with a greenish eye; both flower very early. 'Schneekissen' is a good named white. The rich blue of 'Blue Riband' is marred only by its obtrusive yellow eye.

The primroses with *juliae* blood in them, known familiarly as the juliana primroses, are less dependent on ideal soil conditions than those that are pure *vulgaris*, though they dislike drought as much as any. Familiar old 'Wanda', in bright magenta-purple, must be known to everyone; she can be seen forming unsophisticated strips of colour along cottage garden paths in what seem the most unpropitious conditions. If you cannot take this colour, she comes also in white. Two newer kinds, as yet untried but which look good on the showbench, with neat juliana foliage and abundant flowers are 'Hall Barn Blue' in slate-blue with small yellow eye, and the larger-flowered 'Hall Barn White' which has an acid-lemon eye. *P. juliae* itself has bright purple flowers, and dies down to resting buds for the winter. The *Primula* relative *Cortusa matthioli* enjoys similar conditions, and looks very much like a primula with its tufts of softly hairy, heart-shaped leaves and one-sided sprays of nodding, magenta-pink or white bells on 15cm/6in stems.

As much identified with spring as the primrose is the sweet violet, *Viola odorata*, which grows in hedgerows and woodland edges, most usually in blue-violet, sometimes white. Many selections have been made, such as the splendid violet-purple 'Czar', paler azure-lilac 'Princess Alexandra', pink 'Coeur d'Alsace' and the deeper 'Red Charm', pale 'Skimmed Milk' and the delicious buff and amber 'Sulphurea'. Several other *Viola* species, though scentless, are even more enchanting in flower. Beware the purple-leaved *V. labradorica* and pink-flowered *V. rupestris rosea*; they are rampant spreaders by seed and need to be kept away from a bed of treasures. The scentless dog violets, *V. riviniana* and *V. canina*, pretty in pale lilac-blue, are almost as territorial. But seedlings of the large-flowered white *V. obliqua* (*V. cucculata*) and *V. sororia* (*V.*

papilionacea) are always welcome, as are those of *V. septentrionalis*. 'Freckles' is a pretty thing flecked with violet, by some attributed to *V. sororia*. Then there are the clumpy little vivid yellow violets, which are somewhat energetic seeders and need watching: *V. glabella*, *V. biflora*, and little *V. pensylvanica*.

WILDLINGS OF THE WOODLAND

The anemones, primroses, violets and celandines are virtually the only little plants for cool shade that I propose to discuss here which have been widely selected and developed as named single and double forms. The others, with rare exceptions, are species. Nor are all as small as these; but it may make selection easier if I deal with the plants of this chapter roughly in order of size, from these little treasures that are best tucked into safe corners under the eye to the larger and more muscular woodlanders. Once you have enough of them, of course, even the little things can be self-sustaining; many of the wood anemones, for example, will spread quite quickly to form a colony from which you can dig clumps to start elsewhere, among shrubs and in wilder corners.

There are several *Erythronium* species, of which the European *E. dens-canis* bears as the specific epithet a translation of the common name dog's tooth violet. It is, of course, no violet, but a lily relative, with maroon-mottled, smooth leaves and nodding flowers in shades of pink, purple and, rarely, white. Named forms include 'White Splendour', pale blush 'Charmer', violet-pink 'Franz Hals', 'Lilac Wonder', 'Pink Perfection', 'Rose Queen' and 'Snowflake'. The leafy soil which is presupposed for the plants that find their way into this chapter suits them admirably, and the cheaper unnamed bulbs on offer can be tried in thin grass beneath trees.

Several of the North American species are exquisite, bearing nodding flowers with reflexed, or sometimes starry, petals on slender stems. 'White Beauty' is a hybrid, or perhaps a form, of *E. revolutum*; it increases fast in woodsy soil and is of great beauty with recurved ivory petals and the marbled leaves that have inspired the pet name of trout lily. A hybrid of this and *E. tuolumnense* – itself one of the least elegant with heads of citron-yellow flowers over unmarbled leaves – is called 'Pagoda'; the blooms are sulphur-yellow with rusty markings in the throat. 'Kondo' is similar with darker leaves, and 'Citronella' (attributed to *E. revolutum*) is of the same type again, with wide, nodding blooms, the reflexed petals soft citron within and bloomed with jade on the reverse. *E. californicum* is an easy species with mottled, bronzed leaves and white or cream flowers

marked with tan at their yellow hearts. Easy, too, is *E. oregonum*, with
marbled leaves and white, yellow-centred flowers. With *E. revolutum* we
return to pink; the Johnsonii group includes the deepest pinks, where the
flower is held above dark bronzed leaves. Selections are named 'Rose
Beauty' and 'Pink Beauty', while 'Knightshayes Pink' is as good as might
be expected from the garden of that name. There are other species, both
from North America and from the Far East, but these are the ones likely
to be easy both to obtain and to grow.

In one of the gardens I have made there was a sloping bank of sandy,
acid soil, kept almost permanently moist by springs, and shaded by a
distant cider-apple tree, the house and a tall alder. With ample stone
available – small slabs of sandstone, ideal for low retaining walls – the
bank was modified at the base into two easily accessible terraces and the
soil improved by hefty additions of crumbly, black compost, bracken
mould and leaf mould. If the natural soil had been less sandy, I should
have added some grit as well. Here the erythroniums and anemones and
celandines were planted, one or two of each kind for economy – and here
they quickly bulked up so that they could be tried elsewhere, leaving
space for all the other good things that so enjoyed the cool, leafy soil.

In time, it is possible to have a garden where erythroniums spread
beneath your shrubs as other people have bluebells. I treasure in my
mind's eye the garden of Mrs Amy Doncaster in Hampshire, where
beneath a high canopy of oaks, many fine shrubs, rhododendrons and
others, formed the second layer of cover over countless choice things. By
just such diligence, she had achieved her erythronium woodland, though
there was much else besides.

TRILLIUMS

Trilliums, too, did very well, both in my modest shady terrace and in
Mrs Doncaster's paradise woodland. With the creamy erythroniums,
Trillium sessile grew, its erect maroon petals above the three broad,
marbled leaves contrasting with the pale trout lily. *T. chloropetalum* is
similar, and comes in the same colour range of maroon, pink or white.
The most familiar trillium is *T. grandiflorum*, with pure white flowers of
the habitual three petals, held on arching stems over plain green leaves. It
has double forms, of which the best are as formal as little white camellias;
and an exquisite pink variant. The superficially similar *T. ovatum* ages
from white to pink. *T. erectum* is another species which comes in dusky-
red, but also runs to white, green and yellow – var. *luteum*. This is not to
be confused with *T. luteum*, which has citron-, butter- or green-washed

yellow flowers erect over mottled leaves, so that it looks like a form of *T. sessile*. Another fairly accommodating species is *T. cernuum*, from North America like all these; the pure white flowers fade to pale pink, around contrasting purple anthers. However, as the name suggests, the flowers nod and are somewhat hidden by the broad leaves. Most other trilliums are much smaller, and deserve cossetting with treasures more precious even than these.

Though I can never entirely love the double *Trillium grandiflorum*, the double form of *Sanguinaria canadensis* is most desirable. The blood root – so called from the sap that issues from cut or damaged rhizomes – has beautiful, waxy, pale leaves, and large, pure white, double flowers that last well, whereas the single, lovely though it is, is very fleeting. It is in the poppy family, which is far from exclusively sun-worshipping like the border poppies and the Californian tree poppies, for it includes also several exquisite shade-lovers such as *Eomecon chionanthum*. The dawn poppy has running roots filled with orange-red sap, handsome, large, rounded leaves of bluish tone, and nodding, white flowers with yellow stamens. It should not perhaps have been mentioned here, for it is rather too energetic a spreader among the choice trilliums and erythroniums. The celandine poppy, *Stylophorum diphyllum*, has smaller leaves, somewhat hairy, pale green and rather crimpled, over which are held clear yellow poppies on hairy 30cm/12in stems during spring and summer. Seedlings appear all too rarely. I have never had a single seedling from *Hylomecon japonicum*, which slowly spreads into clumps of fresh green, divided leaves topped by clear yellow poppies, infinitely more refined than the Welsh poppy: which belongs in another chapter, for it is a rampant spreader by seed.

The Himalayan relatives of the Welsh poppy, of course, are the blue poppies – and others – which are so sought after. Here, if I am to stick more or less seriously to my intention of describing the small plants before the taller ones, only *Meconopsis quintuplinervia* just qualifies for inclusion, though at 45cm/18in it is half as tall again as the hylomecon. Reginald Farrer's harebell poppy bears its nodding, lavender bells – described by Farrer himself as 'myriad dancing lavender butterflies' – in spring on arching, hairy stalks over a mat of foliage. Please do not despise it for not matching the pure turquoise of *M. betonicifolia*; it is a most exquisite plant. I am always inclined to plant *M. dhwojii* under my eye also, for I seem to be better at losing it than at growing it. Like many of the Himalayan poppies, it is monocarpic; during the two or three years that it should be building up strength to flower, the rosette is one of the most decorative, of bristly, steel-blue filigree, flecked with purple dots. The flowers should be creamy-yellow in a branched spray on 45cm/18in stems.

MORE ANEMONES

Certain plant families crop up again and again among the plants that we grow in cool, shady gardens. Ranunculaceae has already contributed the celandines and wood anemones, but that is not the end of it. There are more anemones to consider, for a start, as I promised earlier in this chapter. The clear blue, many-petalled *Anemone apennina* grows and spreads well beneath trees in dappled shade – in the garden where I grew up, it formed patches of sky beneath a small grove of silver birches and cobnuts. In earliest spring the furled, ferny leaves start to shoulder their way through the mossy, thin-grassed soil and it is not long before the glossy buds burst open. 'Petrovac' is a very superior form from 'rocky deciduous woods' in Yugoslavia; and there is a white form. *A. blanda* tends to larger flowers and a wider range of colours, including lilac-pink 'Charmer' and the rather aggressive near-magenta, white-eyed 'Radar'. The deepest blue is 'Ingramii', and another good blue is 'Atrocaerulea'; 'White Splendour' has huge, pure white blooms faintly blushing rose on the reverse.

Rarer anemones that are similar to the wood anemone include *A. altaica*, a Siberian species with large, white flowers, veined and backed with blue, over leaves faintly tinged with purple; and the Japanese *A. pseudaltaica*, which has blue flowers. The Italian *A. trifolia* has light green foliage and white or soft clear blue flowers. Another species for which I have a great fondness is *A. multifida* (*A. magellanica*), which has divided, hairy leaves and ivory-cream flowers on strong 15cm/6in stems.

The hepaticas used to be included in *Anemone*, but now have their own genus, and have been separated out into three or four species. *Hepatica nobilis* (*H. triloba*) is found in Europe, Asia and North America, where its three-lobed leaves and blue flowers are to be found in cool, shady positions on calcareous soils. It can be had also in white and pink; while the double forms, in blue, white, and pale or deep pink, are now exceedingly rare. Indeed, each time I have acquired them, they have turned out on flowering to be the ordinary single blue, or on one occasion single white, for which I had paid the price of a double. The Eastern European *H. transsilvanica* (*H. angulosa*) is similar, but larger, while the North American *H. acutiloba* is very like *H. nobilis*, but with more pointed lobes to the mottled leaves. Selected forms or hybrids include 'Ada Scott', and *H.* × *media* 'Ballardii', which is a fine selection from a deliberate cross of *H. nobilis* and *H. transsilvanica*; it has very large, cerulean blue flowers. The newer 'Millstream Merlin', which I have only seen on the show-bench in an Alpine Garden Society's competition, has rich deep blue-violet flowers with an extra row of petals.

STILL IN THE BUTTERCUP FAMILY

The aquilegias or columbines, though in Ranunculaceae, all have the flower structure so familiar in the garden columbine with its clusters of 'doves'. They are generally recommended for sunny positions, but I have grown some species in the more open parts of my cool, shady terraces, including *Aquilegia flabellata* 'Nana Alba', which has waxy, grey-green leaves and short stems bearing fat little creamy-ivory flowers. Another with flowers large for the size of the plant is *A. glandulosa*, in which the Spode blue and white blooms are held horizontally. It seems to prefer a moist, leafy soil and light shade. The fragrant, green and maroon *A. viridiflora* is much slimmer altogether in both leaf and dainty flower; it needs to be planted where you can get close to the blooms and peer into their faces. *Semiaquilegia ecalcarata* is another slight little plant with spurless flowers of sombre madder-purple in spring.

Despite its generic name, which means 'small anemone', *Anemonella thalictroides* is also described by its specific epithet, for this frail little North American woodlander has little thalictrum-like leaves and sprays of white or pink flowers like little anemones, or in 'Jade Feather' little whorls of ivory and green; though it runs mildly at the root if in the loose, leafy soil it prefers, it should perhaps belong in a later section on the shaded rock garden rather than here with the comparatively rumbustious celandines and anemones. *Thalictrum diffusiflorum* is a great beauty in the genus that lent its name to the anemonella; its maidenhair foliage is greyish, the amethyst-blue flowers are nearly 3cm/1in wide, in airy – diffuse – sprays on stems of up to 90cm/36in.

UNUSUAL AFFINITIES

Glaucidium palmatum, the only species in the genus, is a plant which has been shuffled around by the botanists in their attempts to attribute it to the family with which it has most affinities. This has led it to be included in Ranunculaceae, Papaveraceae, Podophyllaceae, and now – according to two different sources both claiming to be up to date – either

Paeoniaceae or its own family Glaucidiaceae. It seems likely that the final word has not been said; but gardeners will continue to covet this exquisite Japanese woodlander for its large, frail-seeming, poppy-like flowers in pale lavender or crystalline white, over large, lobed leaves of *Podophyllum* style. At 60cm/24in, it is rather tall for inclusion among the plants I have so far been describing, but its rarity and beauty mean that few gardeners will wish to relegate it to the back row.

Another plant of similar stature is *Diphylleia cymosa*, the umbrella leaf of North America, so called because of the size of its great two-lobed leaves. This is another plant of uncertain affinities; it has been placed in Podophyllaceae but now resides in Berberidaceae. The heads of small, white flowers are scarcely decorative, but the indigo-purple fruits on reddish stems, held above the leaves, are striking.

HERBACEOUS BERBERIDS

Many of the herbaceous berberids, indeed, are fascinating plants for cool, shady places. Some are well known – the epimediums, for example, of which only the smallest will be mentioned here, for most form excellent ground cover among shrubs and must wait their turn. The only one I shall admit here is *E.* × *youngianum*, a dainty hybrid between two Japanese species which bears white flowers in spring; the best form is 'Niveum', which is also white flowered but shorter in stature at 15cm/6in. 'Roseum' is a selection with lavender-pink flowers.

The species of *Vancouveria* are closely related to the epimediums, and increase in much the same way by slowly spreading rhizomes. In their native habitats of redwood and Douglas fir forests in western North America they grow in deep gloom, but are content in more open conditions of dappled shade in the garden. *V. planipetala* is an evergreen species with tough, glossy leaves divided into rounded leaflets, and tiny, white flowers in open sprays in spring; *V. hexandra* is similar in flower but is deciduous, and slightly taller at 45cm/18in. The most desirable species is *V. chrysantha*, with airy panicles of yellow flowers over biternate, evergreen leaves.

The two species of *Jeffersonia* are of much the same size as *Epimedium* × *youngianum*, though quite different in appearance. *J. dubia* is the Asian species, emerging in spring when the clusters of wiry stems, each bearing a bud that will open to a solitary, cupped, lilac-blue flower, push through the soil before most of the leaves. These are bronzed at first, kidney-shaped with scalloped margins. The North American species, *J. diphylla* or twin-leaf, bears two leaves per stem, each leaf centrally cleft into two segments; they are glaucous-green in colour, while the flowers – opening about a month later than those of *J. dubia* – are pure white.

Rarity and difficulty of cultivation enter into my calculations, as well as size, when deciding whether to include a plant here or later. Thus it is that *Caulophyllum thalictroides*, a berberid with only two commercial sources that I know of in Britain, gets a mention here. At up to 60cm/24in, it is tall enough to grow among shrubs, but it is not the sort of plant of which you are likely to buy quantities, so it could start life under closer supervision, to be moved later. Each stem bears one large, divided leaf somewhat like that of a thalictrum; the small, yellow flowers are unexciting, but the deep blue, berry-like seeds, as big as marbles, are most unusual. Like *Diphylleia* and *Caulophyllum*, *Ranzania japonica* is a woodland plant with rhizomatous roots. Both in the wild and in cultivation it is very rare. The nodding, lilac-pink flowers appear on 30cm/12in stems that burst through the soil before the three-lobed leaves, which are borne at the top of the leaf-stems, unfurl in early summer.

THE UMBRELLA-LEAFS

Podophyllum is a genus that has been given its own family Podophyllaceae, but by others is allocated to Berberidaceae. Without committing myself – for taxonomy is not my subject – I shall describe here the species that I have grown, hoping that the nomenclature I shall adopt is reasonably accurate. There does not, indeed, seem to be much dispute about the only species likely to be commercially available, *P. hexandrum* (*P. emodi*) and *P. peltatum*. The first thrives in moist, shady conditions, where it is very long lived, year after year unfurling its pairs of shiny, deeply lobed, brownish leaves like umbrellas folded from the top of the stem. The nodding, white flowers are followed by glossy red fruits rather like a small, glossy plum-tomato; more plants can easily be raised from the seeds they contain. Var. *chinense* has larger pink flowers, and more deeply divided leaves; var. *majus* is a good large form. The May apple *P. peltatum*, has one lobed leaf to each stem, and nodding, white flowers followed by paler fruits. It is quite a spreader and should really be planted not among these choice woodlanders but between shrubs. I have not grown *P. pleianthum*, which is said to have purplish flowers and deep red fruits.

WOODLAND CYCLAMEN

With these podophyllums, I find myself moving inexorably towards the larger plants for cool shade. It is time to mention some of more modest stature before they become engulfed. Some are determined spreaders by roots or seed, and despite their size are unlikely to be swamped. Such is *Trientalis borealis*, a curious little *Primula* relative with running roots and wiry stems topped by a whorl of small, rather bronzed leaves and starry, white flowers.

The easier cyclamens, too, though small, increase quickly, in their case by seed. *Cyclamen hederifolium* can form tubers the size of dinner plates, but even quite young plants with bead-sized tubers may bear a flower or two, dainty white or pink confections appearing in autumn. The leaves are variable in their marbling and shape. My experience has been that even if you start with pink-flowered forms (as I did, with the gift of two old tubers) you may well find the whites taking over as quantities of seedlings appear. My original tubers were planted at the top of the slope, close to the old cider-apple that provided part of the shade for the little terraces I built; within a couple of years tiny, translucent tubers each bearing one fingernail-size leaf were cropping up everywhere, and I was able to lift and replant elsewhere some hundreds of seedlings each year.

Where suited, the winter-flowering *C. coum*, a complex of related, slightly varying forms, may spread almost as freely. The flowers are stubbier, their colouring often a brighter, deeper rose, as well as white with a carmine nose; the leaves may be rounded and plain deep green, or more or less heavily marbled with silver, while the undersides may be deep red or green. Two other easy species are worth trying in humus-rich soil in light shade (cyclamen addicts will acquire and attempt to satisfy any species offered, but here I am assuming a fondness, rather than a passion, for the genus). *C. purpurascens* has scented, carmine flowers in late summer and marbled green leaves; *C. repandum* bears its elegant, deep rosy-purple flowers with twisted petals over heart-shaped leaves that are only faintly patterned. It is a woodland plant from Mediterranean regions and needs a sheltered corner, as do its forms *rhodense*, almost white with a deep magenta nose, and the pure white *album*; both these last, indeed, are distinctly tender.

DAPHNES

There are some shrublets that deserve inclusion among these small, shade-loving or woodland plants. It is in just such cool, leafy and slightly gritty soil as I concocted for my trilliums and trout lilies and primroses that I succeeded with *Daphne blagayana*. Now you will often read that daphnes like sun, and so it may be, if you want all the flower they are capable of giving. But they also detest dry roots, and will express their dislike, as often as not, by dying. On balance, therefore, I have always tended to give my daphnes a cool position, albeit with open sky overhead, finding that – at least in the south of England – this compromise suits them very well. *D. blagayana* has low, wide-spreading stems that should be tucked up in a leafy mixture, with a flat stone laid here and there to keep them in place and cool. It should then oblige you by producing terminal, rounded heads of creamy, deliciously fragrant flowers in early summer. Where it is happy, *D.cneorum* can make a wide, low mound, the neat little leaves smothered in spring beneath dense heads of sweetly scented, bright pink flowers, most freely borne in an open position; but I always grow its variegated form in light shade, as its vigour is less, and the pale foliage shows up well against a dark, leafy soil.

One of the easiest of the daphnes is *D. retusa*, a slow, neat little evergreen shrub with dark, leathery leaves and heads of fragrant, pinky-purple flowers in spring. *D. tangutica* is half a size larger, at 60cm/24in high and wide. But perhaps the most fascinating, apart from the tinies for alpine house culture, is the winter-flowering, summer-deciduous *D. kamtschatica jezoensis*, with bright yellow flowers in small clusters and fresh green leaves. I have not seen it much over 60cm/24in tall, and it takes a while to get to that size. Having said that, if I were limited to just one daphne it would have to be *D. pontica*, of which more elsewhere (see page 90).

BEAUTIFUL AND BIZARRE

Some fritillaries, in a genus which runs from the obliging crown imperial of cottage gardens to the recalcitrant *Fritillaria recurva* via the familiar snake's head lily, are easy enough for cool, leafy shade and are either beautiful or fascinating, or both. The snake's head lily itself, *F. meleagris*, will naturalize in grass where the soil is not too dry, and in the garden you may find that – as with *Cyclamen hederifolium* – white seedlings will gradually come to equal or dominate the typical, chequered dusky-red. The selected forms, 'Aphrodite' in white and the rarer 'Jupiter', 'Saturnus' and 'Poseidon' in varying shades of purple with the chequering more or less pronounced, are choice enough to grow with the plants of cool shade.

Fritillaria verticillata bears its leaves in whorls, ending in tendrils, and has wide pale creamy-jade bells faintly chequered within, on 60cm/24in stems. The pale lemon *F. pallidiflora* has flowers shaped like sharp-shouldered tulips, hanging on 30cm/12in stems in spring; it dislikes wind, but is otherwise easy to please in soil that does not dry out. The alabaster-green bells of *F. involucrata*, another species happier in light shade, are heavily chequered with terracotta to purple. In *F. pontica* we have something rather different again, green lanterns with snuff-brown tips on 30cm/12in stems. The flared bells of *F. pyrenaica* are mahogany on the outside and burnished gold flecked with brown within; there is also a beautiful form in which the bells are wholly pale green-washed yellow. A plant of subalpine meadows, it seems happy in light or dappled shade and will grow in thin grass. The near-Eastern *F. acmopetala* grows in the wild in open pine woods and corn fields; in the garden, in well-drained soil, it should produce its jade bells with mahogany inner segments, borne a little later and on taller stems than most of the species so far described. But the last of the 'frits' to flower is *F. camschatcensis*, which needs a moist, leafy soil to remind it of its native woodlands. It is a variable plant, of which the most desirable forms are those which increase quickly at the root to form clumps of bright green, whorled leaves topped by hanging, black-maroon bells.

The black fritillary has some of the fascination of the sombre or bizarre aroids which also do well in leafy soils in light shade. One of the most amusing is *Arisarum proboscideum*, often dubbed the mouse plant, for the fat little maroon, long-tailed spathes seem to dive into the foliage like a whole family of mice seeking cover. It is a willing increaser and can be tucked in among shrubs to form a dense carpet of arrowhead leaves. Another easy aroid is *Arisaema triphyllum*, Jack in the pulpit; the green spathes, arching over the spadix, are more or less heavily striped with purple and overtopped by elegant, three-lobed striped leaves. Glossy vermilion berries follow, held in a cylindrical cluster like that of the common lords and ladies, *Arum maculatum*. One of the smaller species, which increases quickly in moist, leafy soil, is *Arisaema amurense*, with five-parted foliage and green, white-striped spathes followed by orange berries.

A. ringens is a much bigger plant, with broad, shiny, three-lobed leaves reaching 45cm/18in above the tightly curled, helmet-shaped spathe, green-striped with chocolate-purple lips. Another that is curled in gastropod fashion is *A. griffithii*, in which the spathe varies from green to chocolate-purple, with frilled edges and a network of white veins: it crouches, sinister, close to the ground, beneath the bold, three-lobed leaves, their deeply incised veins picked out in purple. Even more dramatic is the deep velvety-purple spathe of *A. speciosum*, lightly green or ivory striped, and arching to form a pointed cobra hood above the creamy spadix which trails off into a long, purple string. The leaves, borne on stout 60cm/24in stems with serpentine mottling of brown on green, are three lobed, green margined with rufous-brown.

Some arisaemas are beautiful as well as bizarre. The narrow-waisted, bitter-chocolate spathe of *A. sikokianum* encloses a pure white, broad spadix in spring, before the leaves are fully developed. The same is true of perhaps the most beautiful species of all, *A. candidissimum*, in which the sculptured spathe is pure white, striped with pale pink in the throat and green on the outside. It is a late starter, the spathe suddenly emerging in early summer and soon followed by the broad, handsome leaves. In my experience it is a willing grower, the smooth, rounded corms quickly pupping to make little colonies; or perhaps some of the youngsters are seedlings from the handsome, orange fruits that follow the inflorescence in autumn.

Although the typical arisaema leaf is broad and three lobed, some species present a quite different appearance with leaves that are finely divided. The single leaf of *A. consanguineum* is formed of as many as twenty narrow leaflets terminating in a thread-like tip, borne on tall, brown-mottled stems. The inflorescence is less dramatic than the foliage, a simple green or brownish spathe with a long, thread-like tip; it is often followed by bright scarlet, shining fruits. The green dragon, *A. dracontium*, has similarly much-divided leaves on tall stems, and a very long, yellow spadix protruding from the small, green spathe. The berries are orange.

The arums are distinguished from the arisaemas by their arrowhead leaves, not lobed. The inflorescences, except in the exquisite *Arum creticum* which is a plant for warm soils in full sun, can seldom compare with those of the arisaemas, but the foliage can be very decorative, especially as it enlivens the winter scene when the arisaemas are dormant. The marbled form of *Arum italicum*, known as var. *marmoratum* or *pictum*, has elegant, narrow, spearhead leaves heavily veined and marbled in ivory; it looks well near *Iris foetidissima* 'Variegata' or accompanying a white-flowered *Daphne mezereum*. The orange-red fruits in cylindrical clusters appear in summer when the plant is leafless.

LITTLE LILY RELATIVES

The common Solomon's seal is a charming woodland plant, but rather tall for inclusion here. It does, however, have smaller relatives, of which one of the choicest is *Polygonatum falcatum*, a Japanese species slowly spreading to form a thicket of leafy, arching stems up to 30cm/12in tall, from which the little ivory bells hang in late spring. Graham Thomas recommends growing the form 'Variegatum', in which the leaves are margined with white lightly suffused with pink, with the pink lily of the valley, *Convallaria majalis rosea*, a choice variant much less aggressive than the common *muguet*. Other variegated Solomon's seals, though taller, are so choice as to merit a position under your eye, at least until they demonstrate a willingness to settle. The variegated form of *Polygonatum odoratum*, also known as 'Variegatum', is taller and the leaves are much more boldly marked with cream; they are borne on angled, 60cm/24in stems. 'Gilt Edge' has reddish stems and leaves finely margined with yellow. Other variegated forms are named: 'Grace Barker', 'Silver Wings'. There is a nicely variegated form of *P.* × *hybridum*, the common Solomon's seal of gardens, too, with cream-striped, rather undulate foliage. Both the fragrant *P. odoratum* and *P.* × *hybridum* also have double forms, both called 'Flore Pleno', in which the little, slender, alabaster bells are transformed into tiny tutus. Other Solomon's seals are taller, up to 1.5m/5ft, and must wait to be described.

The related disporums are mostly small enough to belong here. *Disporum smithii* and *D. hookeri* var. *oreganum* are similar, at about 30cm/12in, with fresh green leaves half hiding small, ivory bells in spring. These are followed by orange fruits which may give you self-sown seedlings in the shady, leafy soils the disporums appreciate. The slightly taller *D. sessile* is valued especially for its form 'Variegatum', in which the narrow leaves are striped with white and the flowers are creamy bells. When settled it spreads quite freely and may need watching.

Lily of the valley, *Convallaria majalis*, is much more familiar than these pretty things, and universally loved for its delectable perfume. The type, and the later-flowering 'Fortin's Giant', are too apt to spread into dense, wide clumps to be allowed into the company of the choicer shade-lovers. But the pink form, *rosea*, and the double 'Prolificans' (which is not, actually, a quarter as appealing as the ordinary single), and especially the form with leaves striped in butter-yellow, 'Variegata': these are variants to tuck in among other small treasures. I think I would start the large-flowered 'Hardwick Hall' here, too, until I saw how it intended to behave; the very wide leaves are margined with ivory-green.

The foliage of the clintonias, woodlanders which increase slowly, not aggressively, is similar to that of lily of the valley. The finest species is *Clintonia andrewsiana*, quite tall at up to 60cm/24in, with clusters of rosy-carmine bells topping the stems; they are followed by indigo berries. None of the clintonias is widely available in commerce, but the greeny-yellow *C. borealis* should be slightly easier to come by; it is half as tall, and bears similar fruits in autumn. *C. umbellata* has fragrant, white flowers.

Reineckea carnea has much narrower leaves, rather pale or even yellowish-green in my experience; but then I think my plant is an aberration in more than one way, for it bears its starry, pink flowers in autumn, not when supposed to in early summer. It is the sort of plant described as 'more curious than beautiful', though the slowly increasing, dense clump of pale grassy foliage has its value in contrast to other leaf forms.

Streptopus amplexifolius has rather glaucous, stem-clasping leaves and sprays of greenish-white flowers hanging like Solomon's seal. *S. roseus* is smaller, with dusty-pink bells followed by similar red berries. Then there is *S. simplex*, in which the little bells are cream with the outer segments and the centre mushroom-pink. Yet another offbeat relative of lily of the valley is *Speirantha convallarioides* (*S. gardenii*), which bears fragrant, starry, snow-white flowers in spring above a clump of rich green leaves. The May lily, *Maianthemum bifolium*, is an aggressive little creature with lily-of-the-valley leaves and dainty, ivory sprays of flower in spring; *M. kamtschaticum* is similar, but taller at 20cm/8in and even more of a spreader. Both can be left to cover the ground between shrubs, rather then threatening your smaller, more restrained treasures.

A slow spreader related, and similar, to the Solomon's seals, is *Uvularia sessilifolia*, which forms a thicket of erect stems set with leaves bronzed when young, and narrowly tubular, ivory-cream bells in spring. It has the kitsch pet name of little merrybells; the big merrybells, *U. grandiflora*, is rather taller, and exceptionally pretty with its fresh green foliage and drooping, slightly flared sulphur bells. Var. *pallida* has larger, paler creamy-primrose flowers. Those of *U. perfoliata* are similarly pale, and are borne above the leaves about two weeks later.

TOOTHWORTS AND SHOOTING STARS

Graham Thomas, always ready with an inspired plant association, suggests growing *Uvularia sessilifolia* with *Dentaria pinnata*. This and other species of *Dentaria* have, I believe, now been merged into *Cardamine*. *D. pinnata*, then, becomes *Cardamine heptaphylla*; it forms a clump of divided, fresh green leaves topped by heads of pure white flowers, larger than those of the common, lilac-mauve cuckoo flower, *C. pratensis*. If the colouring of this plant of damp meadows appeals, you could choose its double form 'Flore Pleno', or the very desirable *C. pentaphyllos* (*Dentaria digitata*), with large flowers of clear pink-mauve. *C. raphanifolia* (*C. latifolia*) is taller, at 45cm/18in, and has lavender flowers rather like a small honesty. One of the most enchanting is *C. enneaphyllos*, with creamy-primrose flowers and palely bronzed foliage, a pretty companion for the yellow uvularias, white primroses (or one of the Garryarde seedlings with dark foliage and cream or straw-yellow flowers) and pale creamy *Narcissus* 'W. P. Milner'. *C. kitaibelii* (*Dentaria polyphylla*) is of the same pretty colouring, with whorls of pinnate leaves and nodding, straw-yellow bells. Quite different from all these is *Cardamine trifolia*, a creeping evergreen with dark, trefoil leaves and heads of small, pure white flowers in spring on 15cm/6in stems.

The dodecatheons are plants for leafy soil in shade, with swept-back petals and, often, colourful 'snouts' to the cyclamen-like flower, but the habit is more cowslip-like, with heads of bloom on stout stems, from the arrangement of which they have their common name of shooting stars. There are several species, all similar, with smooth basal foliage; they differ chiefly in colour, from white (such as the miniature *Dodecatheon dentatum*) to the bright rosy-purple of *D. jeffreyi* and *D. meadia* (which has a white form), both up to 45cm/18in tall. One of the best of the middling-sized species is *D. pulchellum*, with pale lilac flowers marked with purple in the throat; the superb selection 'Red Wings' has crimson flowers.

PURE BLUES

In complete contrast to the smooth, spoon-shaped leaves of the shooting stars, *Corydalis* species all have more or less fine, filigree foliage. Some are sun-baskers, some energetic spreaders which must wait until later to be described, some – like the exquisite turquoise-blue *C. cashmiriana* – capricious in captivity. But a few are both well behaved and suited to cool, leafy soils. I have always given just such conditions to *C. cheilanthifolia*, and it has rewarded me well with tufts of ferny, rather bronzed foliage topped by dense sprays of clear yellow flowers. More familiar than this is the shorter, tubbier *C. solida*, which comes in lilac-pink, purple or white, and retires underground to its little tuber shortly after its spring floraison, only unfurling more of its green, divided leaves late the following winter. Even dry shade seems to suit it. The slightly larger *C. bulbosa*, distinguished by the hollow upper surface of the tubers, has finely divided, blue-green leaves and dense spikes of creamy-mauve to deep lilac flowers in early spring.

Pure blue, and the gentle shades of lilac and violet which are very close to the spectrum tint, always appeal. When such cool colouring in the flower is allied to grey-green foliage, as in the Virginian cowslip, *Mertensia pulmonarioides* (*M. virginica*), the combination is irresistible. The shape of the flowers, and their poise, is suggested by the vernacular name, though in fact the bells of the mertensia are more tubular, more nodding than any European cowslip's. It is a woodland rather than a meadow plant, flowering in spring and dying down by midsummer. *M. ciliata* is slightly taller, at 60cm/24in; the pink buds and clear blue tubular bells are set off by glaucous leaves.

The pulmonarias, on the other hand, continue to make good, weed-excluding clumps, especially if you cut them back, leaves and all, after flowering, and then see that they do not go short of water so as to refurnish themselves with fresh foliage for the summer. Many are bulky enough to belong among shrubs, where they can well look after themselves; but I cannot resist describing two species here. *Pulmonaria longifolia* forms a close clump of long, narrow, pointed leaves of dark green much spotted with white; the small flowers, in packed heads, are pure ultramarine-blue. Almost the same lovely colour belongs to *P. angustifolia*, a shorter plant with smaller, blunter, bristly plain green leaves forming a little mat; unlike the other species, it is not evergreen, so in early spring when the sprays of pure blue flowers begin to open the leaves are barely emerging. Selections chosen for their extra blueness are 'Azurea', 'Munstead Blue' and 'Mawson's Blue'. Since neither the lungwort nor the violet has great blobby flowers in which the colour dominates the green of the leaves, you will shock no aesthetic sensibilities if you set this pulmonaria with one of the little yellow violets such as *Viola biflora* or *V. pensylvanica*.

If pure blue seems to appeal to everyone, the muted or slaty blues are perhaps an acquired taste. *Deinanthe caerulea* has nodding, fleshy flowers of just such restrained colouring, borne on reddish stems over clumps of rounded, bristly leaves that need shelter from bruising winds. There is a white form. The small flowers of *D. bifida* are always white, and cannot compare. The waxy, slate-blue, white-centred flowers of *Anemonopsis macrophylla* are described by Graham Thomas as 'meek and forlorn'; they nod in sprays over the ferny green leaves in summer. This lovely thing needs the same sheltered conditions in leafy, cool, moist soil as the deinanthes.

This is just what you should give your *Paris polyphylla*, if you are so fortunate as to obtain a plant. Vastly superior to *P. quadrifolia* which grows in limy woodlands, *P. polyphylla* pushes up a naked 90cm/36in stem topped by a wide whorl of pointed leaves, over which is poised a radiating collar of green sepals below yellow-green petals as fine as thread, held out stiffly like rimless spokes around the prominent, purple knob of the stigma. Graham Thomas tells us that if you can get two clones, it will produce orange seeds as showy as *Iris foetidissima*'s; but most of us would be glad to lay our hands on just one *Paris polyphylla*, let alone two.

Some authorities say we must now call *Aceriphyllum rossii Mukdenia rossii*, which is a double shame, for the unfamiliar name is an ugly one, and the familiar one describes the foliage of this member of the saxifrage family. The umbels of white flowers are borne on 20cm/8in stems in spring before the lobed, dark leaves unfurl. The thick rhizomes slowly spread in leafy, moist soil. If the understated and the offbeat hold no appeal for you, you will care for this no more than, probably, for the deinanthes and *Anemonopsis macrophylla*; but I hope you may come to share my affection for these and other curiosities, so that you may have the same pleasure from growing them as I have.

IRISES IN THE COOL

Most irises like sun, in moist, wet or dry soil according to taste. But I have always grown *Iris cristata* in cool shade, adding a little grit to the leafy mixture. The little rhizomes form a mat from which tufts of narrow leaves arise; the dainty lilac and orange flowers bear a conspicuous crest. There is a wonderful white form with lemon crest. Another of similar construction is *I. gracilipes*, a woodland species from Japan with lilac, orange-crested flowers. The dwarf form of *I. setosa* seems to like similar, or even quite damp conditions; it has slender foliage and large slate-blue flowers on 20cm/8in stems.

My experience of *I. innominata*, and of the Pacific Coast or Californian hybrids, so called, which derive from it and its relatives from western North America, is that they do best in woodsy, retentive, acid soil opened up with a little grit. Some grow quite bulky, but *I. innominata* itself, with hard, narrow leaves in tufts and amber, brown-veined flowers, is of modest size. I used, until matters got out of hand, to sow seed of this and my hybrids each year and raise all the youngsters to flowering size, picking out the smallest and best for choice corners and spreading the rest around, roughly grouped by colours, among shrubs where they make good weed-excluding clumps. And the best, often, are heart-achingly lovely, with butterfly-like blooms in crystalline white, Naples yellow, buff, blush-lilac, aquamarine and amethyst, lavender, violet, and a curious faded fox-brown shaded with madder, all more or less distinctly decorated with pencilling in deeper or contrasting shades. You can buy named cultivars; but why bother, when you can raise such exquisite creatures for yourself from seed?

The time has come for me to gather together loose threads, picking out a few more choice plants for cool shade that, by virtue of their size, their rarity or their beauty, deserve to be grown in the kind of under-the-eye conditions I have been supposing, rather than in the larger context of shrub and woodland areas. Before I do so, let me remind you that in lightly shaded areas, many of the smaller *Narcissus* species and half-height hybrids assort well with primroses and anemones and violets. Creamy 'W. P. Milner' we have met already; it and the pale *triandrus* hybrid 'April Tears' (*N. triandrus* itself seems to need full sun) mix with all the colours, even the pinks. The brighter yellow of *N. cyclamineus*, with its swept-back perianth, comes earlier in the year and needs keeping away from pink or mauve. As well as the familiar 'February Gold' and others – some already mentioned in Chapter I – there are dozens more; the show benches and competitions at spring shows will send you running to your notebook and perhaps even your cheque book, but some of the most enchanting are expensive. This may be no more than a sign of their newness; but it could also suggest that they are difficult to increase, or simply not good garden plants.

Summer and Autumn

With the little pale daffodil 'W. P. Milner', the black-leaved *Ophiopogon planiscapus nigrescens* forms a pleasing contrast; white *Cyclamen hederifolium* for autumn is even more startling against the glossy strap-like leaves, for at this time the ophiopogon is bearing its shiny purple-black fruits also. *Arthopodium candidum* is smaller and hardier than *A. cirrhatum*, proposed as a component of the warmer shady garden; its fawn-pink grassy leaves and little white flowers followed in autumn by black seeds are, as Beth Chatto has noted, charming in combination with the cyclamen and *Ophiopogon*. The other species of *Ophiopogon* with which I am familiar, like the liriopes to which they are closely related, are green-leaved and spread more vigorously, so have no place here. Another dark-leaved plant for cool places is *Saxifraga cortusifolia fortunei* 'Wada', in which the broad, shining leaves are mahogany red, in contrast to the showers of airy white flowers. 'Rubrifolia' is similar; the type has green leaves with maroon reverse.

The ourisias, which are found only in the southern hemisphere, flower a little earlier in summer; some grow naturally in wet soil, and all appreciate coolth in the garden. Both *Ourisia macrophylla* and *O. macrocarpa* form spreading mats of green, leathery leaves topped by heads of white flowers on 30cm/12in stems, and could be rather vigorous for

your cool, shady corners unless you have plenty of space. But the scarlet
O. coccinea is more restrained, its bright green, lobed and toothed leaves
setting off the nodding flowers. It has united with *O. macrophylla* to give
the coral-pink 'Loch Ewe'. A more restrained white is 'Snowflake',
which is *O. macrocarpa* crossed with the diminutive *O. caespitosa* var.
gracilis; the hybrid has good-sized, glistening white flowers, while those
of the smaller parent are also large against the tiny mats of green foliage.
There are other species, all worth acquiring.

LEAVES TO THE FORE

Hostas have become a cult of recent years, and it is impossible for anyone
but an addict to keep up with the latest introductions. The familiar old,
more or less large-leaved species and cultivars are out of scale among the
small plants I am describing, but there are one or two diminutive species
that fit in well here. At the upper limit in size is *Hostas helonioides albopicta*,
which has narrow, strap-like leaves broadly margined in butter-yellow,
and lilac flowers on 30cm/12in stems in summer. Far smaller than this is
H. venusta, with tiny, dark green, heart-shaped leaves and short spikes of
violet flowers; *H. tardiflora* is scarcely bigger, with longer, narrower,
shining green leaves and quite large, violet-mauve bells on dark stems in
autumn. There is a very pretty yellow form of *H. nakaiana*, simply called
'Golden'; the wavy-edged leaves are heart-shaped, the flowers violet.

    Newer hostas that I have fallen for include 'Golden Prayers', with fresh
chartreuse-yellow foliage no bigger than the palm of a child's hand,
holding its colour well through the season; 'Hydon Sunset', with tiny,
broadly lance-shaped leaves of bright lime-gold; and 'Golden Sceptre',
similar but slightly larger and broader in leaf. Of the many blue-leaved
hostas, some are small enough to include here: 'Hadspen Heron', with
narrow leaves, and rounded 'Blue Moon' among them.

    Yellow-leaved hostas make good companions for the pale, fresh
colours of spring: white *Primula denticulata*, *Narcissus* 'April Tears' or the
larger 'Jenny' and 'Dove Wings', *Polygonatum odoratum* 'Variegatum',
white *Dodecatheon meadia* and such like. The blues, on the other hand, set
off the pinks and mauves to best effect, or can join a group of *Primula*
'Wanda' and *Dicentra formosa* 'Stuart Boothman'; keep a watchful eye on
the dicentra, which can spread quite fast when suited despite its slender
looks of ferny, steel-blue foliage and dusky-pink lockets. Again, *Lamium
maculatum* 'Beacon Silver' may prove too keen to spread; but its heavily
silvered leaves and magenta-pink flowers are just right here. The white-
flowered 'White Nancy' has the same pewtered foliage. Much slower

than these is the yellow-leaved 'Aureum', well worth cossetting among the small golden hostas.

TOAD LILIES

So many of the little plants that enjoy cool, shady conditions flower in spring – a reflection of their native haunts in deciduous woodland, very often, where they must hasten to make growth and flower while the light is at its most intense, before the leaf canopy brings gloom to the forest floor – that it is a relief to find some plants at their best in autumn. Although they are mostly rather tall, it is for this reason that I am inclined to describe the toad lilies, species of *Tricyrtis*, here. In any case, not all are tall; and even those that are have flowers of such bizarre and intriguing construction that it is worth having them close at hand. Probably the most common, if commercial availability is any guide, is *T. formosana*, in the manifestation which used to be recognized as a distinct species, *T. stolonifera*, and is now called the Stolonifera group, if it is distinguished at all. It (or they) increases quite freely at the roots; the polished leaves are dark green, and the branching stems reach 60–90cm/24–36in, bearing mahogany buds opening to cupped, starry flowers of sepia tones heavily spotted with mauve, yellow in the throat.

   T. hirta has larger, white flowers blotched and freckled with purple, or entirely white in *alba*, which has pink stamens. Flowering earlier than these, in summer, *T. latifolia* has ochre-yellow flowers mottled with sombre red-purple, and the leaves are mottled also. Another which veers towards yellow is *T. macropoda*, creamy-green or ivory with strong mauve freckling; it flowers in early autumn and, like *T. latifolia*, reaches about 90cm/36in if suited. Two very lovely forms, perhaps of *T. hirta*, are 'White Towers' and 'Lilac Towers'. Both have softly hairy foliage and 60cm/24in stems set with wide flowers; the first is ivory-white, the second, with more substantial blooms, is white heavily spotted with clear blue-lilac.

   Rather different, and singularly beautiful, are the yellow-flowered species in which the segments are less widely spread, giving them a shape rather like shuttlecocks. I shall not soon forget my first sight of *Tricyrtis macranthopsis* growing in the foothills of the large rock garden of the botanic garden in Lausanne, Switzerland. The sheaves of stems set with green leaves arched forward over a rock, as though borne down by the weight of the straw-yellow flowers, which I had to lift to see the brown spotting within. Another of this style is *T. macrantha*; while *T. flava ohsumiensis* has very large, upward-facing flowers of soft yellow over low clumps of pale green leaves.

THE HARDY GINGERS

The members of the ginger family that are hardy in cool temperate zones are few. The cautleyas and roscoeas flower in summer, and do best in leafy, moist soil, equally happy in sun or light shade. *Roscoea cautleoides* sets the tone, with glossy green sword leaves and hooded, sulphur-yellow flowers on 30cm/12in stems. A shorter yellow form is 'Beesiana'. All the cautleyas that I know of are yellow; *Cautleya spicata* is taller than the roscoea and bears deeper yellow flowers in bracts which may be green, but are more striking in maroon. 'Robusta' is a fine form selected for the contrast between the honey-gold petals and deep maroon bracts. The leaves are bold and handsome also in deep green. *C. gracilis* (*C. lutea*) is slighter and smaller with paler flowers. Returning to the roscoeas, we find some species in which the flowers are purple. *Roscoea purpurea* is similar to *R. cautleoides*, but with royal purple flowers; *R. humeana* is of similar rich colouring but is shorter in growth. *R. procera* used to be distinguished as a separate species or as a form of *R. purpurea*, but now seems to have disappeared except as a synonym; the name stood for a handsome form with hooded flowers of white and lavender purple. The smallest is *R. alpina*, pretty rather than striking with short spikes of pink orchid-like flowers.

TRUE ORCHIDS, EASY OR RARE

Some plants must be observed closely, for they are fascinating rather than declamatory. The orchid family has its share of both the discreet and the bold, and none bolder among hardy orchids than *Dactylorhiza foliosa* from Madeira and *D. elata* from northern Africa. In rich, cool soil, where they receive the sun for part of each day, they are easy growers, increasing by natural division of the tubers. The richest and most sumptuous colour belongs to *D. elata*, which bears its long, close-packed, magenta-purple tapering spikes on 75cm/30in stems in early summer. *D. foliosa* is shorter, its purple-pink flowers have a broad, diamond-shaped lip, and its longer, broader leaves are glossy, not matt. Other more modest British orchids can be grown in grass and will be described in a later chapter, though you might wish to keep *D. fuchsii* 'Bressingham Bonus' in a more controlled environment until you had worked up a stock. This is a wild selection of the British spotted orchis, with the usual dark-flecked leaves, and flower spikes of clear violet-mauve.

One of the easiest of orchids for cool, leafy soil is *Bletilla striata*, which in early summer opens rich purple flowers – or white in the exquisite *alba*

– over pleated, deep green blades. They are very different from the lady's slipper orchids, which are rare, expensive and so far impossible to raise from seed. I hesitate, indeed, even to mention them, for all too often the stock that is offered has been collected from the wild, diminishing still further the small colonies that survive. The only way to put a stop to this is for every gardener to insist on cultivated stocks. The European lady's slipper, *Cypripedium calceolus*, is reduced to just one site in Britain, a guarded secret in the figurative and literal sense; for collectors have in the past dug plants in order to see the yellow, mahogany-pouched flowers in their own garden. Even more gorgeous than this is the North American *C. reginae*, which has large flowers, the outer segments white, the pouch soft pink. If you do acquire them, or any other of the species which are occasionally offered, plant them with the crown just below the surface, firm the soil well and make sure that frost does not lift them during winter. Some modest ground cover will protect the slippers from splashes.

The enchanting greater butterfly orchis, *Platanthera chlorantha*, with its winged, long-lipped flowers, is endowed with a perfume of the kind that Christopher Lloyd characterizes as immoral; its natural habitat is scrubby, shady woods, where it grows through the moss. The white helleborine, *Cephalanthera damasonia*, grows in beechwoods on chalk, the ivory flowers gleaming against the cosy brown carpet of leaves. Though the commonest of the genus in Britain, it is not available commercially as I write; you can, however, buy the red helleborine, *C. rubra*. The marsh helleborine is *Epipactis palustris*, which has creeping, shallow rhizomes, and quite large flowers of madder-brown and blush-white in a loose one-sided spray; as its botanical and vernacular names both suggest, it prefers wet soils. Two similar British native orchids with flowers of progressively deeper colouring are *E. latifolia*, a plant of beechwoods, and *E. atrorubens*. But I believe the only one available commercially, as I write, is the North American *E. gigantea*, which has the same slowly creeping rhizomes and narrow basal leaves, with flowers of greenish-bronze, dusky-pink within, the lower lip marked with yellow and orange. None is difficult in cool, preferably lime free soils; once you have sufficient stock, you could try them in your woodland or copse.

TO GROW AMONG SHRUBS

If your simulated woodland margin is large enough to accommodate a few shrubs, then you may wish to grow some of the species of *Codonopsis* here; all seem to do as well in cool conditions as in the more open positions some authors recommend.

Several are sprawlers or scramblers, hence the suggestion of accompanying shrubs; or they can be set at the top of a bank or retaining wall, which will permit you to peer into their strangely marked, more or less flared bells. The foxy smelling *C. clematidea* may get too large, spreading its slender greyish leafy stems widely through its support; the nodding, Wedgwood blue bells are pencilled with saffron and maroon inside. The flowers of *C. convolvulacea* open more widely, showing their periwinkle-blue colouring, a tone shared with the more restrained *C. vinciflora*. The finest form of *C. convolvulacea* is Forrest's form; there is an albino also. *C. ovata* has china-blue bells veined inside with purple and marked at the base within with green and black. The softly hairy *C. mollis* has none of the foxy odour associated with the genus; it has waisted, pale blue bells with reddish striations inside. If offbeat colours appeal to you, try *C. meleagris*, which is non-climbing, and bears large, alabaster green bells striped and chequered with chocolate-brown. Again, there are other species, which if you succumb to the charms of the genus you are certain to seek out.

Grasses and Ferns

I am aware that not a single grass or fern has found its way into this chapter; yet a few of each might qualify for inclusion. The Japanese *Hakonechloa macra*, for example, grows in nature in woodsy soil in shade. Two garden forms are worth planting: 'Albo-aurea', with green and citron leaves overlaid with bronze, and the brighter 'Aureola', which colours best where not too much shaded. In both, the leaves arch in a graceful clump. Mr Bowles's golden grass, *Milium effusum aureum*, is even fresher in its clear chartreuse-yellow colouring; the leaves, stems and airy flowers are all of the same tone. It seeds itself quite freely, but the babies are easy both to spot, in their bright flaxen colouring, and to remove for planting elsewhere. *Holcus mollis* 'Albovariegatus' has creeping rhizomes, mildly invasive but not so tenacious as to be a nuisance, and the narrow blades are more white than green, especially fresh and pale in spring.

All these grasses are soft to handle; I recall how I used to love the plain green form of the *Milium* as a child, on account of its strokeable texture. The small sedge *Carex oshimensis* 'Evergold', by contrast, has tough, narrow, evergreen leaves of bright yellow with green margins, forming tufty clumps that are especially cheerful in winter. The hardiest of variegated grasses is *Molinia caerulea* 'Variegata', its arching, cream-striped blades forming dense, neat tufts topped by feathery, purplish flower heads on pale stalks in autumn. Graham Thomas extols its beauty in winter, when 'faded to parchment tint', but I cannot enthuse about dead grasses any more than about the dead brown leaves of *Polygonum affine* (*Persicaria affinis*).

Little ferns such as the ric-rac, *Ceterach officinarum*, and the wall rue, *Asplenium ruta-muraria*, will grow almost anywhere, though more lush in good, leafy soil than when – as in some gardens I know – their spores land in the crumbling mortar of old walls and grow there. *Blechnum penna-marina* is a little more choosy, though far from difficult; Christopher Lloyd uses it at Great Dixter as a carpet for *Cyclamen hederifolium*, and the two seem to cohabit most equably in rather dry shade, the fern making a dense low carpet of burnished fronds when the cyclamen is dormant. There are some small spleenworts which are dainty and graceful additions to a grouping of little plants for cool shade: *Asplenium adiantum-nigrum*, with thick-textured, glossy green fronds, and *A. trichomanes*, the maidenhair spleenwort, with many small pinnae on black stems.

The true maidenhair, *Adiantum*, includes two small species that are easy to grow and form delightful miniatures remarkably like the greenhouse *A. capillus-veneris*. These are *A. venustum* and *A. pedatum*, both slowly forming carpets of dainty, arching fronds. Only slightly larger, both the oak fern, *Gymnocarpium dryopteris*, and the beech fern, *Phegopteris connectilis* (*Thelypteris phegopteris*), have fresh green, much divided, deciduous fronds. The lacy *Cystopteris bulbifera* is not much taller, at 45cm/18in; the very finely cut fronds have tawny stalks, and the little bulbils that form beneath drop to the ground to make new fernlings, or can be rescued, lined out in a pan and planted elsewhere when large enough to fend for themselves. *C. fragilis* is similar, but makes no bulbils.

The choicer forms of the hart's tongue fern are worth planting among other treasures. *Phyllitis scolopendrium* has sported to frilled and crimpled forms which contrast well with the daintier ferns, or with the broad blades of hostas. Crispa and Cristata are the groups to which these forms belong; there are also some grotesqueries in which the frond divides at the apex. The form of polypody known as *Polypodium vulgare* 'Cornubiense' is a fine, fresh green in summer, and the fronds are much more finely divided than the ordinary polypody which grows in walls and on mossy tree trunks, correctly suggesting that dryness at the root is no threat.

A charming and rather delicate fern, *Davallia mariesii* is known as the hare's foot fern on account of the furred rhizomes that creep across the ground; they look very like the tense, sinewy foot of a hare. The finely dissected fronds grow to about 20cm/8in and are deep bronzed green in colour. But perhaps the loveliest of all ferns for a cool, shady spot where precious things are grown is *Athyrium niponicum pictum* (*A. goeringianum pictum*, *A. niponicum* 'Metallicum'), in which the divided fronds are flushed with dove-grey and pinkish-maroon on wine-red stems. It combines beautifully with *Helleborus lividus*, in which flower and leaf echo the grey and pinkish tones, *Anemonopsis macrophylla*, and the choicest pink wood anemones or *Primula* 'Guinevere'.

III

Shade and Moisture

Most gardeners learn early that shade can help to compensate for lack of moisture, enabling you to grow candelabra primulas and astilbes in cool corners when they might fry in the sun. But shady gardens may be damp, too, and where the sun can filter through for part of the day, these and other moisture-loving plants can reach lush dimensions unknown in drier gardens. Though many would flower with more freedom in full sun if the soil were moist, they will put up a fair show in lightly shaded places.

The season opens with the kingcups and globe flowers, yellow and white bog arums, the drumstick primula and *Primula rosea*. *Caltha palustris* is the common marsh marigold or kingcup, a name evoking the wide, shiny-petalled, buttercup-like flowers opening in early spring. There is a discreet little white form, and an assertive yellow double, 'Plena'. The rounded, polished leaves are fairly efficient weed-excluders, always a useful attribute in moist soils where weeds luxuriate and can be hard to remove except with an attached squelch of soil. Though its leaves are larger, *C. polypetala* is not perhaps so trustworthy as ground cover, for it has rooting stems rather than forming solid clumps, so that it is apt to be hunting new ground all the time without paying due attention to its original quarters. Planted at the water's edge, this kingcup's stems will even spread over the surface. The flowers, too, are larger, and open earlier still than those of *C. palustris*. Except for the white marsh marigold, and white *C. leptosepala*, the kingcups should be kept well away from *Primula rosea*, which has flowers of insistent pink at the same season and is better set among quiet companions, as it might be *Salix hastata* 'Wehrhahnii'. This stocky little willow slowly makes a shrub wider than high, with stout, dark brown stems, contrasting with the fat,

47

white, cotton-woolly catkins in spring. Later, as the glaucous-backed leaves start to expand, the catkins burst into fuzzy yellow candles.

Kingcups are declamatory, even brazen flowers, their petals mirror-bright like the buttercups, their relatives. Many globe flowers, though also related to buttercups, are more subtle in their appeal. *Trollius europaeus* is the common globe flower of damp, subalpine meadows, its pale citron, cupped and incurved blooms held on 60cm/24in stems in spring. Though they may be bigger, bolder, brighter, few of the hybrid cultivars with blood of the Asiatic species can rival it, though I have a soft spot for *T.* × *cultorum* 'Alabaster', its name aptly suggesting the translucent ivory tones of its globes. 'Canary Bird' is a fresh lemon-yellow, and pale yellow 'Earliest of All' usually lives up to its name. Deeper and warmer in colour are 'Fireglobe', 'Salamander' and 'Orange Princess', their colouring derived perhaps from *T. chinensis*, in which the outer petals form a bowl around the central cluster of narrow petaloid stamens like little tongues of flame; 'Golden Queen' is a familiar cultivar and 'Imperial Orange' a newer one every bit as good. The paler, clearer yellows are beautiful with 'blue' rhododendrons, the orange globe flowers with the coppery young leaves of astilbes, and vivid azaleas. The later-flowering *T. yunnanensis*, which has wide-open, not cupped flowers, of vivid yellow with green reverse, is an ideal companion for the deepest inky-black forms of *Iris chrysographes*. These moisture-loving irises, allied to the Siberian irises which flower on taller stems, have dainty blooms pencilled with gold scribblings to echo the bright *Trollius*. Later again comes *T. stenopetalus*, at midsummer; it is like a larger, paler *T. yunnanensis*.

You will need plenty of space for the bog arums, for although in their early spring season of flower they seem restrained enough, the leaves that follow are massive smooth paddles as much as 1.2m/4ft long and a third as wide. The pointed arum flowers of *Lysichiton americanus* are clear yellow; they have a curious odour, rather like cheap instant coffee, not unpleasant from a little distance. The fruits that follow are distinctly smelly. The white counterpart of this from the Far East, *L. camtschatcensis*, is a little smaller and smells nicer; hybrids between the two are creamy or primrose in flower and extremely desirable. They seed themselves freely in the soggy soil or shallow water that best suits them. The name skunk cabbage, sometimes attributed to the bog arums, in fact belongs to *Symplocarpus foetidus*, a plant as smelly as both its vernacular and botanical names suggest; but the brownish flowers squat at ground level in early spring, and the odour does not carry so far as the bog arums', so the skunk cabbage is not as antisocial as it might seem, and it has handsome leaves (finer than a cabbage's, more like a hosta's).

PRIMULAS FOR MOIST SOILS

Early summer is the season for many moisture-loving irises and primulas. Though all primulas are tempting (except the execrable manmade polyanthus and primroses with colossal, crudely coloured blooms) none is more so than *Primula sikkimensis* and its allies. Over rosettes of narrow leaves, these Asiatic species offer for our delectation fragrant, hanging bells of soft pale yellow, tender lilac or ivory, on white-powdered 60cm/24in stems. The gentle sulphur-yellow *P. sikki-mensis* itself is one of the easiest. *P. alpicola* is milk-white, or primrose in var. *luna* and lavender in *violacea*, which turns grey after pollination. The deeper wine-red *P. secundiflora* has a one-sided flower head, and is preferable, if you need this colour, to *P. waltonii* which is promiscuous, its claret tones infecting the offspring of the other species. That said, one of the most exquisite alleged *P. sikkimensis* I ever saw was presumably the result of an illicit union with *P. waltonii*, for it was of sultry lilac, dusted with creamy powder.

A true *P. sikkimensis* is the ideal companion for the black, gold-scrawled forms of *Iris chrysographes*. To digress a little, I once thought it would be entertaining to plant with the darkling iris a willow with black catkins, having been told that *Salix gracilistyla melanostachys* grew slowly to 90cm/36in or so. I gave it a place on a sloping, half-shaded bank of sandy soil, moist with springs, above the damper pond-side where the iris grew and the pale primulas. Within two years, the willow was 2m/7ft tall and 3m/10ft across; though I could not complain about the quantity of its little black catkins that turn to rust and then gold as the anthers develop.

Though it is not a sikkimensis primula, and flowers later, I want to bring in *Primula viallii* here, for it needs similar conditions, is similarly apt to be less than wholly perennial (though some losses are undoubtedly due not to early senescence but to theft, in gardens that are open to the public), and is quite as desirable. Many people, on first encountering it, do not believe it to be a primula at all, for the flowers are arranged on 45cm/18in stems in dense, poker spikes, crimson-scarlet in bud opening to light violet, a combination of colours that just avoids civil war at the stage when the upper flowers are still in tight bud and the lower fully expanded into a cylinder of mauve. Nothing goes with this primula: by which I mean that it is so striking as to merit a setting where nothing else is going on except the green of foliage and the sparkle of water. Perhaps, though, I would make an exception for *Rheum alexandrae*, choicest of rhubarbs, with glossy green leaves like broad, blunt spearheads, and an in-florescence composed of a tapering spire of large cream bracts piled one upon the other, in early summer. Or perhaps I would repeat a planting that worked well in my first garden, where the backdrop for *Primula viallii* was a willow of middling size, *Salix elaeagnos*.

A WILLOW PARASITE

The hoary willow, as *S. elaeagnos* is sometimes called, is distinguished by its dome-shaped outline and slender, dark red-brown stems set with long, needle-slender leaves, grey-green above and white-felted beneath, the silvery undersides delightfully revealed when the foliage is ruffled by a breeze. On the roots of my plant I established a colony of the parasitic toothwort, *Lathraea clandestina*. A true parasite, this has no leaves at all, first appearing very early in the year as a collection of molar-like bumps in the leafmould. Soon these creamy knobs unfold into hooded, crocus-purple flowers 5cm/2in or so in height, lasting for several weeks until masked by the willow's summer leafage. It is no more difficult to establish this fascinating thing than any other plant of more familiar habits; only a different technique is called for, and some seed. You merely scrape aside the soil until you have bared a root or two of the prospective host, wound the bark of the root and place the seeds on and around the wounded area, then cover over carefully with soil. Eighteen months later there should be flowers, and the little colony should increase rapidly thereafter. It is also possible to dig a sod of soil in which *Lathraea clandestina* is already settled, and transplant it to the roots of another host willow.

BEWARE OF CLASHES

Where the candelabra primulas are suited, they can quickly seed into great masses; you need to beware, however, the potentially vile clashes that can oocur if magenta-crimson and orange primulas meet. They can swear among themselves as violently as mauve-pink rhododendrons with orange and ochre azaleas. But keep them in their own segregated colour ranges, with supporting foliage of the right tones – as of blue-glaucous hostas with the pink and crimson candelabra primulas, acid-yellow hostas with the orange – and all will be well.

One of the earliest, and easiest, opening from late spring, is *Primula japonica*, typically candelabra in the whorled arrangement of its crimson-purple flowers, though the stems are shorter at around 45cm/18in, and the whorls correspondingly less widely spaced, than in other species of like colouring. 'Miller's Crimson' is a steady old strain of clearer tones, which, like 'Postford White', comes true from seed. A newer white strain is 'Fuji'. The whites might seem suitable to mix with orange primulas, but they often have a pink eye, adding to their charms and disqualifying them for association with sunset-coloured companions of any kind. Nameless *P. japonica* hybrids often include intermediate pinks, some of which are very pretty. Following these comes the more dignified *P. pulverulenta*, in which rich magenta-crimson flowers are set off by mealy-white stems. The Bartley strain is enchanting in a range of pale pinks from shell to salmon.

Confusingly, several candelabra primulas flowering in early summer have specific names beginning with 'b'; it is well to keep the stocky, rosy magenta, yellow-eyed *P. beesiana* and the less mealy but otherwise similar *P. burmanica* well away from clear orange *P. bulleyana*. Apart from blue-toned hostas, bold foliage contrasts come from *Rodgersia pinnata* 'Superba', with horse chestnut-like leaves of burnished bronze and plumes of rich pink in summer, reaching up to 90cm/36in. *R. aesculifolia* is a bigger plant, with bronzed leaves and tall, foaming steeples of ivory or creamy-pink flowers; *R. sambucifolia* is slighter and shorter, with distinctly pinnate leaves and milky sprays of summer flower. If you have the space, add *Rheum palmatum* 'Atrosanguineum', its great jagged leaves crimson as they emerge and remaining burgundy-backed until the tall, frothy spires of bright cherry-red open in early summer. They can grow as much as 1.8m/6ft tall, and you will need at least this much lateral space to accommodate the great pile of foliage of this ornamental rhubarb. 'Ace of Hearts' is a smaller variant that I have not grown, with crimson-tinted foliage and pale pink flower plumes.

The grassy or sword-like foliage of irises adds another outline, as it might be of the *Iris chrysographes* hybrid 'Margot Holmes', its claret flowers marked with lemon; or the *I. sibirica* cultivars 'Helen Astor' in rosy-plum with white veining, rich purple 'Emperor' and 'Caesar' or velvety 'Tropic Night'. Still pursuing the same colour theme, pink meadowsweets add summer flower of crushed strawberry or cerise. *Filipendula purpurea* flowers first, its large divided leaves forming a plinth for the flat heads of tiny vivid flowers, glowing in the shadows. A week or two later it is the turn of *F. palmata*, with no less handsome foliage and pale flowers, reaching their fullest expression in 'Elegantissima'. If a plant of 1.2m/4ft is too large, plant the dwarfer 'Nana'.

A willow of extreme silvery grace that, once established, is apt to spread rapidly by suckers in a most unwillow-like manner, *Salix exigua* makes a tall fountain of upright stems set with narrow, white-silvery leaves. (It grows equally well in dry soils in sun.) It is best set among lower companions – the smaller meadowsweet, for example, not the taller ones – so that its characteristic outline is not blurred. It is in complete contrast to the stiff, mounded outline, much broader grey leaves, and general stoutness of aspect of S. *hookeriana*, another willow that is native of western North America.

Where space is limited, S. *lanata* is a better choice, a satisfying foliage plant with quite large, rounded, silver-felted leaves; the catkins are long yellow candles. 'Stuartii' is a selection that is even more compact, with smaller leaves but larger catkins still. The slender stems of S. *repens argentea*, set with little, oblong, grey leaves, give an entirely different effect from the stocky S. *lanata*; here the catkins are nothing special. Somewhere between the broad and the narrow style of willow leaf come the neat S. *helvetica* and S. *lapponum*. These willows lose little of their grey feltiness in light shade, but are unsuited to really dark corners.

THE SUNSET SHADES

Primula bulleyana is not the only, though it is the tallest, orange candelabra primula, at 90cm/36in or so. *P. chungensis* has tangerine, red-tubed flowers borne in the usual candelabra whorls, and *P. aurantiaca* has tawny-orange flowers on 30cm/12in stems, while *P. cockburniana* is smaller again, as dainty as a candelabra can be, with rich orange flowers. Much bigger and brighter is the amazing, potent orange-vermilion 'Inverewe', a sterile hybrid that must be increased by division. These sharp colours need careful placing; ivory-white and cream assort well, as do the fresher greens and chartreuse to lime yellows, and deeper tawny or mahogany tones, as of the moisture-loving *Euphorbia palustris* or marsh spurge, *E. sikkimensis* and *E. griffithii*.

The marsh spurge starts to display its bright acid-yellow bracts from late spring on 90cm/36in stems, matching in height, though exceeding in bulk, *Primula bulleyana*; later it fades to lush green before dying down in autumnal tones of fire and flame. *Euphorbia sikkimensis* is at its best in early spring as the vivid scarlet-crimson shoots emerge; the leaves in summer are soft green and the flower heads are the usual chartreuse-yellow. With its spreading roots and tall stems it is a rather untidy plant. The very similar *E. schillingii* makes a more compact clump needing no support, and has the same sharp lime-green colouring to the bracts, above bold, dark foliage with white midribs, but is not so bright in spring. *E. griffithii*, by contrast, takes these rich tints to its early summer bracts, varying from coppery-red to tangerine, the green leaves enlivened by pink midribs. 'Fireglow' is a selection with especially bright bracts, but more than usually questing roots, particularly in light soils; 'Dixter' seems better behaved, and has luscious, dark foliage flushed with maroon as a backing for deep orange bracts.

A fern such as *Matteuccia struthiopteris*, the ostrich plume fern, adds fresh green shuttlecocks of finely cut fronds; it is a walker, spreading quickly in the moist soils it appreciates, though with more restraint than the sensitive fern, *Onoclea sensibilis*. Here the lettuce-green, arching fronds are divided into broad pinnae, which at the first onset of autumn frosts turn to russet, hence the vernacular name; it is perfectly hardy at the root. The most magnificent of water-loving ferns is the royal fern, *Osmunda regalis*, a tall plume of rich green fronds unfurling from tawny croziers and dying away in autumn in lemon and tan. The interrupted fern, *O. claytoniana*, is so named on account of the curious arrangement of the fertile and the sterile portions of the spore masses occurring along the fronds; it is as tall, at 1.2m/4ft, as the royal fern, but less bulky in maturity. The cinnamon fern, *O. cinnamomea*, is at first thickly dusted with spice-brown indumentum, emerging from downy youth to the fresh green of maturity. I like to see it in company with an unusual willow, *Salix fargesii* (*S. moupinensis* is very similar), which has large, deep glossy green, strongly veined leaves, and stout, sealing wax-red winter buds on shiny, red-brown stems. Ultimately reaching 3m/10ft or so, it is slow growing, and may be scorched by late spring frosts; so that a lightly shaded position, with its implications of shelter, suits it well. It is perfectly winter hardy in the British climate.

BOLD LEAVES AMONG THE REDS AND YELLOWS

Foliage contrast of a different kind, for this group of chartreuse, tangerine and brick-red tones, comes from *Rodgersia podophylla*, with bold, web-footed leaves that are at first copper-tinted, especially where touched for part of each day by the sun; later they turn to a deep or bronzed green before ripening to metallic coppery-mahogany in late summer. The flowers, if they happen at all, are creamy plumes, of not much account.

A vertical accent is given by the emerging spears of *Iris pseudacorus* 'Variegata', their primrose-yellow, longitudinal stripes remaining fresh and bright until the yellow flowers open in summer, when the leaves fade to green. Though its vernacular name is yellow flag, it is unrelated to the sweet flag, *Acorus calamus*, which is an aroid. With its sword-shaped leaves, this looks more like a rush than an aroid; 'Variegatus' is fresh and bright in cream striped on green. It has a much smaller relation in *A. gramineus* 'Variegatus', which looks like a dense little clumpy grass with

15cm/6in blades of dark green striated with cream; the newer 'Oborozuki' is striped with acid-yellow on green.

The plant that used to be known as *Rodgersia tabularis*, and is now called *Astilboides tabularis*, adds a softening, tender green note in its big, rounded leaves, scarcely lobed at the edges. Why it should be called by a name that suggests a resemblance to an astilbe I have no idea, for even the plumy ivory flowers borne in summer are not very like, and nothing could be more unlike the finely cut leaves of astilbe than these leafy dinner plates. At ground level, a form of meadowsweet, *Filipendula ulmaria aurea*, spreads its sharply lobed leaves in a textured carpet of bright chrome yellow – if you get the recipe right. It needs a moist soil, certainly, and a modicum of shade; too much and it turns to green, too little and the edges of the leaves will crisp in the sun. It is also essential, if the foliage is to keep its freshness all season, to decapitate the flowering spikes as soon as they show signs of reaching upwards.

The best of the variegated bamboos belongs here, for its soft-textured blades are broadly striped with citron-yellow, brightest when the plant is set in a sunny position but still quite acceptably cheerful in light shade, where it grows to about 90cm/36in. It used to be known as *Arundinaria viridistriata*, but we must now get used to calling it *Pleioblastus viridi-striatus*. If you have the space for some shrubby components, the right note for this scheme of citrus tones from lime to orange comes in the form of *Cornus alba* with greenish-yellow foliage, known simply as 'Aurea'; it thrives in moist soils like all its kin, and has reddish winter stems after the leaves have fallen. The golden alder, *Alnus incana* 'Aurea', is more inclined to make a small tree, pretty not only in fresh gamboge young leaf, the colour holding well through the summer, but also in the tawny-yellow of its bare winter stems, and coppery-red catkins in spring.

YELLOW WITH BLUE

If orange is not much to your taste, perhaps the yellow candelabra primulas will appeal more. *Primula prolifera*, with its orange buds opening to bright yellow flowers, and rich green leaves, assorts well with the group just adumbrated. According to the taxonomists, *P. helodoxa* is now part of *P. prolifera*; but as a garden plant it differs in its softer, buttery colouring from green buds, and mealy-white stems up to 90cm/36in tall, half as high again as *P. prolifera*. It has a sweet fragrance. Furthermore – which cannot be said for many of the candelabra primulas – it appears to come true from seed. The ever popular combination of blue and yellow can be had if you set this with Siberian irises, their blue just shaded with lilac or purple so that the contrast is softer than if you mix *P. helodoxa* with Himalayan blue poppies. (I did this once, and found it too potent to live with, though it was immensely popular with garden visitors.)

Since the plant breeders turned their attention to Siberian irises, there are a great many cultivars, and I shall probably be castigated for daring, often, to prefer the older kinds. 'Perry's Blue' and 'Heavenly Blue' are mid-blue, 'Ottawa' and 'Cambridge' paler, while 'Flight of Butterflies' is a newer, rich blue with white, blue-veined falls, and 'Papillon' a paler shade. White Siberian irises include 'Snow Queen' and 'White Swirl', the latter with fresh yellow at the heart of the flower, while 'Lime Heart' is white with a more acid tone at the centre. All appreciate moist soil, and sun for a few hours of the day rather than constant shade. A smaller iris of similar style and needs is *Iris versicolor*, in purple or – var. *kermesina* – rich wine-red scrawled with white. More to my taste is *I. forrestii*, very fetching in its clear lemon, tan-pencilled flowers among bright green narrow leaves. *I. kerneriana* is of similar soft citron colouring, with beautifully formed flowers, the falls narrow and recurving. At 45cm/18in it is smaller still and deserves a special position.

Summer at the Streamside

The irises that most need damp soil are the yellow flag, *Iris pseudacorus*, Japanese *I. laevigata* – which will even grow in shallow water – and the taller, flatter-flowered, calcifuge *I. ensata*, the name we must learn to use in place of the familiar *I. kaempferi*. *I. laevigata* comes in lavender and in white, always with full flowers on 45cm/18in stems; the leaves are broad light green swordblades, very decorative in 'Variegata' which is striped with cream. The two species have hybridized, resulting in 'Rose Queen', a taller plant than *I. laevigata* with well-formed dusky lilac-pink flowers. *I. ensata* flowers most freely in sun, but I have successfully grown both the purple and the white forms in a partly shaded spot in very moist soil. Modern cultivars have been developed further and further towards the large, clematis-like style of flower in which some of the grace of the wide, drooping falls is lost; but they are undoubtedly magnificent, ranging in colour from white and ethereal lavender to rich velvety violet, from almost shell pink to royal purple.

WHERE PINK DOMINATES

The way I aim to write about plants is the way I use them in the garden; that is, building upon colour themes, planning for seasonal groupings and succession, considering leaves as well as – often before – flowers. In a scheme where shades of pink dominate, the early spring flowers of a saxifrage-like plant, *Darmera peltata* (*Peltiphyllum peltatum*), many little, pale pink stars set in rounded heads on reddish, naked stems arising from rhizomes like elephants' trunks, are followed by rounded leaves like a smaller, darker version of *Astilboides tabularis*. The broad, almond green leaves of *Salix gracilistyla*, a willow of medium height and spreading habit, are preceded in spring by pussy catkins of softest grey-pink; at least, this is what I have always called *S. gracilistyla*, but I now learn it is correctly *S.* × *stipularis*. *S.* 'Eugenei', by contrast, has very narrow leaves of sombre green backed with glaucous tones, on slender upright stems bearing in early spring many small, grey-purple catkins.

Summer brings the foam-soft texture of *Astilbe*, the flowers held in upright or elegantly arching plumes over finely cut foliage. Emerging in coppery-crimson, mahogany, snuff-brown and metallic green, so textured that the visual and tactile imaginations are tantalized, the leaves alone are a delight. By the time the flowers open, the feathery image is complete. The very smallest would be swamped by *Iris ensata*, let alone by some of the robust foliage plants already proposed. Thus tiny *Astilbe glaberrima* var. *saxatilis* has bronzed, filigree foliage and miniature sprays of pink flowers, of a scale to grow with the ankle-high, dwarf form of *Iris setosa*, a pretty creature with narrow leaves in neat clumps, and butterfly flowers of slaty-blue (the ordinary *I. setosa* looks well with yellow primulas). The foliage of *Astilbe* × *crispa* 'Perkeo', 'Lilliput' and 'Gnome' is slightly reminiscent of *A. simplicifolia*, dark and crinkled like some tiny fern; they flower in late summer to autumn in shades of pink.

ASTILBES MOVING UP IN SIZE

The forms or hybrids of *Astilbe simplicifolia* are a size or two larger, forming clumps of finely dissected foliage, more or less bronzed, up to 45cm/18in wide, topped by airy, arching sprays of flower on stems of 30–45cm/12–18in. They are in scale with some of the neater hostas that have become so popular, the blue-toned *Hosta* × *tardiana* hybrids. *Astilbe* 'Bronze Elegance' has flowers of pale dawn pink, while 'Dunkellachs' is of richer salmon and 'Atrorosea' comes in warm skin-pink. 'Sprite' is a charmer in softest shell-pink and 'William Buchanan' contrasts crimson-maroon foliage with ivory sprays. 'Praecox Alba' is a clean white with greener foliage, especially subtle with *Hosta undulata undulata* of the spiralling, pointed leaves, green with a broad central stripe of ivory. *Astilbe simplicifolia* itself is shorter than these at 15cm/6in, with frilled, toothed but undissected leaves and foamy-white flowers.

The most familiar astilbes are the taller hybrids, available in varying colours and mostly reaching between 90 and 120cm (3–4ft). White astilbes tend to have green foliage: 'Bridal Veil', shorter-growing 'White Gloria', and 'Professor van der Wielen', with arching, not erect, plumes. 'Irrlicht' has unusually dark foliage for a white, while 'Snowdrift' is a promising newer cultivar derived from this, with fresh green leaves and vivid white plumes. The 'Professor' has counterparts in deep pink 'Straussenfeder' ('Ostrich Plume') and shell-pink 'Betsy Cuperus'; all three may now be hard to obtain, but should be preserved for their distinctive grace. More straightforward pinks include 'Bressingham Beauty', a good lusty grower of rich colouring, and softer pink 'Venus'. 'Peach Blossom' is a pretty clear pink, though given the marked difference in visual texture of an astilbe from the flower of a peach tree, I don't much care for this as a name. 'Amethyst' and 'Hyacinth' lean well towards the lilac-mauve tones implied by their names, and 'Jo Ophorst' is stiffer and deeper tinted.

The least effective colours in shade are the deep reds, which also tend to have the most richly coloured foliage: short 'Fanal', brighter, 'Fire', rosy 'Federsee', coral-scarlet 'Koblenz' and garnet-red 'Glow'. Several other hybrids are named after German cities: 'Dusseldorf' in cerise and 'Köln' ('Cologne') in pink, with stark white 'Deutschland'. 'Rheinland' is short and neat in bright pink and 'Europa' a well-endowed paler pink of much the same height, 60cm/24in or so. All the pinks, from shell to amethyst, and the whites, look charming in a streamside glade with the white trunks of birches and the graceful leafage of the bamboo *Sinarundinaria nitida* beyond. The same setting would become *Aruncus dioicus*, the goat's beard, a handsome plant something like a supremely well-fed astilbe, with a great pile of finely cut leaves, over which at midsummer huge plumes of countless, tiny, creamy flowers last, alas, only for a short while before turning brown. The goat's beard comes in male and female forms, the males more feathery in flower, the females quite ornamental in seed but apt to reproduce themselves all too freely. There is an exceptionally fetching form called 'Kneiffii', half the size of the type and with still more finely divided leaves composed of thread-fine green segments.

SCOPE FOR STRONG CONTRASTS

Pretty though such a scheme of cool greenery, pink and white may be, there is nothing to compare for freshness in the moist and shady garden with *Primula florindae*, the giant cowslip of Tibet. The big leaves make an effective blanket against weeds, and are overtopped in summer (after the main primula season) by tall stems 60–90cm/24–36in high, each bearing at the apex a nodding cluster of pale yellow bells dusted with white and as delectably scented as the humbler European cowslip. It seeds itself around most obligingly, but sometimes, and perhaps vexatiously, runs to art shades of rust and copper and tan, buff and pale tangerine. Beautiful as these are when examined individually, they can corrupt the integrity of a stand of the pale citron type.

If you like emphatic contrasts, and can keep the red intruders at bay, emulate Graham Thomas's grouping of *P. florindae* with purple *Lobelia* × *gerardii* 'Vedrariensis'. Softer harmonies come from the purer blue of *L. siphilitica*, or from the water forget-me-not, *Myosotis palustris*, which spreads its pale blue flowers along the streamside or pool's edge in early summer; its more compact selection 'Mermaid' has a longer flowering season. The brooklime, *Veronica beccabunga*, is a British native waterplant with fleshy leaves and spikes of blue flowers; a pleasant thing in an unemphatic way.

The astilbe season continues into late summer with *Astilbe chinensis pumila*, an energetic spreader if happy, making a ferny carpet topped by tight, branching spikes of bright mauve seen on close inspection to be touched with scarlet, rather as shot silk suddenly gives glints of unexpected contrast; though the astilbe spikes, nubbly in bud opening to a stiff fuzzy plume, are textured like no shot silk I ever saw. Its much larger cousin *A. chinensis taquetii* 'Superba', is three times as tall, at 1.2m/ 4ft, its late-summer spires of flaunting magenta on sepia stems under-pinned by dark, wrinkled leaves, less angular and sharply cut than the little fellow's. Pale citron, as of *Lysimachia ciliata*, is recommended by Graham Thomas as an emollient; more effective, I think, is to revel in the astilbe's assertive purple as Christopher Lloyd does, setting it with pink hydrangeas, the double blue *Geranium pratense* called 'Plenum Coeruleum', and *Rosa glauca* (which in shade, as I shall later attempt to persuade you, is a most fetching shade of dove-grey.) But the rose, of course, must not have a soggy soil about its roots.

Christopher Lloyd's previous ploy with this astilbe was to pair it with the strong yellows of *Ligularia* × *hessei* and the shorter *L.dentata* 'Desdemona'. These are as content in a squelchy soil as any astilbe, but other difficulties, he recounts, manifested themselves: slugs, and the sheer discomfort of two fierce colours fighting it out. For the same reason, I cannot do with Graham Thomas's suggested companions for the ligularias, red-purple *Lobelia* × *gerardii* 'Vedrariensis' or purple phloxes. But Mr Thomas is often acclaimed, and with reason, as one of the most sensitive gardeners of our time; so it is only right to pass on such suggestions so that you may try them for yourself.

ONE-COLOUR GROUPS WITH YELLOW DAISIES

My own preference with these and other ligularias is to set them with plenty of cool greenery and some sharper yellows, so that their flaunting egg-yolk or saffron daisies come as the climax in a single-colour range. Both *Ligularia* × *hessei* and 'Gregynog Gold' are tall – 1.8m/6ft in rich damp soil – and have great heart-shaped leaves below a broad spire of summer flower. 'Desdemona' and 'Othello' are shorter, though still bulky plants; curiously, they are very similar, both with big, kidney-shaped leaves of bronzed green backed with rich plum-maroon, and wide clusters of large orange daisies. I should have expected 'Desdemona', a blonde, to be green leaved and paler in flower, but there you are. *L.stenocephala* flowers several weeks earlier; similar in flower, it has large, rounded, tooth-edged leaves.

Of the species and cultivars with rounded leaves, I have a great weakness for *L. veitchiana*, for the 1.5m/5ft flowering spike is composed of clearer yellow daisies assembled into a narrower plume. They are immensely popular with butterflies, and unlike the purple of buddlejas their colouring does not clash with the tawny tortoiseshells and commas. *L. wilsoniana* is similar. Even more desirable is *L. macrophylla*, which flowers later, towards the end of summer, its narrow spires of yellow daisies soaring over a rosette of grey-green leaves shaped like some huge dock.

If a plant that stands man-high in flower is too tall for you, there is a smaller species in *L. hodgsonii*, which has toothed, kidney-shaped leaves and clusters of daisies that vary in colour from canary-yellow to warm orange; deeper-toned flowers go with leaves bronze-tinted on the reverse. Another species, *L. przewalskii*, has foliage deeply cut into segments, so that it gains in elegance what it lacks in boldness of leaf. The basic leaf outline is triangular; the flowering stems are black, and the narrow spike of clear yellow daisies reaches 1.8m/6ft. 'The Rocket' is a popular, and for once aptly named, selection.

Any one of these ligularias, according to taste and available space, could join the group already adumbrated in which yellow primulas are joined by spurges, irises and the yellow-leaved dogwood. The yellow flag, *Iris pseudacorus*, is an invasive self-seeder, but handsome in bright yellow flower and strong green sword leaves; a softer colour, pale citron, belongs to the curiously named *bastardii*, while 'Golden Queen' is an unmarked rich yellow selection. All should have their seedheads cut off before the seeds fall, or you will quickly have nothing but irises, and the wild form at that. 'Holden Clough' is a hybrid with yellow flowers veined and scribbled with brown.

A different style of yellow daisy from the ligularias, perfectly content in a darkish corner with stodgy soil, is *Rudbeckia fulgida* 'Goldsturm', one of the best of this group of canary-yellow, black-eyed Susans, the pet name deriving from the central black cone in the wide-eyed flowers. There is a double rudbeckia, if you will, *R. nitida* 'Goldquelle' – but as the charm of the coneflowers lies precisely in the contrast of ray florets and cone, a double is a waste of space. In the very tall 'Herbstsonne', over 2m/7ft when in flower, the high central cone is green in contrast to the long, clear yellow rays. With *Inula hookeri* we have yet another version of yellow daisy, a fast spreader with rather coarse foliage, valued because of the sharp, unripe-lemon of its fine-rayed daisies, which open from white-whiskery, spiralling buds.

Given ample space and a willingness to curb its territorial ambitions, you could add the yellow-striped *Spartina pectinata* 'Aureomarginata', a tall and graceful grass. If this is too invasive for you – and it must be said that in moist soil it travels at an alarming rate, so that you may be speared by its insistent sharp runners at some distance from the original clump – then the hardy papyrus, *Cyperus eragrostis*, might do instead. The grassy green leaves form a splayed rosette from which arise the flowering stems bearing green umbels decorated with jutting green leaves arranged like the spokes of a wheel, but of different lengths. The galingale, *C. longus*, is taller, at 1.2m/4ft, and has browner flower heads to echo the coppery tones of *Rodgersia* leaves. Warmer, sharper tones of bright orange come from the moisture-loving lilies, *Lilium pardalinum* and *L. superbum*, both with tall stems bearing vermilion-orange, spotted turk's caps in summer.

COPPERY TONES

The coppery terracotta *Iris fulva* is of the right colour for this scheme, but will need placing where larger plants cannot choke it out, for it is only 60cm/24in tall. It flowers after other damp-loving irises, in high summer; the only other of this type to share its season is its own hybrid, *I.* ×

fulvala, in which the velvety fox-red colouring is muted to madder-purple with a yellow centre. Sunset and fiery colours belong also to some of the monkey musks such as 'Whitecroft Scarlet', which is on the orange side of red, or 'Wisley Red' in deeper velvety tones; 'Shep' is canary-yellow freckled with tan, and 'Inshriach Crimson' deep blood-red. Different growers give different recipes for success with these little *Mimulus* hybrids, some recommending full sun, some part shade; though all but one agree on the need for moist soil. My best successes with the monkey musks have always been in damp soil in fleeting or dappled shade.

The taller, sticky-leaved *M. lewisii*, usually rose-pink, has a warm orange-red variant called 'Sunset' which may no longer be available, though I was growing it only a few years ago and thoughtlessly lost it in moving from one garden to another. *M. cardinalis* in red (or sometimes yellow) is taller still, at 90cm/36in. Be warned that *M. luteus*, fetching though it is with its bright canary-yellow flowers, is a rampant sprawler in wet soil; the related *M. guttatus* is better behaved, and its yellow, monkey-faced flowers are usually splashed with mahogany, so much so in the cultivar 'A. T. Johnson' that only a yellow margin remains. 'Hose in Hose' is an unusual shade of soft tan with one flower inside the other.

For a real eyeful of hot colours, these yellow and orange flowers are accompanied by the scarlet lobelias, hybrids of the North American cardinal flower *Lobelia cardinalis* and of the Texan-Mexican *L. fulgens*, which has beetroot-dark leaves. The real *L. cardinalis* has green leaves topped by a tall spike of vivid sealing wax-red flowers in late summer; its most famous offspring is 'Queen Victoria', with the richly coloured foliage of the Mexican parent but flowers of no less refulgent a scarlet. 'Bees Flame' is similar. These older hybrids are said to be a little tender (though I believe many losses are due to slug damage in spring, not frost damage in winter); newer hybrids from Canada have been bred specifically for hardiness, and some excellent things have resulted from the search for a fuller, richer spike of larger flowers. In the scarlet range, there are 'Will Scarlett', 'Brightness' and 'Huntsman' to choose from.

COMPANIONS FOR LOBELIAS

We have been dealing with a good many muscular, space-hogging plants, so it is a relief with the lobelias to come back to something of more modest size, suitable for any garden with a patch of moist soil (indeed, they will do in an ordinary border so long as it is not too dry). What other plants of restrained growth may we assort with the lobelias? A pretty, variegated sedge, *Carex siderosticta* 'Variegata', has broad, short blades

heavily striped with cream, just the emollient needed for the fulgurant
lobelias; lemon day lilies add fragrance. Related to the yellow ligularias,
Senecio smithii is a plant from southern Chile and the Falkland Islands,
where it cowers from the wind in wet ditches. The leaves are shaped like a
dock's, but are a richer, shining green, and the fat daisies in 1.2m/4ft
spires are white, not yellow.

For another note of green and white, add *Houttuynia cordata*. Though it
is quite a spreader in moist soil, it is lowly enough to do little harm, and its
dark green, pointed, heart-shaped leaves are pungently scented, rather
like Seville orange peel with a hint of something throat-catching behind.
The single-flowered form is rather insignificant, but the double 'Plena',
with its little cones of white in summer, is pretty. There is a variegated
form called 'Chameleon', which achieves the 'best' – that is, the most
hectic – colouring of yellow and green and pink and red in sun. I would
not give it garden room, myself.

Back to lobelias, for something more dignified. These also offer
another range of colour, from pink to deep ruby-red, assorting with the
astilbes that follow crimson candelabra primulas among white-
variegated or glaucous hostas. From palest to deepest in colour, 'Russian
Princess' is a clear pink, 'Cherry Ripe' cerise, and 'Dark Crusader' a
sumptuous velvety garnet-crimson with dark foliage. These are shades
that assort well with the pink forms of bee balm, *Monarda didyma*: clear
rose 'Croftway Pink', candy-pink 'Melissa' with deeper buds, or paler
'Beauty of Cobham', in which the whorls of hooded flowers are held in
purplish calyces. The newer Zodiac series promises well: violet
'Aquarius', deep purple 'Scorpio', rosy 'Pisces', and deep pink 'Libra'
with tawny bracts. 'Capricorn', is crimson-purple, and another good
richly coloured bergamot is 'Mahogany', with very dark bracts.
'Prärienacht' ('Prairie Night') is of *M. fistulosa* extraction and less insistent
on moist soil; the flowers are, as the name suggests, rich purple, though
on the redder side of the colour than a midnight sky. The colours of
Mimulus ringens, a slender musk, are those of earlier night, a cool blue
from which all the but the last lingering red of sunset has gone.

The purple loosestrifes, *Lythrum salicaria* and its cultivars, grow in the
wild in boggy soils: 'purple' suggests something more restrained than
their assertive shocking pink, as in 'Brightness', 'Lady Sackville' and
'Robert', or vivid magenta of 'The Beacon' and 'Feuerkerze'
('Firecandle'). *L. virgatum* is more slender, and shorter at 90cm/36in; 'The
Rocket' is well named, evoking the aspiring slender candles characteristic
of the lythrums, while 'Rose Queen' has less of purple in her pink tones.
They last long in summer, and after the flowers fade the plant often dies

away in autumn in bonfire colours. I like to soothe the exclamatory spikes of *Lythrum* with *Polygonum campanulatum* (which some botanists are now calling *Persicaria campanulata*), an overground colonizer spreading a carpet of soft-textured, pointed, ribbed leaves backed with fawn felt, over which 90cm/36in stems bear branching heads of many tiny blush-pink bells for weeks, from summer into autumn. It is at its best in light shade.

Most of the knotweeds, indeed, whether you call them *Polygonum* or *Persicaria*, prefer a moist soil in light shade. Some are too big and aggressive to include here, belonging in the wilder parts of the garden; but others, with bottle-brush or poker spikes, are better behaved and long-lasting in flower. Following the bistort, *Polygonum bistorta,* which flowers in early summer, the rather neater *P. milletii* bears its crimson spikes over a long season. *P. bistorta carneum* is of the same style in pink, good with a medium-sized hosta such as *Hosta lancifolia*, which has dark green, pointed leaves and rich lilac-violet flowers. The poker flowers of *P. amplexicaule* are more tapering, and range in colour from the white of 'Album' and blush of *oxyphyllum* to the half-height (60cm/24in), crimson-red 'Inverleith' and deep ruby *atrosanguineum* or the brighter 'Firetail'. 'Arun Gem' has, instead of vertical spikes, little tassels of shocking pink nodding gracefully on 60cm/24in stems; they turn disgracefully to brown on fading. All the form of *P. amplexicaule* make generous clumps of dock-like leaves.

Summer into Autumn

Late summer is the season of a most unlikely candidate for the damp garden, *Artemisia lactiflora*. Unusually for a genus of sun-baskers with silvery foliage and insignificant flowers, this is a lush perennial with tall plumes of creamy flowers on 1.8m/6ft stems over rich green, sharply lobed leaves. Its colouring fits it for associations in which blue, violet or yellow flowers feature, but it will look merely grubby near cleaner whites. Several monkshoods flower at the same season and their sultry indigo or navy blue is just right for the artemisia. It is a matter of choice whether you grow the bugbanes, *Cimicifuga*, and the monkshoods with pink and crimson and purple flowers or with the cooler shades of yellow; the white or ivory of *Cimicifuga* and the dusky or violet-blue of most monkshoods assort equally well with either.

Aconitum napellus is the common monkshood of Europe and Asia, a poisonous plant also known as wolf's bane, which conjures the imagination straight back to the middle ages. It is tall, at 1.5m/5ft, with light indigo–purple flowers (or soft skin–pink in *carneum*) of the typical hooded, secretive shape, in late summer. Richer colours, deriving from this and other species, belong to shorter-growing hybrid cultivars such as violet-blue 'Bressingham Spire' and midnight-dark 'Spark's Variety'; 'Newry Blue' is of marine-blue colouring and as tall as *A.napellus* itself. 'Blue Sceptre' and 'Bicolor' are both blue and white, and 'Ivorine' is a delicious, shorter creamy-ivory, flowering earlier, in summer. They all have good foliage, polished dark green and deeply cut. The leaves of *A. carmichaelii* are no less handsome, which is well, since you have to wait until early autumn for the flowers, typically hooded but borne in short spikes and of paler amethyst-blue. 'Barker's Variety' is a true-seeding selection and 'Arendsii' is of richer violet-blue, very fine with *Polygonum amplexicaule* or, in a different setting, with *Kirengeshoma palmata*. 'Kelmscott' is another tall (180cm/6ft) deep blue.

The cimicifugas mostly have attractive, ferny leaves, but with one possible exception would not be grown as foliage plants alone: the slender, white bottlebrushes are elegant in their late summer or autumn season, bringing lightness to cool, shady corners of the garden. The first to flower is *Cimicifuga racemosa*, its pure white, branching spikes on 1.5m/5ft stems opening over divided, fresh green foliage; good with pink meadowsweets and *Hosta fortunei hyacinthina*. The slightly later-flowering var. *cordifolia* has, as its name implies, less ferny foliage; the stiff spikes are formed of brown buds that open to flowers of not so clean a white, though the green-washed cream of some forms is quietly appealing.

Flowering a little later again, *Cimicifuga dahurica* differs in its wider, open-branching sprays of white flowers on 1.8m/6ft stems over dissected leaves. Two of the finest species flower in autumn: *C. simplex*, the smallest of the genus, and *C. ramosa*. This last has ample, much divided foliage forming a ferny plinth for the 2.10m/7ft stems that branch into a foam of pure white, narrow bottlebrushes each 30cm/12in or more in length, contrasting with the deep blue helmets of *Aconitum carmichaelii*. Even more desirable is the dark-leaved form 'Atropurpurea', but this, for the best foliage colour, needs an open position with moist soil; too much shade will fade the sultry metallic tones to a rather dirty green. No doubt, even though it promises to be duskier still, the same will be true of 'Brunette'. *Cimicifuga simplex* has two graceful cultivars, 'White Pearl', its snowy, arching bottlebrushes turning to handsome, lime-green seed heads, and the beautiful 'Elstead Variety', last of all to flower and very distinct in its purple stems and buds opening to creamy-white wands enlivened by pink stamens.

KAFFIR LILIES

Among the last flowers of the season are the satiny-crimson or pink flags of *Schizostylis coccinea*, the kaffir lily. This South African irid thrives in any fertile soil that is not too dry, preferably where the atmosphere remains moist also; but it does very well in a damp soil or even in shallow water, flowering freely in light shade. The first to flower, as early as the end of summer, is rosy-pink 'Tambara', followed by the old favourite 'Mrs Hegarty' in paler pink. Paler still is 'Pallida', the nearest to white until the true albino *alba* was introduced; in this the crystalline whiteness of the petals is enhanced by a green heart. Its only fault is that the flowers are rather small, in contrast to such modern cultivars as pink 'Jennifer' and 'Sunrise' or clear-toned 'Zeal Salmon'.

Now that we know the kaffir lily does throw albinos from time to time, we find new white cultivars reaching the market; 'Snow Maiden' is the name given to one such, which I have not yet grown, and it has sported back to the pale 'Maiden's Blush'; both are said to have an exceptionally long flowering season in late autumn and winter. 'Professor Barnard' is a deeper sulky pink. Closing the kaffir lily season are pink 'November Cheer' and 'Viscountess Byng'. The original wild kaffir lily is deep glistening crimson; 'Major' is an old cultivar with wider, brighter flowers and 'Cardinal' is a newer scarlet selection. All increase fast in damp soil and can be split yearly, if need be, to make new clumps. Even a newly purchased plant in a container may well bear several crowns and give you six, a dozen or more for the price of one. If you like positive, clean-cut contrasts, set the scarlet kaffir lilies near the evergreen water figwort, *Scrophularia auriculata* 'Variegata', which has deckle-edged leaves heavily splashed with cream, decreasing in size as they ascend the 60cm/24in stems; and be sure to deflower the figwort rigorously to keep the foliage fresh.

For Wider Spaces

At intervals in this chapter I have mentioned plants of generous dimensions or territorial ambitions; but I have yet to give word-space to the real thugs and giants of the moist, part-shaded garden. *Gunnera manicata* is surely the largest perennial that can be grown in cool, temperate gardens, a massive plant with huge, rough, rhubarb-like leaves on rasping, prickly stems, and flowerheads like broad brushes of many tiny, red-brown flowers. The leaves on a mature plant in rich, moist soil can stand tall enough for you to shelter beneath. It is tolerant even of jungle-dark shade, where indeed its imposing bulk looks singularly appropriate. *Inula magnifica* needs a boggy soil and a less shaded spot than the *Gunnera*, if it is to produce its 15cm/6in wide, bright yellow, narrow-rayed daisies in late summer on 1.8m/6ft stems. The leaves are broad and ample, smothering anything that ventures within their wide reach.

With either of these plants, the huge grass, *Miscanthus sacchariflorus*, can hold its own, the long arching leaves held on bamboo-like 3m/10ft stems forming non-invasive clumps. At that height, it is more of a maker than a taker of shade; its value lies equally in the sound and movement of its rustling, fluttering blades, in contrast to the static monumentality of the *Gunnera*.

Both moisture and some shade are essential to *Senecio tanguticus*, for even in the wettest soil the sharply cut leaves wilt disconsolately in hot sun. The roots, which look very like Jerusalem artichokes, are busily invasive; the flowers are tall, handsome steeples of yellow daisies turning to blond fluff in seed. Even more aggressive is the winter heliotrope, *Petasites fragrans*, and its kin. However tempting it may seem when bearing its dense heads of mauve, fragrant daises in late winter, the winter heliotrope is likely to be cursed when its roots have invaded other plants. By roadsides it makes wide sweeps of rounded, handsome foliage; let it stay there, for in all but the largest gardens it becomes a worse weed than anything it may have been intended to smother. The butter bur, *P. hybridus*, is a size larger and just as far-reaching; the flowers are white in a ruff of pale green.

Largest of all and correspondingly most threatening is *P. japonicus giganteus*, with leaves that may be as much as 1.2m/4ft across; the green and white flowers emerge from the bare soil in early spring. Having warned you of the risk you may be taking if you plant any *Petasites*, I must admit that they may have their place. In a garden I once cared for, there was a sloping bank beneath trees, always soggy from unchannelled springs and too dark for most plants to thrive. *P. japonicus* did a fine job there, and being bounded by stony paths was relatively easy to keep from escaping to the more manicured parts of the garden.

INVASIVE GRASSES

There are thugs among the ornamental grasses, too. *Glyceria maxima* 'Variegata' will grow in anything from shallow water to a dry border, but is at its best in damp soil, where it will fast grow into clumps of graceful, cream-striped leaves, flushed with pink in spring and early summer, and again in autumn. It looks well with the larger astilbes in pink and white, or in a planting on the grander scale it might accompany *Eupatorium purpureum*, which bears its wide, flattish heads of fluffy, old-rose flowers in autumn on dark stems as tall as a basketball player. 'Atropurpureum' is a duskier and slightly stockier selection.

The gardener's garters, *Phalaris arundinacea picta* 'Picta', is invasive also, but can be forgiven for its white-striped blades, lighting up shady corners. There are in fact two variegated forms, the other – 'Aureovariegata' – with creamy-primrose striations, quite distinct early in the year but slowly fading to near-white through summer. Both turn to parchment in winter. *Carex riparia* 'Variegata' is a sedge, not a grass; it is dainty and graceful, but invasive, with long, narrow leaves striped or wholly white, and spikes of brown at midsummer. At only 60cm/24in, it is half the height of the gardener's garters.

COLOURED WINTER STEMS

You will need a good deal of space to do justice to the willows and dogwoods that are grown primarily for their coloured winter stems. They enjoy boggy soil, and will grow in shade that is not too dense, so long as it is the shade from deciduous trees, so that in winter the low rays of the sun may light up the coral-red, yolk-yellow, black or acid-green stems. Both the willows and dogwoods are the better for being quite ruthlessly pruned in spring, to ensure a supply of the young shoots which give the brightest colour. Whereas the dogwoods (which are described in Chapter VIII) are best stooled – that is cut virtually to ground level in spring – the willows are often better pollarded and allowed to form a short trunk from which spring the long wands that you annually cut back. This has the advantage of allowing you to grow other plants up to the willow trunk, making for more interest in spring and summer than the rather boring leafage of the dogwoods.

With one or two exceptions, the coloured-stem willows are definitely better massed, though even a singleton, if carefully placed, makes for winter interest in the damp garden where most plants go to ground during the colder months. Sheaves of red and yellow stems are provided by forms of *Salix alba*; orange-scarlet 'Britzensis' and yellow *vitellina* are two that are readily available. Of several willows with purple, white-bloomed stems, *S. irrorata* has the most alluring name, meaning 'bedewed'; it is very similar in garden effect to *S. daphnoides* and *S. acutifolia*, of which 'Blue Streak' is a good named selection. You will need a lot of space for *S.* × *laurina*, which has blood of *S. caprea* in it and shows tremendous hybrid vigour, producing red-purple, bloomy stems and an abundance of snowy-white catkins in midwinter. *S.* 'Erythroflexuosa', on the other hand, needs encouragement to produce plenty of its bright yolk-yellow ringlets: the stems are twisted like a smaller, brighter version of the familiar *S. matsudana* 'Tortuosa'. In *S. babylonica* 'Crispa', it is the leaves that are curled, like little ram's horns, on semi-weeping stems. I have found it more than usually susceptible to fungal disease causing dieback of whole branches, and it has no particular charms in winter.

With the willows and dogwoods, if you want to build on the winter theme, both *Kerria japonica* and *Leycesteria formosa*, not commonly thought of as damp-loving plants, will do well if not actually in a bog, and add brighter pea-green stems in winter; while *Stephanandra tanakae*, after its maple-like leaves fall in autumn, reveals the cosy fox-brown of its stems. *S. incisa* is smaller, and its slender stems are markedly zigzag; the crisp little leaves are smaller and neater, too. Both are very fresh in their summer greenery, though the off-white flowers in little flat heads are hardly showy.

IV

The Native Woodland

In chapter I, I assumed that you had a garden where the shade to grow your woodland plants had to be created. Here I am making the opposite assumption: that you have an area of existing, wild woodland that you want to tame, but not transform, because you like its character and do not want to alter it. As before, I must qualify that word 'woodland': it could be no more than a copse, or conceivably just one tree that is already large enough to form a canopy and beneath which some sort of community of native plants has already formed. Just what those plants are will vary from area to area, with soil and climate and aspect; and, of course, will vary still more from country to country. In suggesting ways to embellish without betraying your wild woodland, I shall not restrict myself to plants that are native to any one country (I write, of course, from an English standpoint) but will include any that, to me, seem capable of settling into a natural community of plants without violating its integrity. Ultimately, the decisions you reach will be subjective, arrived at ideally by studying the natural associations that already exist, or that you see in other, similar areas of woodland, and building on them.

Before you can plant anything, you need to assess the site itself as well as the plant community. Do you need to let in more light? This can be done by selective felling, in a group of trees: but before you bring out the chain saw, look at the shapes of the trees and their state of health; consider whether the remaining trees have flexible or brittle wood; bear in mind the direction of the prevailing wind, and whether at any season the wind is likely to come from another quarter. Remember, too, that you must be able to get at your plants, for even a 'natural' woodland will need some maintenance; so you will need to devise a system of paths. Another way

69

of letting in more light is to remove selected branches, rather than whole trees. Letting in more light will usually let in more rain as well, which is likely to benefit your underplantings; the soil beneath a dense canopy can become extremely dry.

Some trees can be brushed up to make a taller trunk, raising the canopy; others can be carefully thinned. Low-branching trees such as, for example, many maples, or multi-stemmed trees, seldom benefit from brushing up. But there may be some large shrubs that could be turned into small trees, by removing branches at ground level to leave just one, or a few, main stems with a spreading canopy above. You will be pruning not only to let in more light, if it is needed, but also to enhance the branching structure of your trees: do not rush it, but carefully consider each tree as an individual, visualizing its appearance after removing the branches you decide are likely to be superfluous, before you actually apply the saw. You also need to bear in mind how each cut will influence the future growth of the tree. This applies just as much to mature trees from which you are removing the clutter as to young ones which you hope to guide into the mature form you desire. The study of your woodland with thinning and pruning in mind should be done in winter, when you can see the whole branch structure of the trees. If you can so long restrain yourself, a whole year should elapse before you do anything rash, so that you also have a summer to consider the canopy when the trees are in leaf.

Consider, too, as you wander through your wildwood, any natural incidents such as streams or springs and rocks, as well as trunks worth revealing for their handsome, buttressed roots or attractive bark, or colonies of mosses or ferns; keep what you can as features, and allow them to influence the design of your paths. Ascertain the type of soil: its level of acidity or alkalinity, its underlying structure – clay, sand, loam – and whether it tends to dryness or is kept moist by underground water or springs. Most shade-loving plants do best on mildly acid soils but will grow well enough where the soil reaction is neutral; some need it decidely acid; few actually demand alkaline soils. The soil under conifers is usually acid and sometimes sour, and the shade is very dense; under oaks, rowans, maples and birch soil is usually somewhat acid; ash and beech often indicate an alkaline soil. The plants that have already established themselves will give further pointers to soil type.

By now you should have a reasonable idea in your mind of the *genius loci* of your woodland: that amalgam of factors which go to make it what it is, and which must be respected if you want to keep it looking natural. It is time to start clearing, so that you can make such additions to the understorey as you think appropriate. It is a waste of time to try to clear the whole area, unless it is small enough to maintain right from the start; generally, it is better just to clear the space for one season's planting and let those new inhabitants of the woodland settle in and grow large enough to be self-supporting, and weed-suppressing, before you tackle another area. Otherwise, you may find that what you thought was a nicely bramble-free copse returns, after twelve months, to something as wild as before, with all your treasures lost beneath the renewed undergrowth.

SPRING IN THE WILDWOOD

The chief season for woodland gardens is spring. Some of the plants you can add without destroying the untamed nature of a wildwood have already been suggested in Chapter II: wood anemones, celandines, primroses, violets. The ordinary white or pink-flushed *Anemone nemorosa* is the one to start with, or perhaps one of the vigorous blues such as 'Robinsoniana'. Wood sorrel, *Oxalis acetosella*, is another little white or blush-flowered woodlander that spreads freely; the smooth trefoil leaves are a fresh green. From western North America comes *O. oregana*, a larger plant with leaves like a big, smooth clover, and good-sized, deep pink flowers over the expanding foliage in spring. The common celandine, *Ranunculus ficaria*, should be acceptable enough here, and you could add its giant form 'Major'. The wild primrose, *Primula vulgaris*, varies slightly in colour from cream to butter-yellow, and comes also in white; the bright colours of highly bred primroses, to my eye at least, have no place here, and if you once introduce them you will find all manner of horrid seedlings of muddy magenta-pink threatening to overrun the lovely pale wildling. Sweet violets in blue and white can look after themselves, and so can the dog violets in paler blue, *Viola riviniana* and *V. canina*; they have no scent, but spread carpets of colour among the trees. *V. rupestris rosea* is a mid-pink violet which is also an energetic colonizer; the bright yellow *V. pensylvanica* and *V. glabella* can also cope with semi-wild conditions and spread by seed. You could add the purple-leaved *V. labradorica purpurea*, another self-seeding spreader; it makes a pretty contrast among clumps of the common snowdrop, *Galanthus nivalis*. You can hasten the spread of your snowdrops if you lift some of the clumps just after flowering, divide them, and distribute the bulbs to clump up again in their new stations.

Bluebells, currently called *Hyacinthiodes non-scripta*, hardly need any assistance to increase; they seed very freely, as anyone who has tried to remove them from an area where they are unwanted will have discovered, for the seedlings will keep coming up for years. The pale blue, starry-flowered *Scilla messenaica*, though less than half the size, seems just as ready to spread a haze of colour in spring. The white-flowered, garlic-smelling *Allium triquetrum* flowers much later; it is almost as free-seeding, and very pretty with nodding, green-striped bells on triangular stems. Much choicer than this is the Lent lily, *Narcissus pseudonarcissus*, which flowers in early spring; typically, it has a soft yellow trumpet and paler, rather twisted perianth segments, and it is invariably much smaller than the gross modern cultivars. In the wild it seems to grow equally well in the open, in meadows – often near the hedges and in moist valleys – as in deciduous woodland. Most crocuses, on the other hand, need the sun; but the free-spreading *Crocus tomasinianus* is happy in light shade where its little, slender, buff and mauve flowers are borne just as generously as in the open. Variants in deeper purple, red-purple or white seem every bit as easy.

Lily of the valley, if it likes you, will quickly spread into a mat of fresh green leaves among which the little white bells appear in late spring. The related *Maianthemum bifolium* is shorter, and has a white, fluffy flower in place of the bells; but it is no less energetic a spreader in cool soils. The taller Solomon's seals are also well able to look after themselves. Largest of all is *Polygonatum biflorum*, which in cool, humus-rich soil may reach 1.5m/5ft, with fresh green leaves and alabaster bells in proportion in late spring. The European *P. multiflorum* is half the size; more often seen is its hybrid with *P. odoratum*, known unimaginatively as *P. × hybridum*. As with almost all Solomon's seals, the stems arch gracefully, and beneath the horizontally poised leaves little clusters of green-washed white bells hang in late spring. The odd one out is *P. verticillatum*, a taller plant in which the narrow leaves are held in spaced whorls on the erect stems; the little bells hang beneath each whorl. *Smilacina racemosa* is a related plant forming good clumps of foliage very like the ordinary Solomon's seal, topped by upright spikes of creamy, fluffy flowers with a delicious fragrance; the lesser *S. stellata* is not half so good, and spreads energetically in light soils.

EASY FERNS AND GRASSES

Ferns, and fern-leaved plants, contrast well with the Solomon's seals. In the wildwood, the ferns that spread by underground rhizomes into a colony of fronds can be allowed their head in a way that might be unacceptable in more gardened areas. Some ferns will settle down in dry, rooty areas that could otherwise be difficult to fill; these will be described later, in Chapter VIII. The oak fern and the beech fern, respectively *Gymnocarpium dryopteris* and *Phegopteris connectilis*, are small and fragile-seeming; they have already been proposed as suitable inhabitants of a cool and shady border of choice woodlanders, but as quite rapid runners they could as well be planted in wilder surroundings. *G. robertianum* is another dainty, spreading fern with fresh green, lacy fronds. Other filigree ferns of running tendencies include *Hypolepis millefolium*, a New Zealander that looks like a diminutive bracken and is almost as invasive; and the very similar *Dennstaedtia punctilobula*.

The hard fern, *Blechnum spicant*, is a clump former, and a very pleasing one with leathery, ladder-like fronds of dark green radiating around the erect fertile fronds. It will not grow on lime soils. Although it does not run, the hart's tongue fern, *Phyllitis scolopendrium*, can increase quite fast by spores; the broad curved blades are in striking contrast to the lacier ferns. The polypody, *Polypodium vulgare*, is another fern that is easy and tough, a spreader with matt, divided fronds which come new in summer and last through the winter.

The lady fern, *Athyrium filix-femina*, is delicate in appearance, with finely cut, pale green fronds; but as tough and adaptable as they come, and happy to spread around by casting sporelings, often in the most unlikely places. The male fern, *Dryopteris filix-mas*, also grows wild throughout the cool, temperate regions of the northern hemisphere, and earned its name from the more robust, sombre appearance of its evergreen, shuttlecock fronds (which die away in winter in exposed areas). It is as ready as the lady fern to put up with drought but is at its best in moist, not boggy, soil. Both the male and the lady ferns run to fancy forms, which do not belong in the wildwood. But other species of *Dryopteris*, such as the broad buckler fern, *D. dilatata*, are easy; this one has spreading, broad, deeply cut fronds. The hay-scented buckler fern, *D. aemula*, is so called from the aroma of the fading fronds; it is an elegant, evergreen fern of more upright habit than the broad buckler fern. There are more, but I must keep the best for my Eden in woodland, where I will also describe the shield ferns.

By way of contrast to the lacy ferns, bold rounded leaves are an obvious choice. Less so, perhaps, are some of the grasses and sedges. Mr Bowles's golden grass, *Milium effusum* 'Aureum', is welcome wherever you plant it; its soft butter-yellow blades are charming among darker greens, and it seeds itself mildly. It is not really a ground-cover plant, *pace* Graham Thomas; but the woodrush, *Luzula sylvatica* (*L. maxima*), is a determined spreader forming a thick carpet of broad, hairy blades under trees; its variegated form, in which the leaf margins are discreetly edged with cream, is slightly more restrained, but still a bit of a thug. Such plants need pairing with others that can hold their own, or they can be planted to cover a difficult bank or inaccessible streamside and left to do the job. The woodrush will grow even in deep shade.

Covering the Ground

There are other plants that, if all you want is to cover the ground with something less hostile than brambles, can be left to get on with the task. Ivy, of course, will often be doing the job anyway, and you could introduce, for still greater effect, the Irish ivy, *Hedera helix* 'Hibernica', a ground cover of generous proportions with wide leaves and a wide-ranging habit. Other ivies, with fancy names, belong in more gardened surroundings, unless you have a mind to try *H. colchica*, the Persian ivy, in its plain green form, for its enormous leaves.

Lamium galeobdolon 'Florentinum' ('Variegatum'), the yellow arch-angel, must have earned much opprobrium from gardeners who succumbed to Margery Fish's enthusiasm for the plant and put it among border flowers; but in an impossible corner where little else will grow it comes into its own, spreading both above and below ground to form a silvery-sheeny carpet spangled with yellow deadnettle flowers in early summer. I recall a hazel copse in Shropshire, which petered out in a steep-sided ditch that had been used as a dumping ground for weeds; the archangel had entirely filled it, smothering even the worst rejects from the garden. Graham Thomas, in his book *Plants for Ground Cover*, gives its dimensions as 30cm/12in tall by 2.7m/9ft wide; on the evidence of the Shropshire ditch, that sounds modest. 'Silberteppich' ('Silver Carpet') is said to be non-invasive, but its more heavily platinum-flecked leaves belong in tamer surroundings. The smaller *Lamium maculatum*, with dark green leaves centrally striped with white like a badger's face, is more manageable; its flowers are purplish pink. Selections from this are decidedly garden-worthy and are described elsewhere. The bastard balm, *Melittis melissophyllum*, is a deadnettle relative, not so effective at weed suppression, but pretty in its way with clusters of white flowers striped with mauve – or all white in the variety *albida*.

The greater periwinkle, *Vinca major*, and the rose of Sharon, *Hypericum calycinum*, are both vigorous and efficient ground covers for lightly shaded places. The periwinkle produces its wide, slate-blue flowers during spring and early summer and increases by rooting stems; the summer-flowering hypericum is more insidious, spreading below ground. The flowers are large for the genus, yellow saucers filled with a showy boss of red-tipped stamens. The taller, smaller-flowered *H. androsaemum* increases freely by seed; checking commercial availability of the plants I write about I was surprised to find it listed by so many suppliers, since I would scarcely waste space on it except in the wildest corners, for all that it flowers over a long summer season. *H. inodorum* 'Elstead' is a much finer thing, an upright shrub of shoulder height at the most, with small but abundant clear yellow flowers in clusters and bright coral-red fruits. Even its bright-leaved form 'Summergold' would scarcely be out of place, though in full sun its acid yellow is rather hectic.

A WORD OF CAUTION

I mention *Pentaglottis sempervirens*, the evergreen alkanet, more by way of warning than recommendation. Its marine-blue flowers are handsome, but the leafage is coarse and scratchy, and it is both invasive, by seed, and hard to eradicate, with roots reaching far down into the subsoil. There is little point in planting something to exclude weeds which is itself a bad weed. *Trachystemon orientalis*, like so many of these blue flowers of spring, a member of the borage family, is a better bet for wide spaces, even in dense shade; its large hairy leaves appear after the starry flowers. The indigo-blue *Buglossoides purpureocaerulea* (*Lithospermum purpureo-caeruleum*) is slightly more clubbable; it spreads by flinging down rooting runners in much the same way, though at more modest rate, as the archangel. Unlike the purer blue *Lithodora diffusa*, it is perfectly happy both in shade and on limey soil, provided it is not too dry.

Euphorbia amygdaloides var. *robbiae*, on the other hand, copes with anything, even the darkest, driest corner, which it will fill with rosettes of dark green leaves on upright stems, topped in spring by erect sprays of chartreuse-yellow bracts. Its roots run underground, so that it needs to be kept away from anything you value; I once inherited a rhododendron which had been invaded, and had to resort to herbicides, painted on leaf by leaf, to subdue the spurge. The wood spurge itself, *E. amygdaloides*, is not so much of a weed excluder, but very appropriate in wilder, woodsy corners, with yellower flowers over green leaves or, in the handsome form *rubra*, mahogany-purple contrasting boldly with the lime-yellow inflorescence. Again, on account of its invasive ways rather than its ground-covering ability, I may mention *E. dulcis* here; a rather insignificant thing with small leaves and short stems of greenish flowers in early summer, it comes into its own in autumn when it turns to apricot, orange and crimson. Its selection 'Chameleon' has dusky-brown leaves, but will lose some of its colour in shade. Still in the green and yellow idiom, *Salvia glutinosa* is a coarse and leafy thing which, unexpectedly for a sage, is perfectly happy in half-shaded, rough places; the hooded flowers in spikes up to 1.2m/4ft high are pale yellow and last for weeks in summer.

Some gardeners have inherited the Japanese knotweeds, *Polygonum cuspidatum* and *P. sachalinense* (also known as *Reynoutria japonica* and *R. sachalinensis* or as *Fallopia japonica* and *F. sachalinensis*). Planted by our misguided forefathers, who admired their tall hollow stems topped, in autumn, by airy plumes of creamy flower, they are among the most invasive weeds known to man, at least in temperate regions. Nothing seems to deter them; I once tried burying the roots beneath eight feet of cheesy clay, excavated during the construction of a new driveway, but they bobbed up again quite unbothered. The only way to control them seems to be to resort to herbicides; and to keep on, and on, until at last, if you are persistent and lucky enough, they will give up. *Reynoutria japonica* var. *compacta* is said to be less aggressive, and it is pretty in its way with late heads of tiny, white flowers turning to deep pink and then to crimson seeds. I wonder . . . I did plant *Polygonum weyrichii* (*Persicaria weyrichii*) and had no particular trouble with it, and valued it for its good clumps of large, pointed leaves topped by sprays like some generous, creamy-white buddleia, followed by dark seeds. *P. molle* and its variety *rude* are similar.

Late summer to autumn is the season, too, for the biggest and most rumbustious of the so-called Japanese anemones, *Anemone tomentosa* (*A. vitifolia* 'Robustissima'), which has the usual spreading roots, only more so, and large lobed leaves, greyish beneath, topped by branching clusters of mauve-pink saucers. From summer to autumn *Geranium procurrens* will provide a succession of purple-magenta flowers; the leaves have jagged edges and are borne on rooting stems that will quickly cover a wide area, swarming about the anemone and the knotweeds or half climbing into any nearby shrub.

MORE MANAGEABLE COVER

If you want ground cover of a less aggressive nature, yet still able to cope with wildish conditions, there are plenty of plants to choose from that will look appropriate in your untamed woodland. I should not hesitate to plant *Brunnera macrophylla*, which has heart-shaped leaves expanding to their largest size after the sprays of vivid blue forget-me-nots have faded in late spring. Blue-eyed Mary, *Omphalodes verna*, is another forget-me-not-flowered, carpeting plant that is at its best in cool soil in shade; the tufts of heart-shaped leaves are topped by sprays of bright blue or white flowers. It is the first of the genus to flower; following it later in spring comes O. *cappadocica*, with larger, sky-blue flowers. 'Anthea Bloom' has been selected for its softer blue flowers over slightly greyed leaves, and there is also a white form.

The largest of the lungworts, *Pulmonaria mollis*, has good, deep blue flowers, though they tend to fade towards purple; the long, bold leaves are soft velvety green and make wide clumps. It is a much more muscular plant than the common spotted lungwort, *P. officinalis*, which is also known as soldiers and sailors or as Joseph and Mary on account of the flower colouring: the little bells open in spring, at first bright pink fading to lilac-blue. A better plant, and just as well able to look after itself, is *P. saccharata*, with boldly platinum-spotted evergreen leaves and pink flowers fading to blue. There is an increasing number of selections of each: white forms ('Sissinghurst White' is a good form which may belong to *P. officinalis*), another variant of *P. officinalis* called 'Cambridge' and one of *P. saccharata* called 'Barfield Pink'. 'Mrs Moon' is a good selection of *P. saccharata*; the heavily silvered 'Margery Fish' is a form of the related *P. vallarsae*. Flowering earlier than all these is *P. rubra*, which has unspotted, soft-textured, clear green leaves and coral-red flowers that do not change in colour as they age. I have not seen either 'Redstart', a selection made by The Plantsmen (Eric Smith and Jim Archibald), or 'Bowles's Red'; but as both E. A. Bowles and The Plantsmen had an exceptionally good eye for a plant, they are likely to be worth acquiring.

All the comfreys are easy-going, shade-loving plants that will make useful cover beneath trees or shrubs; some of them, being like the lungworts and omphalodes in Boraginaceae, share the borage tendency to blue flowers. *Symphytum* × *uplandicum* is a big, coarse plant, but valued where space permits for its pure blue, tubular bells in late spring. A more petite comfrey is *S. caucasicum*, which bears narrow bells of pale sky-blue; its counterpart in deep crimson is *S.* 'Rubrum', but this has not the allure of the Caucasian species. 'Hidcote Pink' and 'Hidcote Blue' are hybrids of *S. ibericum* (*S. grandiflorum* of gardens); the variegated forms appeal to some but have no place in the wildwood. *S. ibericum* itself is pretty, forming a low mat of pointed, green leaves just topped by nodding, creamy, tubular bells.

There is ever something appealing about a flower that nods. The water avens, *Geum rivale*, forms clumps of rounded leaves topped, in late spring, by modest Tudor rose flowers of subdued coppery-rose on reddish stems. 'Leonard's Variety' has creamy-pink flowers with a tangerine flush, and 'Lionel Cox', perhaps a hybrid, has primrose-yellow

bells in fox-brown calyces. There is also a delightful white form of G.
rivale, faintly tinged with lemon green. Much more of a weed than this is
the herb bennet, G. *urbanum*; but the cross between the two, unimaginatively called G. × *intermedium*, was described by Reginald Farrer in
almost reverent prose, valuing its 'large, wide, rosy-salmon blooms'.
The master's verdict notwithstanding, I incline to growing it in the
wilder areas, where it can indulge as much as it wishes in its free-seeding
ways, producing a range of colours from clotted cream and lemon to
terracotta, peach, and raspberry-pink. It seems that, as well as banishing
evil, the herb bennet (the name derives from medieval Latin *herba
benedicta*) exercises a benign influence as a parent. A chance seedling from
G. × *intermedium* is Beth Chatto's 'Coppertone', which she describes as
'translucent pale apricot'.

Flowering in early spring, *Pachyphragma macrophyllum* has heads of
small, pure white flowers, after which the circular, glossy green leaves
make solid cover all season. The handsome, rounded, deeply lobed leaves
of *Peltoboykinia tellimoides* are at first mahogany-red; the creamy flowers
in spring are incidental to the plant's value as a good ground cover in
shade. The flowers of the asarums are still less noteworthy, incon-
spicuous little brown bells hiding beneath the leaves, yet the evergreen
foliage is pleasing and their quiet colonizing ways earn them a place.
Asarum europaeum has rounded or kidney-shaped, glossy leaves forming a
low, spreading mat; A. *canadense* is similar, while the Californian A.
hartwegii, with marbled foliage, and A. *caudatum* have bolder leaves
lacking the polished surface. The asarums are known as wild ginger, on
account of the flavour of the rhizomes, which can be candied.

THE COLONIZERS

Woodlanders with small leaves may make just as good a job of covering
the ground: sweet woodruff, *Galium odoratum*, is one, a rampant spreader
with whorls of bright green leaves and heads of starry, white flowers in
late spring. The small, fleshy leaves of *Claytonia sibirica* also form weed-
excluding carpets, over which the tiny blush flowers float in spring. One
of the most determined carpeters in woodsy soil, with pushy shoots that
will scuttle along in moss or among the leafy litter of the forest floor, is
Cornus canadensis. From these wide-ranging roots little erect stems, no
more than 15cm/6in, hold up clusters of leaves like a little dogwood
tree's, and miniature dogwood flowers with white bracts, followed by
orange-red, clustered berries.

Then there are plants which, whether perennial or not, seed around to make colonies. Of these, I have a fondness for *Geranium robertianum* in both its typical pink and its two albino manifestations, 'Celtic White' and the more robust, red-stemmed *album*; the rosettes of finely divided leaves have a characteristic, slightly acrid but not unpleasant smell. *G. lucidum* is a wildling with tiny, pink flowers and pretty, polished, fresh green rounded leaves. *Corydalis lutea* is more permanent, with pale green, filigree foliage and little heads of tiny, spurred, cool yellow flowers from spring until autumn; even more appealing is *C. ochroleuca*, with green-washed white flowers over slightly greyed leaves. They both grow to about 30cm/12in. The taller *C. scouleri* has mauve flowers in spring and is more of a spreader than a clumper. The Welsh poppy, *Meconopsis cambrica*, increases fast by seed, its clumps of fresh green, divided leaves topped by single poppy flowers typically of clear citron, or sometimes tangerine.

Tellima grandiflora definitely belongs among the ground-covering plants, for its spreading clumps are good at excluding weeds. The rounded, hairy leaves turn to coppery tones in winter; in the form *rubra* the copper deepens to crimson, and the little, creamy bells of the type, that open in late spring, are tinted with pink pigment also. It is a more substantial, and less graceful, plant than the tiarellas. The foam flower, *Tiarella cordifolia*, is an efficient weed-masker, and extremely pretty with it; the little, spreading carpets of lobed, hairy leaves are topped, in spring, by soft, airy plumes of creamy blossom. In the more restrained *T. wherryi* the sprays are taller and pinker in bud; *T. polyphylla* has leaves with conspicuous purple veins, and feathery spikes of palest pink flowers. *T. trifoliata* has the longest season of flower, all spring and summer bearing airy, white plumes over a plinth of foliage. *Mitella breweri* is like a miniature tellima, with little, rounded leaves forming a small but determined carpet (it spreads also by seeding around) topped by tiny, green-white flowers in summer. There are three or four other odd little species you might want to seek out. I cannot, somehow, love the related pick-a-back plant, *Tolmiea menziesii*; its hairy, ivy-shaped leaves are very nondescript, not to say weedy, and its variegated forms, measled all over with yellow, simply make a bad thing worse. It is, though, better than many of the weeds which might otherwise be occupying its space.

WOODLAND GERANIUMS

Several geraniums do splendidly in cool shade as well as the herb Robert already described, and help to extend the season into summer. Among the early starters that prefer shade, *Geranium* × *monacense* (*G. punctatum*) is valued in spring not only for its nodding, muted purple flowers with maroon pointel, but also for the fresh primrose-yellow of its unfurling leaves, on which five maroon spots stand out distinctly. Later, the leaves fade to green and form weed-excluding clumps. *G. nodosum* is even more of a shade-lover, with glossy green leaves and a long spring-to-autumn succession of small, lilac-pink flowers. The mourning widow, *G. phaeum*, earns its name from the sombre colouring of its very dark maroon-purple, nodding flowers, with reflexed petals; it is a taller plant, at 60cm/24in, than *G.* × *monacense*, and comes also in white – not a stark white, more an absence of colour – and slate-blue, in the form known as var. *lividum*. 'Lily Lovell' is a delightful selection in warm lavender-mauve.

The pungent *G. macrorrhizum*, which we have already met clothing the ground beneath *Prunus sargentii*, is equally tolerant of full shade. Chalky pink *G. endressii* is just as good at excluding weeds, and is also evergreen; it has a long season from summer to autumn. 'Wargrave Pink' is a cleaner pink. Still more adept at covering the ground is the *endressii* hybrid 'Claridge Druce', now classed with others of its kind under *G.* × *oxonianum*; it has greyer foliage than its parent, and bright magenta-pink flowers all summer. Each clump will grow to about 90cm/36in in width. 'Thurstonianum' is an oddity, with squinny purple petals, giving it the look of a wildling. Silvery pink 'A. T. Johnson' and the warmer, faintly veined 'Rose Clair' are now considered to be hybrids in this group also, rather than selections of *G. endressii*.

Incidents of Flower

One of the most typical flowers of European woodlands is the foxglove, the biennial *Digitalis purpurea*, which also comes in white, as well as the exquisite primrose and apricot forms which are lovely enough to merit individual care in more gardened surroundings. Having said that, if you are prepared to grovel among the copious seedlings that all foxgloves produce, in order to uproot any that have a trace of purple on the leaf stalk, you can ensure that your pale strains continue unsullied by the purplish-pink type from year to year; and they do light up a dark corner most beautifully. The grosser manifestations extolled by seedsmen under such threatening names as *gloxiniiflora*, or even the Excelsior hybrids with their large flowers blaring at you from all around the stem, have no place in untamed surroundings. But there are some perennial foxgloves that you could well grow here. The most unsophisticated is *D. lutea*, with ivory-primrose 'gloves' to fit the tiniest fingers, held in slim steeples; the green leaves are smooth, not wrinkled like the common foxglove. It is virtually perennial, and increases freely by seed. The nodding bells of *D. grandiflora* are much larger, and seem bigger still for being borne on short 60cm/24in stems; they are pale buff-yellow with freckles of brown among the whiskers within the bell. The narrow leaves are evergreen. *D. davisiana* is similar, but the plant I had by this name was rather leafier and taller, and its colouring slightly closer to pale citron.

A plant that has some of the poise of a foxglove is *Campanula alliariifolia*, also known as 'Ivory Bells', which quite well describes the nodding flowers held all along the 45cm/18in stems over soft-textured, pale green, heart-shaped leaves. It seeds itself mildly. The same cannot be said for *C. latifolia*, which bears violet-blue or white tubular bells along 1.2m/4ft stems in summer; it is a terrific seeder. Selected forms are 'Brantwood' in richer violet, and pale amethyst 'Gloaming'. If you do not want them to take over, cut out the spikes as the flowers fade and before the seeds have time to ripen, which they do with amazing rapidity. A spreader by underground roots rather than seed, *C. takesimana* was until recently classed as rare; gardeners who, putting their faith in this assertion, planted it in a special corner soon found that it is quick to take over. In wilder corners it can be allowed to run around, for the large tubular bells are beautiful in blush-lilac heavily spotted with mahogany.

There are few lilies that I should wish to consign to the wildest corners of the garden; but I might make an exception for *Lilium pyrenaicum*, a leafy plant that is powerfully fragrant – almost too much so for close quarters – and has yellow (*aureum*) or tawny-red flowers. If you are so lucky that the martagon lily, *L. martagon*, will thrive and increase for you, then try it by all means, for it has the discreet looks that belong in untamed plantings, the nodding, dusky-pink turk's caps held on 90cm/36in stems. It grows here and there in the cooler corners of the meadows around our Swiss chalet, and is scythed down each year with the hay; but it seems undeterred by such harsh treatment. The white form is exquisite and I doubt if anyone would banish it from the garden to the wood. If my woodland were in North America, then I should be thinking of *L. canadense* and others; but their extreme grace and elegance also qualifies them for the paradise woodland.

WHITE FLOWERS IN THE SHADOWS

Having said that the albino martagon is too good for the wildwood, it is true that white flowers show up well in dark corners, and if their character is suitably untamed, their white not too stark, they might as well lighten the woodland. *Ranunculus aconitifolius* is usually grown in its double form, which I will recognize at the appropriate moment; in cool soil among trees the single-flowered wildling is charming in its spring season, with wide flights of white buttercups over bold, leafy clumps of divided, dark green foliage. Var. *platanifolius* is extra good in leaf and flower alike. The snowdrop anemone, *Anemone sylvestris*, is a much smaller plant of about 30cm/12in, with running roots, divided hairy leaves and fragrant, nodding white flowers with yellow stamens. The seed heads that follow are well described by E. A. Bowles as 'like lumps of cotton-wool . . . very white and ornamental'.

The milky fuzz of bloom borne by *Eupatorium rugosum* (*E. ageratoides*) and the similar *E. fraseri* comes in autumn, when most of the woodland flowers are long over; though not strictly woodlanders themselves, they do well in dappled shade, and the nettle-like (though non-stinging) foliage is fresh green in summer. The only astrantias I have ever been able to enthuse about are *Astrantia maxima* and perhaps the little dusky-crimson *A. carniolica rubra*; the ordinary *A. major* seems to me just the sort of plant that should be tucked away in some odd corner. The structure of the flowers, a collar of bracts around a central cluster of tiny florets, is amusing, but the rather dirty greenish-white colouring lets it down. Var. *involucrata* is an improvement, with an extra-large ruff; 'Shaggy' is a fine selection of this chosen by Margery Fish. The choicer meadowsweets needing moist soil have received their dues already; in the wilder woodland the lusty *Filipendula rubra* can spread its wide clumps of jagged leaves and tall (1.8m/6ft or more) stems topped by huge, creamy-pink flower heads in summer. 'Venusta' is the pinkest in flower. *Lysimachia clethroides*, with its curious grey-white flowers packed into spikes formed like shepherd's crooks opening in late summer, is another plant that never seems to me to have quite enough quality for the border; it is leafy, and the roots travel.

TALLER TERRITORIALS

It is not so territorial as the yellow loosestrife, *Lysimachia punctata*, which quickly makes a mass of leafy columns set with bright yellow flowers and should be left in some out of the way corner that you do not want to have to garden. Much finer than this is *L. ciliata*, of which the emerging foliage, in spring, is milk-chocolate coloured, and the spires are formed of nodding, not staring, flowers of soft lemon. It runs, but manageably. The little creeping Jenny, *L. nummularia*, is of course a busy ground coverer, with circular leaves (bright gamboge yellow in form 'Aurea') spangled with yellow cups in summer.

The greater celandine increases by seeding very freely, but in wild places is always welcome for its fresh green, divided leaves and flights of yellow flowers. Despite its vernacular name, *Chelidonium majus* is quite unrelated to the lesser celandine, but is a member of the poppy family. Some columbines are almost as free-seeding; plants of the 'Hensol Harebell' strain, derived from a cross between blue *Aquilegia alpina* and the variable *A. vulgaris*, are always welcome in their shades of cobalt-blue, blue and white, or less often of pale pink or lilac, pure white, or deep plum-red, and the flowers are less dumpy than the granny's bonnets of *A. vulgaris* itself. They assort well with the pink cowparsley, *Chaerophyllum hirsutum roseum*, a lovely thing with ferny leaves and heads of soft lilac-pink flowers on shorter stems than the wild cowparsley. Another pink umbellifer that is similar, flowering in summer, is *Pimpinella major rosea*. Cowparsley itself is, of course, very pretty if you can view it dispassionately; in a vase, with pink tulips, you can forget its weediness and admire its white delicacy of line. Sweet Cicely, *Myrrhis odorata*, is lovelier still, with aromatic, finely dissected foliage and creamy-white umbels in early summer; but she, too, is well able to spread her favours around by means of her abundant, dark brown seeds, every one of which seems to germinate if left to itself.

The potato family, which can fill our bellies with food, our conservatories with beautiful flowers and our sunny walls with showy climbers, has some good things for the woodland garden, too. *Physochlaina orientalis* looks well with the early geraniums; it forms a leafy clump with sprays of lilac, bell-shaped flowers. The scopolias are rather coarse, but I have a soft spot for them; the leaves at flowering time are restrained enough, so that one can examine the little, tubby bells of greeny-yellow or brown, and if later they are too exuberant, that scarcely matters in the wildwood. Names to look out for include *Scopolia carniolica* and its variants *hladnikiana* and *podolica*.

FOR WOOD AND GARDEN

Just because a plant gets a mention here does not mean that I always think it inferior to those that seem to belong in more gardened areas. It is a question of style, not of quality. Thus it is that among the heucheras (relatives of the tiarellas and tellimas) there are some I should admit to the wilder areas, and others that I should keep for the domesticated garden; yet, if I were forced to choose between them, I think I would rather do without the latter. Certainly the bright colours of *Heuchera sanguinea* and its hybrids have no place in the 'natural' woodland. The alum root, *H. americana*, is valued for its foliage, the beauty of which is expressed in its other vernacular name, satin leaf; for the rather ivy-shaped leaves are touched with metallic-copper glints on dark green when young, and though the bronze tones fade, the sheen does not, except on the forms distinguished as 'Purpurea' (*H. rubescens* of gardens) in which the upper surface is coppery-red and the reverse deep mahogany. The inflorescence is no more than a spray of minute, greenish flowers in early summer. 'Greenfinch', a selection of the poker-flowered *H. cylindrica*, was chosen for the creamy celadon-green of its large spikes, over fine clumps of lobed, dark green leaves. It flowers after the satin leaf, but before *H. villosa*, which has large, soft green, maple-like leaves topped by open sprays of cream flowers in late summer, coinciding – as Graham Thomas reminds us – with the willow gentian.

This, *Gentiana asclepiadea*, is not a temperamental lime-hater for the rock garden, but a graceful and easy perennial that will look after itself in cool soils in part shade, forming generous clumps of arching 90cm/36in stems set with sheaves of ultramarine trumpets. There is an exquisite albino, of that quality of whiteness that seems to be washed with cool green waters; and selected forms such as azure 'Phyllis' and marine-blue, white-throated 'Knightshayes'. They all increase by seed, though to keep the named kinds true to form you must take cuttings.

So much of the woodland flora bears its flowers in spring that the willow gentians are doubly welcome in their late season. They could be joined by the baneberries, which are grown far more for their intriguing fruits than for their insignificant flowers. They have dissected foliage, making a plinth for the spikes of berries, bright shining red in *Actaea rubra* and polished black in *A. spicata*. *A. erythrocarpa* is taller, with smaller, claret-red berries. Most fascinating is *A. alba* (*A. pachypoda*), twice as tall at 90cm/36in, in which the small, white berries are held in spikes on fat, scarlet stalks. Unfortunately, all the baneberries are poisonous, so it is perhaps well to keep them in a safe corner of the woodland rather than too easily to hand in the garden. Another berrying plant which assorts well with the willow gentian is *Coriaria terminalis* var. *xanthocarpa*. A semi-shrubby plant which will behave in a herbaceous manner in many gardens, it has attractive, fresh green foliage forming arching fronds which turn to apricot and tangerine in autumn. Before that, in late summer, the petals of the flowers thicken to form long sprays of translucent amber fruits. The type is scarcely less attractive with its black fruits, and there is also a red-berried variant with fruits as bright and juicy-looking as redcurrants. If this unusual shrub appeals to you, you may wish to try some of the other species, including the ground-covering, red-fruited *C. japonica*, the low, ferny, suckering *C. thymifolia* with minute, black fruits, and purple-berried *C. napalensis*.

THE WINTER WOODLAND

Even in late autumn and winter the deciduous wild woodland need not be bereft of interest. Trees with handsome bark, or with buttressed roots, come into their own when most of the vegetation has died down. Their silhouettes are more clearly seen when the leaves have fallen; the slender twigs of birches stand out in a haze of purple-brown against the wintry sky. And on the forest floor, if that is not too grand a term to give to the modest woodland I am assuming, incidents such as a clump of *Helleborus foetidus*, black of many-fingered leaf, may stand out, the steepling clusters of jade-green flower, each little bell edged with maroon, opening at midwinter. The stiff, green blades of *Iris foetidissima* set off the bursting pods filled with bright orange seeds. Do not assume from their specific names that these plants will fill the wood with evil odours; neither smells bad unless bruised (when it serves you right) and some forms of the hellebore have deliciously fragrant flowers, their perfume floating on the cold air to surprise you.

No odour attaches to the Chinese lanterns, *Physalis alkekengii franchetii* and the more modest *P. alkekengii* itself; they are similar, with orange-red, papery lanterns following the unshowy, creamy flowers. As they both run at the root, and are nothing to look at until the lanterns colour, and will grow quite happily in shade in any soil short of a bog, the wilder corners are ideal for them. Much the same is true of the poke weeds, *Phytolacca americana* and the smarter, Chinese *P. polyandra* (*P. clavigera*). Taller, at 1.2m/4ft, than the Chinese lanterns, they are leafy plants, both smelly and poisonous, but handsome in autumn. The first has spikes of white flowers that turn to gleaming mahogany berries; the second has pink flowers, and enhances its autumn display of black, polished fruits with foliage that dies in tones of yellow among the bright crimson stems.

Shrubs and Climbers

As well as the understorey perennials, you may wish to add a few shrubs to your woodland. The same criteria will apply: nothing too domesticated or sophisticated in appearance should be allowed into the wild woodland. That does not mean limiting yourself to snowberries and elders; though both have their uses. *Symphoricarpus albus laevigatus* is the common snowberry, an amazingly tolerant shrub that will grow in the darkest corners, under the drip of trees, in rooty poor soils: and still produce a crop of its pure white fruits like soft marbles. Almost as good tempered is the coral berry, *S. orbiculatus*, which has purple-pink fruits, much smaller but freely borne in packed clusters. Avoid, in this context, its variegated forms (I should avoid them in any context, but some people admire them). The hybrid between this and *S. microphyllus* is *S.* × *chenaultii*, of which the selection 'Hancock' is a dwarf, ground-covering shrub with blush fruits deepening to purple on the exposed side. The next generation of hybrids, in which *S.* × *chenaultii* is united with *S. albus laevigatus*, are a little more pernickety about soil, and more stay-at-home; which may well be an advantage. Collectively known as *S.* × *doorenbosii*, they come in varying colours of berry: 'Mother of Pearl', with fruits of white flushed with rose-pink, 'White Hedge', of upright habit, and its lilac-fruited companion 'Erect', and pink 'Magic Berry'. All the snow-berries tend to hang on to their fruits until they turn disgustingly soft and brown at winter's end. The more restrained cultivars could be used near the wood's edge, as a link between the wilderness and the garden proper.

ELDERS AND BRAMBLES

Certain forms of elder could be used in the same way. The common elder, *Sambucus nigra*, is a big shrub or small tree with smelly, fly-dispelling foliage on pithy stems, and flat plates of lacy, creamy flowers, used to impart their sweet muscat perfume to gooseberry fool or elderflower 'champagne'; they are followed by clusters of many small, juicy, purple-black berries which, with added raw sugar, ginger and cinnamon, make the highly effective old-fashioned cough remedy known as elderberry rob. There are thus plenty of reasons for growing it, where space permits; furthermore, it is an adaptable shrub, happy in the shade of trees and draught-resistant. Seedlings appear with too much eagerness, and should be removed while still small if they fetch up in the wrong places.

Some of the garden forms of the common elder are pleasant things, still with that touch of wildness; even the yellow-leaved 'Aurea' is restrained in colour, unless baked in full light (in too much shade it is virtually green). 'Guincho Purple' ('Purpurea'), too, is not of the hard, metallic purple-brown of so many shrubs bearing similar epithets, but a quieter shade of dark green overlaid with matt purple, deepest on the young growths. The flowers are often faintly pink-flushed. One of the most appealing of elders, fit for any company, is *laciniata*, in which the pinnate leaves are finely divided into dissected fronds; 'Linearis' ('Heterophylla') is more of a curiosity than a beauty, with the leaflets reduced to mere threads of green. There is a modestly cream-variegated cultivar, 'Marginata', of no especial merit, and the brighter 'Aureomarginata': their colouring disqualifies them from the wild woodland. Still less appropriate is 'Pulverulenta', in which the leaves are flecked and mottled with cream until hardly any green remains. The red-fruited *S. racemosa*, which is so spectacular in the Alps in autumn, is not much inclined to fruit if grown in shade, though it is handsome in spring when filled with bold heads of creamy flower. Far more striking that this, however, is *S. canadensis* 'Maxima', which bears great, wide, convex plates of white flowers in summer; the foliage is correspondingly luxuriant, especially if encouraged by hard pruning each spring.

The genus *Rubus*, which includes the hated brambles that can so quickly infiltrate neglected woodland with their barbed, snaring stems, also gives us a couple of vigorous species worth introducing to the wood. *R. odoratus* and *R. spectabilis* both form suckering thickets of tall stems, the first unarmed, with peeling, pale bark, the second finely prickly. The leaves of *R. odoratus* are soft-textured and palmate, and the fragrant flowers are bright rose-purple; *R. spectabilis* has trifoliolate leaves and vivid magenta flowers opening earlier, in spring. Both have reddish, edible fruits. The thimble berry, *Rubus parviflorus*, is of similar suckering habit, with shreddy bark on thornless stems, velvety pale green, maple-shaped leaves, and wide, white flowers like dogroses, followed by large, edible, if not especially tasty, red raspberries. *Rubus tricolor* is an evergreen sprawler, with long, lax stems, red-furred, not prickly, bearing polished, dark green leaves with white on the reverse, white flowers of no great moment in summer, and – sometimes – red fruits. It is one of the few plants that will cope even with dense shade, as of beech trees, though you should not expect much in the way of flowers there.

The pheasant berry, *Leycesteria formosa*, is so named because pheasants are fond of its black-purple, toffee-flavoured fruits, hanging in clusters from the burgundy-red bracts which earlier set off the white flowers. In winter the leafless, hollow stems keep their sea-green colouring until browned at their soft tips by frost; the whole shrub can be cut hard back in spring to make a new fountain of bloomy stems. Seedlings crop up everywhere with excessive enthusiasm.

PALE–FLOWERED SHRUBS

The shrub I grew up calling *Osmaronia cerasiformis*, the oso berry, is now to be known as *Oemleria cerasiformis*. A tall suckering shrub, it has arching sprays of fragrant, ivory-white flowers in early spring, when it looks rather like a pale flowering currant; the foliage is glaucous-tinged. *Ribes alpinum*, which is a real currant, is extremely shade tolerant, but not much of a shrub with its nondescript twiggy habit and dirty greenish flowers. Much more respectable flowers belong to *Rhodotypos scandens*, a kerria relative forming a spreading clump of erect stems set, in late spring and summer, with white flowers of dogrose outline, followed by glossy black fruits. *Kerria japonica* itself does well enough in shade, but only the single-flowered form would be admissible in woodland; its canary-yellow flowers are much prettier than the harsher yolky yellow of the double, which has been contemptuously dismissed by one garden maker and writer, the idiosyncratic George Schenk, as 'that floral meatball'.

Some of the viburnums look well in open woodland. The guelder rose, *Viburnum opulus*, is a common shrub of hedgerows and woods, where its white, lacecap flowers shine out in summer and its translucent fruits like redcurrants in autumn gleam among the richly tinted autumn leaves. A form with amber fruits, 'Xanthocarpum', is even more beautiful. The Asiatic *V. sargentii* is larger in leaf and in fruit; it is surpassed by the selection 'Onandaga', which has young growths of mahogany-red and crushed strawberry-pink. *V. acerifolium* also has maple-like leaves, as its name asserts; the fruits are dark blood-red to purple, and the autumn foliage of rich crimson matches their sombre tones.

Several other North American species could be tried, if obtainable: *V. lentago*, of upright habit with polished leaves flaring brightly in autumn, and creamy, late-spring flowers turning to fruits like tiny damsons; *V. dentatum*, the arrow-wood, with white flowers; *V. prunifolium*, with edible black fruits among richly coloured, dying foliage to follow the white spring flowers; *V. cassinoides*, in which the leaves unfurl in bronzed metallic tones, subduing to dark green as a background for the ivory flowers at midsummer and blazing out in crimson and flame in autumn; *V. trilobum*, a guelder-rose type with scarlet fruits that ripen in summer and last all winter.

In acid-soiled woodland, some of the more discreet azaleas will not look out of place, their flights of small, pale flowers on airy branches adding lightness to the late spring or midsummer scene. *Rhododendron arborescens* is the sort of azalea I mean; a deciduous shrub with glossy leaves, often glaucous beneath, and fragrant, white or blush funnels at midsummer or later. The swamp honeysuckle, *R. viscosum*, is sticky-flowered, the narrow white funnels delectably perfumed with spicy undertones; it is a smaller shrub than the first and flowers at much the same season. *R. vaseyi* flowers a month or two earlier, before the foliage (which often flares up in bonfire colours at leaf-fall), the wide, pale pink blooms freckled with tangerine. And the yellow *R. luteum*, the Pontic honeysuckle azalea, is at home anywhere on acid soils, from the wildest to the most manicured plot, which it fills with heavy, swooning perfume at flowering time.

SELF-RELIANT CLIMBERS

In a natural woodland, climbing plants are apt to use shrubs and the lower limbs of branching trees to hoist themselves towards the light. Honeysuckle or woodbine does this with such vigour that it may strangle its host. The common honeysuckle of European woodlands is *Lonicera periclymenum*, valued for the sweet fragrance of its creamy-yellow or burgundy-purple flowers all summer; 'Belgica' is said to be earlier flowering, and 'Serotina' later and redder. For a truly early-flowering honeysuckle, plant *L. caprifolium*, which has perfoliate upper leaves (*L. periclymenum* does not) and fragrant, creamy flowers sometimes touched with pink at midsummer. Even more rumbustious than these is the semi-evergreen *L. japonica*, with perfumed flowers opening white and aging through creamy-primrose to Naples yellow.

The wilder corners of the woodland are where *Polygonum baldschuanicum* (*Fallopia baldschuanica*) belongs, for here, if you have a sizeable tree of no great merit, you can allow it its head, when it will fill the host's entire canopy with its massed sprays of tiny, creamy-pink flowers in autumn. Unlike the Japanese knotweeds, which I warned you against earlier in this chapter, it ramps only upwards, not below ground. The climbing bittersweet, *Celastrus orbiculatus*, is almost as vigorous, and, provided you have a pair, male and female, or the hermaphrodite form, should bear in autumn and winter on the bare, twining stems, its spindle-like capsules that split to reveal shining red seeds against a yellow lining. There are other species, but most gardens can cope with only one at best, a reality faced by nurserymen, who seldom list them. The related *Tripterygium* species are of the same stamp, but even rarer in commerce.

SOLID EVERGREENS

A great deal of what I have described, whether understorey plantings or shrubs or climbers, is deciduous or herbaceous; and of the evergreen, ground-cover plants, not all look respectable in winter once the canopy of leaves above them has gone and they are exposed to the elements. (I write, of course, of chilly northern gardens.) Some self-reliant evergreen shrubs can make all the difference to the winter scene in your woodland without destroying its untamed character. In an English woodland where the hand of man has not been felt, ivy and holly and, rarely, spurge laurel (*Daphne laureola*) would be the only evergreens, unless in an area where box grows wild.

Whether or not the spurge laurel, with its yellow-green flowers in spring, grew in my woodland, I should add *Daphne pontica*, a low and spreading evergreen with lustrous, broad, pointed leaves and posies of lime-yellow flowers endowed, in the evening hours, with a heavenly, free-floating perfume. And I should save its dark berries, rub off the pulp and immediately sow the seeds, to make more and more, for my woodland, for shady beds by a much-used door or window, and indeed for just about anywhere in the garden that it could be persuaded to grow. In the chilly dampness of a northern woodland, holly, *Ilex aquifolium*, gleams darkly, the polished surface of its leaves reflecting what light there is. The little matt-surfaced leaves of box, *Buxus sempervirens*, give a wholly different texture; in shade, and with discreet pruning, it can be allowed to develop into a thin and graceful shrub quite different from the stodgy mass of a clipped box hedge.

On a much larger scale, the cherry laurel, *Prunus laurocerasus*, is perfectly happy in shade and could be allowed to grow loose and large to make a windbreak – and a visual interruption – in a woodland of appropriate scale. In time, with encouragement, it will turn itself into a tree. On acid soils the often despised *Rhododendron ponticum* can, given plenty of space, be planted to make a drift of colour in spring and a solidity of foliage all year; the rather pinkish mauve of its flowers, disastrous in the gardened woodland where rhododendrons of purer colour are valued, is perfectly in tune with the muted purple of foxgloves. Other rhododendrons of appropriate toughness and wildling looks are described in Chapter VIII.

In this whole chapter I find I have made no more than passing reference to moss, though at all seasons, and perhaps especially in winter, a mossy carpet may be the most beautiful and the most appropriate cover for the soil beneath your trees. Moss and shade go together, as anyone who has tried to make a good lawn beneath trees can testify. A walk through your local woodland is likely to reveal a great variety of mosses of different textures, shades and patterns, from the kinds that look like tiny fern fronds massed together to the close-packed kinds like thick-pile plush or clipped velvet. It used to be that weeds had to be removed by hand from a carpet of moss, but – provided you have no ethical objections – it is now possible to maintain a good deep-pile moss without weeds (that is, without non-moss) by watering it from time to time with a dilute solution of paraquat. This destroys all green things that it touches, except, for some reason, moss. Incidents in your mossy carpet should be used with discretion: a rock, a clump of ferns, a cluster or two of early-flowering, early-dormant woodlanders such as clintonias. Fallen leaves in autumn should be gently raked off.

Finally, though it should be unnecessary to say so, no wild-woodland gardener should think of introducing to his copse or wood all the plants I have described; where the aim is to improve on nature without seeming to do so, restraint is all.

V

The Woodland as Eden: on Chalk and Lime

BEAUTIFUL as the natural woodland may be, there is ever the temptation to add exotics, until the *genius loci* is quite overwhelmed by the foreigners. It may be wiser, knowing oneself to have this tendency, to decide from the outset that the woodland area is to become a tree-shaded Eden, where plants from all lands grow in harmony and beauty.

The first thing to realize is that this will require a good deal of management. Trees grow, mature and die; as they increase in size the shade beneath them deepens from the dappled light and shadow of young trees to the mossy, deep shade of mature forest, where only the falling of a senescent tree allows, for a while, the sun to strike the forest floor once more. In a span of fifty years, two generations, a new plantation becomes a dimly lit grove. Even on the small scale of a garden, thinning – by removing entire trees, or by judicious branch reduction – is necessary as time goes by if the carefully created plant community is to remain as intended. You will need to maintain a balance, at all times, between the mature trees forming a canopy overhead, the glades where more light enters, and the young trees that will represent the next generation of mature canopy.

Wherever the climate and soil permit, the Eden in woodland is usually given over largely to rhododendrons. It is all too easy to become addicted to the genus, and to grow almost nothing else; and that being so, I want to leave them until later. Specifically, I want first to consider some of the host of other lovely things that can grow in soil unsuitable for ericaceous plants; for nothing is more infuriating to the gardener on limy soil than to be confronted with the words of an author who assumes that everyone's garden has a pH of 5.5 or so.

In the paradise woodland, many of the small plants that I have already

92

described in Chapter II could well find a home. The chief reason for dealing with them separately, apart from the need to make chapters of manageable length, is that small plants can all too easily get smothered by taller ones; a poultice of hosta leaves or of pulmonaria, or an invasion of the determined roots of epimediums, will finish off the tiny things unless your eye is on them all the time. But plants that can run away from trouble, such as the wood anemones, are safe enough and can be encouraged, if that is your wish, to spread into wide patches such as you would probably not permit in the more intimate surroundings adumbrated in Chapter II. I cannot tell you precisely what you should or should not plant in your wood; ultimately, it is your decision, for only you know how much space and time you can give over to it, how watchful you are prepared to be over the smaller plants that might be under threat.

In the paradise woodland, groupings of plants that would look selfconscious in the wildwood are acceptable. The aim is not to make groups that look as though they have happened naturally, but to show nature what she ought to be doing if she had her design wits about her. Careful appositions of foliage seldom seem to occur to the old lady; she is too busy encouraging her children to run to flower so that they can perpetuate themselves. Yet some masterly hand – call it the hand of God, if you will, or evolution, or chance – has created the spears of *Luzula sylvatica*, the broad blades of hostas, the ferny fronds of dicentras and pale dinner plates of *Astilboides (Rodgersia) tabularis*, and there is nothing to say that you cannot group them beneath a cut-leaved maple in an interlocking group, all swarmed about with a carpet of variegated ground elder or pale pink *Lamium maculatum*, if you want to.

Shrubs for Lime Soils

Though many of the shrubs that grow best in the dappled shade of woodland demand an acid soil, there are those that do not, and many of them are ample consolation for the inability to grow pieris and kalmias and their kin. If you want declamatory foliage, as bold as many a rhododendron, you need go no further through the catalogues than A for *Aucuba japonica*. There is much more to aucubas than the spotted laurel of dingy London gardens, an image which the shrub seems to have difficulty outliving despite the availability of several beautiful cultivars with not a measle between them. 'Hillieri' is a female clone (given a husband, females bear sealing-wax-red berries the size of a small cherry) with large, polished, dark green leaves; 'Crassifolia' is a squatty male form with fat, dark leaves. The willow-leaved cultivars are even more good looking: *longifolia* is female, brighter in leaf than her male counterpart 'Lance Leaf', while female 'Salicifolia' is especially good with slim, glossy leaves on green stems and a heavy crop of fruits. All the aucubas are incredibly easy-going, coping with draughts, rooty soils, and perpetual gloom; but given leafy soil and a sufficiency of moisture they will reward you.

Anyone with a passing familiarity with windowbox planting will know that *Skimmia japonica* 'Rubella' is a standby for the shaded side of London's tall buildings. The genus has much more to offer than this cultivar, appealing though it is with its cones of cherry-red winter buds, opening in spring to bunches of yellow-anthered, white flowers scented like lily of the valley. For berries, 'Nymans' is one of the best, a rather open dome with narrow, pointed leaves leaving the abundant clusters of scarlet berries clearly seen; for fragrance, the old 'Fragrans' is still unbeaten, a neat, leafy mound with flowers less red in bud than 'Rubella' but more powerfully and persistently fragrant. Where a smaller plant than this is needed, 'Ruby Dome' is a good choice, a shapely hummock about 60cm/24in high and twice as wide, with leaves bronzed and buds reddened during winter where the sun touches them, though not so red as the name suggests. Though skimmias are almost as accommodating as spotted laurels, in limy soil in sun they bleach at the edges and appear chlorotic, but usually retain their green good looks in shade.

Philip Brown (who gave me most of the skimmias I have grown, including some unusual cultivars of diminutive size) considers that the whitish edging to the leaves derives from exposure, starvation, aging, or simply the whim of the plant, but that an occasional dosing with magnesium sulphate solution will help. Like spotted laurels, skimmias come in separate sexes ('Fragrans' and 'Rubella' are both male, the first a better pollinator than the second); a gardening friend who taught me much about shrubs and trees used to say that with skimmias, as with humans, the right proportion is about seven females to one male. Feminists might rage at such male chauvinism, but it all depends what you want your skimmias for. I happen to think that the flowers are more worth having than the berries, which always look to me rather unnatural, as though they had been stuck on the plant by a props department that had run out of the right size of shiny red bauble; so I should probably reverse the ratio anyway.

FRAGRANCE ON THE COLD AIR

First choice, on that basis, would be *Skimmia* × *confusa* 'Kew Green', a hybrid of *S. laureola*. Low, wide and spreading, it has bright green, pointed, aromatic leaves, with cones of green-white flowers in spring: good with green hellebores, *Ribes laurifolium* and *Oemleria cerasiformis* in a harmony of ivory and jade. There is confusion in my mind between *Skimmia laureola* itself and *S. anquetilia*; the first is said to be deliciously aromatic, the second rank-smelling. We are told also that the smelly one is actually *S. laureola* of gardens. As smell is so intensely subjective, I am far from sure that I have them straight. I acquired, some years back, two plants – male and female – of what was said to be *S. laureola*; they travelled home in the car with me and filled it with an odour that was both strong and agreeable; but it might have been 'rank' to someone else. Both sexes made glossy-leaved domes that reminded me more of *Daphne pontica* than of the more familiar skimmias. They were settled in beneath a cut-leaved beech, with other green and white flowers. *Danaë racemosa*, which is related to, and resembles, butcher's broom, but is infinitely more elegant, belongs here, too, for its arching green stems set with narrow cladodes form graceful fountains of foliage, lucent green all year, like some evergreen bamboo. *Ribes laurifolium*, a low and spreading evergreen shrub with large, leathery leaves, bears its nodding sprays of alabaster-white currant flowers in early spring; snowdrops and a group of white *Daphne mezereum*, upright in habit and always full of flower along the bare branches, joined the ribes and the skimmias, epimediums, *Arum italicum marmoratum* and a sweep of sarcococcas.

The sarcococcas, winter-flowering evergreens, like the skimmias, bleach to a chlorotic yellow in full sun, but make lustrous clumps in the shade. *Sarcococca humilis* is low and far-reaching in its suckering way; the pointed leaves are polished dark green, and the tiny almost colourless tassels of flower are fragrant. *S. ruscifolia* is a size larger in height and leaf, differing also in bearing red fruit, not black; *S. confusa* is similar, with tapering leaves, perfumed creamy flowers, and black berries. One of the best in leaf is *S. saligna*, but it is rather tender, and scarcely scented. As an all-rounder, the finest is probably *S. hookeriana digyna*, which has elegant, narrow leaves on erect stems forming a thicket, the tiny, creamy-pink flowers filling the cold air with fragrance. The best form of this is 'Purple Stem', with dark stems and petioles.

MAHONIAS TALL AND LOWLY

The beauty of the lower-growing mahonias lies in the pattern of their foliage. In this, the least satisfactory is the Oregon grape, *Mahonia aquifolium*, which could well form an ingredient in wilder woodland. For our more polished copse, 'Apollo' is a fine selection. The variant or hybrid of the Oregon grape which I know as 'Toluacensis' or as *M. aquifolium* 'Heterophylla' differs in its less compact growth, the branches set with leaves composed of up to nine narrow, wavy-edged leaflets that turn from green to burnished mahogany and burgundy-red in winter. Another cultivar, now considered to be of hybrid origin, is 'Moseri', which has some of the poise and appeal of a nandina, the holly-like leaflets varying in colour, when young, from muted bronze to bright apricot and tangerine, fading to apple-green before lapsing into the puritan dark green of maturity; it often shows coral-red tints in winter. *M. aquifolium* also enters into the parentage of 'Undulata', a taller shrub than its parent with lucent dark leaves, wavy at the margins; the flowers are the expected yolk-yellow, stubby clusters in spring. More striking is the plumy, chrome-yellow floraison of *M. repens rotundifolia*, which departs from mahonia tradition in the smooth, not spiny, edges of the rounded, sea green leaflets. *M. pumila* is of similar colouring, but prickly; it is a neat, little shrub with large bunches of bloomy berries to follow the yellow spring flowers. *M. repens* itself slowly suckers to make an ankle-high carpet of matt-green leaves. It is not so good as *M. nervosa*, another restrained, suckering colonizer which has polished leaflets of firm outline as though stamped from metal; dark green in summer, they often flush crimson in the cold weather.

The firm decorative pattern of these little, slow mahonias is echoed in large by the tall species, the best of which should be ample consolation for any gardener lamenting his inability to grow rhododendrons. A mature and flourishing *M. japonica* needs no excuses about soil or climate; it is good enough for any company, with its generous mounded habit, bold deep green leaves forming a strong pattern of spiny leaflets, and arching sprays of clear yellow bells, scented like lily of the valley. The more tender *M. lomariifolia* is more striking still but always has the look of an alien, especially once run up to a leggy monster with each stem topped by a rosette of laddering, spine-edged leaflets of tropical magnificence. In winter the ruffs of foliage are topped by clustered candle-spikes of deep yellow flowers.

Hybrids between these two larger species, collectively *M.* × *media*, are hardier than *M. lomariifolia* and have foliage intermediate between the comparatively few broad leaflets of *M. japonica* and the many narrow divisions of *M. lomariifolia*; the leaf surface tends more to the matt texture of the latter than the smooth *M. japonica* style, and the inflorescences also are nearer to the fern-leaved parent, being mostly stiff, upright, many-candled clusters of scarcely scented, close-packed, yellow flowers. 'Charity' is the most widely grown, but by no means the best; 'Buckland' and 'Lionel Fortescue' are as good as one might expect from their eponymous raiser; but I would choose, of this group, 'Winter Sun', for its half-upright spikes of yellow flowers are distinctly fragrant. None of the mahonias is at its best if cluttered up with other plants. The little fellows can join other forest-floor plants (with due regard for their modest rate of growth) to form varied patterns of foliage; the big chaps can stand as bizarre isolates in a glade , or with the simplest of plantings: spears of *Iris foetidissima*, bergenia paddles, or just a carpet of moss.

The mahonias are not the only berberids that can bring a touch of alien sophistication to a shaded garden. *Nandina domestica*, a shrubby plant with elegantly divided, non-prickly foliage tinged with coppery-red in spring and again in autumn, on unbranched canes, is less evidently related, and indeed its common name of sacred bamboo more accurately suggests its appearance, if not botanical affinities. (I am aware that some botanists find it sufficiently distinct to merit its own separate family.) Selections are chosen for extra brightness of leaf – 'Firepower' – or for dwarfness. The type grows to about the height of a man, and might double that if it likes where you plant it; so 'Nana Purpurea', of dumpy habit with red-flushed foliage, and 'Pygmaea', which is not much more than knee-high, are useful for small spaces. In high latitudes nandinas tend not to flower very freely, still less to fruit, unless in exceptional summers; but where there is plenty of ripening sun, even in lightly shaded places they may bear their creamy plumes.

FOLIAGE INSTEAD OF RHODODENDRONS

The flowers of *Trochodendron aralioides* are green, and open in late spring. People who expect flowers to be big and bright (and this includes many rhododendron buffs, else why should we still see such masses of 'Cynthia', 'Pink Pearl' and 'Britannia'?) are unlikely to swoon over this noble shrub. Its leaves are pale, fresh apple-green, with scalloped edges emphasized by the narrowest of red-brown margins, poised in whorls on long stalks. Painfully slow to get started (quicker if seed-raised than if grown from a cutting), it will in time make a large shrub, tolerant of most soils except thin chalk and looking its best in the play of light and shade

beneath an open canopy of trees. Similar conditions, in leafy soil, suit
Illicium anisatum,the very sort of thing disappointed rhododendron
species aspirants should grow if their soil is on the alkaline side of neutral.
Here is an evergreen, aromatic shrub, slowly bulking up, well set with
varnished, thick-textured, pointed leaves of rich green to set off the
many-petalled flowers of pale, translucent yellow in spring. Give it pale
epimediums for company.

Many viburnums are shade plants, including that darling of landscapers, *Viburnum davidii*. This is a plant for which I have an irrational
hatred, perhaps simply because it is over-used, perhaps because it has the
same irretrievably smug look to it that makes me despise, also, *Hebe* ×
franciscana 'Variegata' and even poor little *Rhododendron yakushimanum*. I
can recognize their qualities – exception made of the hebe – but I cannot
love them. But if you want a low, wide-spreading, evergreen shrub with
bold, deeply nerved foliage and, if the spirit moves it, berries that are too
small and not quite blue enough to earn admiration, then *V. davidii* it is. It
is tough and will grow virtually anywhere; you need at least two clones,
probably more, to ensure a reasonable crop of fruits, and that is another
good reason to give it a miss, for who wants more than one *V. davidii*? I
believe, incidentally, that it is functionally rather than structurally
unisexual and that planting 'male' and 'female' as offered by certain
nurserymen is no guarantee of fruits.

Its cousin, *V. cinnamomifolium*, is another thing altogether. Similar
foliage, but of thinner texture and more polished finish, decks a much
larger, and entirely non-smug, evergreen shrub that relishes a half-
shaded, sheltered corner. The flowers are similar off-white clusters and
the little fruits are indigo-black; the leaves are the thing. The lugubrious
V. rhytidophyllum is bigger again, and looks in leaf a bit like a chastized
rhododendron; done well, it can look splendid, the long corrugated
leaves sub-glossy above and greyed beneath. Only their poise, which
recalls Eeyore in his most despondent moods, is against them. The best
thing you can do with *V. rhytidophyllum* is to inherit a large specimen,
prune it up, not down, with all the aesthetic restraint at your command,
and enjoy the resulting tree, which will bear clusters of beige, felty buds
from earliest spring, opening to an anticlimax of ivory flower. A sexually
active pair will produce red and black fruits, but with *V. rhytidophyllum* as
with *V. davidii*, though for different reasons, one is enough for most
gardens. The variegated form is a monstrosity that should have been
strangled at birth, though some people profess to admire it.

These viburnums trail far behind others in my own rating of the genus.
How could anyone not fall for the entirely desirable *V. henryi*? Swiss

garden centres habitually offer large specimens, already as tall as I am; I long to take them all home. More or less upright in growth, more or less open-branched, *V. henryi* bears narrow, pointed, deep green, lacquered leaves and, at midsummer, nubbly white cones of flower that might be made of crochet, followed by sprays of fruits that start red and age to black, both colours at once in each cluster. A hybrid of this with the deciduous (and desirable) *V. erubescens* is dubbed *V.* × *hillieri* 'Winton'; less wholeheartedly evergreen, less elegantly slender in leaf, it earns admiration for its coppery unfurling leaves and burnished winter colouring. Unexpectedly, *V. harryanum* is a middling-sized, evergreen shrub with dark, coin-sized leaves in threes, and small white flowers in spring. Deciduous viburnums are many, and I think must wait, lest we get indigestion. Besides, with two notable exceptions that in any case will not stand lime, they earn a place for flower, not foliage, and that gives them on the whole a supporting, not a starring, role.

VICTORIAN EVERGREENS

Laurels are almost as synonymous with dusty Victorian shrubberies as aucubas, yet *Prunus laurocerasus* has various manifestations which I should not hesitate to use in a planted woodland on alkaline soil, unless it were a very poor and shallow chalk. The ordinary cherry laurel is a big, muscular shrub with bold, dark green foliage that glitters in the dappled light of a copse; it is tough and tolerant, standing wind, shade, even drip from overhanging branches. In spring, if left to grow free, it bears sprays of not quite agreeably smelling creamy flowers that are followed by fruits like little cherries, turning from red to black. In woodland, however idyllic it is intended to be, I would not plant the variegated 'Marbled White', and I can think of nowhere I would plant the distorted monstrosity that is known, in a bizarre slander on camellias, as 'Camelliifolia'. But 'Magnoliifolia' is another matter, with the biggest, glossiest leaves of any cherry laurel.

At the other end of the scale is 'Otto Luyken', a dumpy shrub with narrow, polished dark leaves on upright stems; as much of a landscaper's pet as *Viburnum davidii*, yet more tolerable. Better still, if you need something low, wide and deep green as efficient year-round ground cover, is 'Zabeliana', long and slender of leaf and very free with its creamy flower spikes. I used it once in a dark corner where an ugly wall met, at an awkward angle, a bank of clay that had the consistency of processed cheese; 'Zabeliana' quickly spread a fan of branches over the horrid stuff, its lacquered leaves reflecting every scrap of light.

The Portugal laurel, *Prunus lusitanica*, never runs to such magnificence of leaf as the best cherry laurels, but is a shrub of greater charm, and fully tolerant of chalk. It flowers a few weeks after the cherry laurel, the little ivory, fragrant blossoms held in long, slim spikes contrasting with the dark burnished leaves on claret-red petioles.

Good evergreen foliage belongs also to the genera *Osmanthus* and *Phillyrea*; the first also has discreet, but deliciously fragrant, flowers. Even in the darkest corners *Osmanthus decorus* will make a broad dome of up to 3m/10ft, with bold, glossy leaves and little, white flowers in spring. The holly-leaved *O. heterophyllus* is equally shade tolerant; you could, if you wish, use its variegated forms ('Variegatus' with ivory-margined leaves, gilt-edged 'Aureomarginatus', or broad-leaved, white and green 'Latifolius Variegatus') in place of the plain, polished green of the type; but you might, like me, find them fussy rather than appealing.

So far as I know, no one has insulted *O. armatus* or the similar *O. yunnanensis* with variegations; their long and narrow, leathery leaves, armed with neat fierce teeth along their margins, need no such embellishment. Both have the poignant fragrance, in flower, typical of the genus: *O. yunnanensis* in late winter, *O. armatus* in autumn. The hybrid *O. × fortunei* flowers also in autumn; its foliage is like some bold and beautiful holly's. By comparison with these, the most familiar species, *O. delavayi*, is unexciting in leaf; its little clusters of tiny, white, spring flowers are delectably scented, but are abundant only if the shrub receives enough light. *O. × burkwoodii*, a hybrid of this with *O. decorus*, falls between the two, with larger leaves than the first, and clusters of fragrant, white flowers in spring. It is very popular, but I find it faintly unlikeable. By contrast I am fond of *Phillyrea latifolia*, which is despised by many because it has little, off-white flowers; but it is a handsome, glittering evergreen with elegant sprays of abundant, small, polished leaves.

DARK BACKGROUNDS FOR WINTER FLOWERS

Dark evergreens such as these earn their keep not only for their year-round beauty, but also as contrasting companions for shrubs that bear their flowers on bare branches. A corylopsis, say, that is seen against a background of sombre green carries twice the impact of a forlorn specimen lost among other leafless shrubs or standing lonely in a grassy, winter-drab glade.

Although the epithet *Corylopsis* means *Corylus*-like, these shrubs resemble the common hazel-nut tree only in leaf; though the clusters of soft yellow, cowslip-scented blossoms might be remotely likened to short, much-magnified catkins in their elegant, drooping poise. It is a genus recently revised by the botanists, so that with the exception of *C. pauciflora* (which dislikes lime, so must wait until the next chapter) and one other, I have had to relearn all the names I first mastered. *C. sinensis* 'Spring Purple', which has young leaves delightfully flushed with soft purple, used to belong to *C. willmottiae*, a species with soft lemon flowers which is now referred to as *C. sinensis sinensis*; *C. gotoana*, distinguished by its pink-flushed young growths and glaucous-white leaf reverse, is now sunk in *C. glabrescens*, which has more pointed leaves less distinctly white beneath; *C. platypetala*, with densely packed, palest primrose flower spikes, has become *C. sinensis calvescens*; and the delicious, erect *C. veitchiana*, with large tassels of lemony-primrose, red-anthered flowers and strong cowslip perfume, is cumbered with the name *C. sinensis calvescens veitchiana*.

Of the species that are not calcifuge, given a fair depth of leafy soil, only *C. spicata* still bears its old name; it is a spreading, hazel-like shrub with long, narrow, drooping spikes of clear yellow: showy, quite, but lacking the charm of *C. veitchiana*. With their conspicuous yet dainty blooms opening in spring, just before the leaves unfurl, the species of *Corylopsis* can be set among the lowly woodland flowers of spring in some delightful combinations. Spread a sheet of soft blue *Anemone apennina* beneath them, or risk the more piercing tones of *Chionodoxa sardensis*.

VIBURNUMS FOR EVERY SOIL

As spring fades into summer, the genus *Viburnum* once again comes to the rescue of the shade gardener with alkaline soil. Like the hydrangeas which follow them in high summer, some viburnums come in lacecap or in sterile, snowball variants. The lacecap forms of the guelder rose, *V. opulus*, have already been proposed as candidates for the natural woodland garden; here, in the woodland in Eden, the snowball *V. opulus* 'Roseum' ('Sterile') might be your choice. As tough and hardy as the type, it decks itself, at midsummer, with globes of tender jade maturing to ivory-white. The sterile form of *V. plicatum*, the Japanese snowball, has larger spheres of white flowers borne a month or so earlier, but lasting long, each branch arching with the weight of the double rows of snowy clusters. 'Grandiflorum' has larger flower-heads still, the white florets faintly rose-flushed. Whereas the guelder rose makes a big shrub both upwards and outwards, *V. plicatum* characteristically grows sideways, increasing its height by piling layer upon layer of horizontal branches.

The wild type is known as *V. plicatum tomentosum*, and bears, in late spring, foaming lacecap flowers of ivory and pure white. The tiered branching is still more distinct in the lacecap cultivar 'Mariesii', in which the ray florets are large, so that the pleated, fresh green leaves are almost hidden beneath the snowy cloth of flower. 'Rowallane' and 'Lanarth' are less markedly horizontal in growth; the first often bears showy clusters of small, red fruits in autumn. For tender colour in place of all this dazzling white, choose 'Pink Beauty' in which the ray florets blush as they age. As for placing these viburnums, they should not be in deep shade, for they will scarcely flower; but where they are only lightly shaded, the sun reaching them for part of each day, all will be well. They appreciate coolness at their roots, and a humus-rich soil. They do not enjoy chalk, but are not by any means lime-haters. With enough light, you can expect them to colour in characteristic tones of deep wine-red in autumn: the foliage of 'Mariesii' is especially apt to die magnificently.

Much less familiar than these is *V. sieboldii*, a tall shrub or even a small tree, with foliage of freshest apple-green, and creamy flowers in early summer followed by pink fruits that ripen to indigo-blue. The leaves are bronzed on unfurling in spring and sometimes again in autumn. I have already briefly mentioned *V. erubescens*, which is just slightly tender, and appreciates the shelter of woodland, though its form *gracilipes* is tougher. Unusually, the blush-white flowers are borne in long panicles; they are fragrant, and open after midsummer, followed by plentiful red fruits aging to black.

A shrub that is usually extolled for its fruits rather than its flowers is *Decaisnea fargesii*, a tall and rather slender shrub with large, pinnate leaves. The fruits are exciting, it is true, for they look like indigo broad-bean pods; but the flowers are enchanting, sprays of narrowly flared, chartreuse-green bells. Semi-shade and a soil that is moist rather than dry suit this Chinese shrub.

Most magnolias prefer a soil at least neutral if not acid, and for that reason I have chosen to describe them all together among the other shrubs and trees of acid soils. But the chalk or limy garden can grow magnolias, too, provided they are the right kind. Among the summer-flowering group, *Magnolia wilsonii* and its hybrid offspring *M.* × *highdownensis* are perfectly happy even on chalk, while for spring *M.* × *loebneri* would be the best choice, for it begins flowering with laudable precocity unlike its equally lime-tolerant parent *M. kobus*, which seldom flowers until into its teens. The apparently ubiquitous *M.* × *soulangeana* is scarcely lime tolerant, from which we may deduce that more gardens are blessed with a neutral or acid soil than their owners believe when they fail to establish an uprooted heather plant from the Scottish moors or a rhododendron that is asked to move straight from the peaty nursery bed to a hostile clay.

On neutral or alkaline soil, you may get hydrangeas to grow but you cannot expect blue flowers, though if the pH is 6.5 or less you can help an undecided hydrangea to turn blue by scattering, in late autumn, aluminium sulphate among the stems, watering it in thoroughly. You need about half a kilo/1lb. for a medium-sized bush. If there is some lime in the soil so you achieve not blue but a dirty mauve, water each bush twice at intervals of a fortnight, in spring, with a solution of Epsom salts (about 60gm/2oz. per 10 litres/2gals per bush). On very alkaline soils the iron needed by the hydrangeas to retain their lush green good looks may be locked up; if the foliage turns yellowish and the bush looks wretched, a foliar feed will usually help. In a woodland setting the lacecap hydrangeas are more beautiful than the mopheads, which have the same kind of artificiality, of colour at the expense of dignity, as hardy hybrid rhododendrons, only more so; for they last for months from summer onwards, a wallop of colour that fast becomes indigestible.

One of the first lacecaps to flower, opening soon after midsummer, is 'Lanarth White', bearing an abundance of pure white flowers among foliage that is rather yellow, especially on lime soils. It is usually more successful in sun, at the edge of a woodland clearing perhaps, than in shade. 'Veitchii' follows, and is better suited to a shady position, forming a tall shrub, its white ray-florets usually rather triangular, for they normally have three sepals where 'Lanarth White' has four or five. 'White Wave' is a big and lusty shrub with large, wavy-edged ray-florets. Of coloured lacecap hydrangeas, 'Mariesii Perfecta' is a big seller on account of the name by which it is better known, 'Blue Wave'. It does not in fact 'blue' very readily, and many must be the gardens where a pink or lilac hydrangea is growing, planted by someone expecting clear azure colouring. 'Mariesii' itself is even less likely to come blue, and certainly not on limy soils, where it is a pretty pale pink, with well-shaped flowers rather fuller of sterile florets than the usual lacecap but far from so opulent as a mophead. The brightest is 'Geoffrey Chadbund', a cultivar of moderate growth with deep red lacecap flowers. All these are derivatives of the wild *Hydrangea macrophylla*, and are greedy feeders, wilting dismally in the heat or when the soil is drier than they like.

A moist, rich soil is also the recipe for success with the *H. serrata* cultivars, hardier, often smaller, and more decidedly shade-loving than

the *macrophylla* types. 'Bluebird' is widely offered and popular, on
account of its name no doubt; it does 'blue' more readily than many, or
can be grown as a pretty and free-flowering lilac or pink lacecap on limy
soils. 'Diadem' is paler in colour, with leaves often red-flushed where the
sun strikes them. The cultivars that change colour as they age are more
predictable: both 'Rosalba' and 'Grayswood' open white and gradually
deepen to crimson regardless of soil pH, so that for weeks the bushes
present a varied play of colour from white to pink to ruby. Of the two,
'Grayswood' is the brighter and the more floriferous, the ray florets
finally an intense dusky crimson, deepest where the sun strikes them.
Little *H. involucrata* is a pretty shrub but not very hardy, with white ray-
florets opening very late in the season. It has a sweet little double form,
'Hortensis', with bubbly ivory and blush flowers.

For the same reason that I exclude mophead hydrangeas of *macrophylla*
extraction from the woodland garden, *H. paniculata* 'Grandiflora' is
banished. But the lacy variants of this species are entirely acceptable.
Because of their tough constitution, they are described in Chapter VIII. A
more muscular plant even than *H. paniculata, H. heteromalla* and its
variants in the Bretschneideri group, together with var. *wilsonii* and var.
xanthoneura, formerly regarded as separate species, are sturdy shrubs that
will even make small trees in woodland. All bear creamy lacecap flowers
at midsummer: 'Snowcap' is a fine, white-flowered selection very
tolerant of dry soils.

Despite its name, *H. arborescens* is much less tree-like than these,
forming a smallish shrub with rather pale green leaves; botanists have
recently reorganized this species, too, to include others formerly
considered distinct, such as *discolor* and *radiata*. The form of *H. arborescens*
usually seen is 'Grandiflora', a mophead in the sense that each inflorescence is formed of massed sterile florets, but for all that not too
obtrusive in a wooded setting, for the heads are fairly small, and the
individual florets much smaller than the hortensias'; at first chartreuse-
green, they open to cream before fading again towards green. 'Annabelle'
is a huge-headed variant to be kept away from informal settings. Var.
discolor is what we used to call *H. cinerea*, so named on account of the
dusty-grey backing to the leaves; its form 'Sterilis' has creamy-white
globes in place of the lacecaps of the type. In var. *radiata*, the reverse of the
leaves is white-felted, a truer white even than the ivory of the fragrant
flowers that are borne in wide heads in summer.

Still more name-changing has afflicted the rough-leaved hydrangeas of
which *H. villosa* is the best known. Now *H. aspera* var. *villosa*, it is a
wonderful shrub at best (which means obtaining a good form, not always

easy in the absence of distinguishing names), often billed as the hydrangea that is blue in all soils. This is to stretch the definition of blue well beyond even the shades usually accepted as 'nurseryman's blue', for *H. villosa* (as I will call it for brevity) has lacecap flowers of warm lilac: that is, of a colour with a good deal of pink in it, even if nearer to blue than to true pink. Disliking both wind and spring frosts, it thrives in sheltered woodland, as do its allies *H. aspera* var. *strigosa* which flowers even later, in autumn, and var. *rosthornii*.

Even deep shade suits the great velvet-leaved *H. sargentiana*, which has stems as bristly furred as the calyx of a moss rose, and flowers like little purple turtles, the sparse white florets stuck like feet on a humpy aggregation of deep mauve fertile florets. Wind is its enemy, for the huge leaves are easily bruised and torn. Despite attempts to lump this, too, in with *H. aspera*, I believe it still retains its separate specific status. With all the name changes that have beset the genus – or more specifically us gardeners, who grow them and hope to be up to date in what we call them – one species has remained blissfully unaffected: the oak-leaved hydrangea, *H. quercifolia*. Here is a smallish shrub with leaves like oak – one of the American species with pointed lobes rather than the blunter English oak – which can be splendid in autumn in rich but not jazzy shades of copper and mahogany and crimson. The summer flowers are loose and lacy confections of white, sterile florets among the usual tiny fertile flowers.

White lacecaps belong also to the most familiar of the climbing hydrangeas, *H. petiolaris*, which will receive its dues when I come to shaded walls; suffice here to mention that it will also shin up a tree trunk in a wooded setting, or can be simply left to get on with life on the flat, when it will gradually mound up into a shrub much wider than high.

The Understorey: in Place of Weeds

If your woodland area admits enough light to give you flowers on these summer-blooming shrubs and climbers, then it will certainly grow a fine crop of weeds on any bare ground between them. This is a clear signal to plant perennials of your own choice, not nature's, in their place. The chapter on cool shade already gives you a long list to choose from, but there remain some of the larger perennials and bulbs, and the more energetic ground covers that seem better suited to the gardened, rather than the wild, wood.

Thus the epimediums, which seem to me too beautiful in leaf and in finely drawn flower to relegate to a wild corner, though the larger species can certainly hold their own against most weeds during years of neglect, once established. Cool and shady positions suit them best, but they will come to no harm if they grow into the sun during the course of their slow but determined root increase. The evergreen *Epimedium perralderianum* is especially valuable among deciduous shrubs, for the bold, polished, toothed leaves of fresh green are handsome all year. In early spring come flights of small, bright yellow, almost spurless flowers, borne on 45cm/18in stems so that they just overtop the foliage. *E. pinnatum colchicum* is virtually evergreen, with bronzy or brighter winter tints, and vivid yellow flowers in spring. Their hybrid, helpfully called *E.* × *perralchicum*, has foliage similar to *E. perralderianum* and the sizeable flowers of the other parent. Any of these could set the tone for a fresh yellow grouping that would carry on through spring and early summer with *Euphorbia polychroma* 'Major', Welsh poppies, and a double buttercup: tall branching *Ranunculus acris* 'Flore Pleno' with tight little rosettes, or the lower, larger-flowered *R. constantinopolitanus* 'Plenus' (*R. speciosum plenus*). A less familiar evergreen epimedium is *Epimedium pubigerum*, which has tiny, cream or blush flowers in tall, airy sprays at the usual early spring season. Its offspring with *E. alpinum*, *E.* × *cantabrigiense*, is almost as tall, with small, muted red and yellow flowers over evergreen foliage.

Other epimediums are deciduous, and add to their dainty spring flowers the appealing colours, dusky pink, terracotta or bronze, of the unfurling foliage, tints that are often repeated in autumn. *E.* × *rubrum* is one of the smaller epimediums, perhaps two thirds the size of the muscular *E. perralderianum*, but just as easy and willing, with coppery-red young leaves turning to clear green, overtopped by little, crimson, white-spurred flowers. Even more delicious is *E.* × *versicolor* in all its manifestations. The yellows are the more vigorous, soft yellow 'Sulphureum' and 'Neosulphureum', which you can distinguish by the number of their leaflets: 'Sulphureum' has as many as nine, against the usual epimedium ration of three. The original cross with its pink tints in both flower and leaf is charming with the small-flowered pink daffodils which are now being raised: 'Foundling', 'Lilac Charm'. 'Sulphureum' is soft enough also in colour not to clash with pink, or can join other pale beauties with lovely leaves such as the smaller Solomon's seals, *Corydalis ochroleuca*, hostas with pale variegations, and ferns.

By contrast *Epimedium* × *warleyense* should be kept clear of pink or mauve or lilac, for its little flowers are tangerine-orange over fresh green leaves that are less densely weed-excluding than some. *E. alpinum* is the likely source of the reddish colouring; it is a pleasant little thing with crimson and yellow flowers, a dozen or so on 20cm/8in stems, looking a

Rhododendron 'Pink Lady Rosebery': Lower Coombe Royal, Kingsbridge, Devon

Magnolia wilsonii: Lukesland, Devon

Galanthus 'Magnet': Rodmarton Manor, Cirencester, Glos.

Kalmia latifolia 'Ostbo Red': Coldham, Ashford, Kent

Pernettya mucronata (above): The Level, Pillowell, Glos.; *Hydrangea sargentiana (below)*: Coldham

Paris polyphylla: Coldham

Rodgersia podophylla and *Carex siderosticta* 'Variegata' (*above*): Coleton Fishacre, Kingswear, Devon; *Hosta fortunei albopicta* (*below*): The Level

Lonicera tragophylla: Coleton Fishacre

Rudbeckia fulgida sullivantii 'Goldsturm' (*above*); Coleton Fishacre; *Viola* 'Jackanapes' (*below*): The Level

Mitraria coccinea Lake Puye form: Savill Gardens, Egham, Surrey

Primula 'Inverewe' (*top*): The Level; general view at Steadstone, Dumfries & Galloway (*above*)

Senecio smithii: The Level

Trollius 'Canary Bird' and *Meconopsis betonicifolia* (*above*), and *Astilbe* 'Irrlicht' and 'Fanal' with *Carex elata* 'Aurea' and *Hosta fortunei hyacinthina* (*below*): The Level

Arisaema candidissimum: Hidcote Manor Garden, Chipping Campden, Glos.

Polygonum bistorta 'Superbum' and *Gunnera Manicata* (*above*): The Level; *Orchis latifolia* (*below*): Savill Gardens

Meconopsis grandis GS 600: The Level

little like a small version of its offspring *E.* × *rubrum*. The other half of *E.* × *rubrum* is the splendid *E. grandiflorum*, with a name that tells us it has the largest flowers. It comes in a range of colours from rich pink or dusky lilac to white, always with long spurs, held on 30cm/12in stems above the small leaves. Selection is not hard, for the names reveal the colour: 'Rose Queen', 'White Queen', sultry *violaceum*, 'Crimson Beauty'. Even longer spurs belong to yellow-flowered *E. davidii*.

WELL OUT OF THE WIND

Dicentra is a genus apt to crop up again and again whenever shady gardens are under discussion, as it has already, and will again, in these pages. Here in the woodland idyll, in cool soil with shelter from wind, is the place for *D. macrantha*, a perennial of exceptional grace and dignity with dissected leaves and long, hanging lockets of soft honey-yellow, held on 45cm/ 18in stems in spring, that is, rather earlier than the more familiar bleeding heart and its smaller cousins. Two of the less familiar *Meconopsis* species thrive in similar conditions, and will cope with some lime in the soil so long as it is leafy and moist. *M. chelidonifolia*, as its name suggests, has lobed leaves recalling those of the greater celandine; the tall, branching stems, up to 1.2m/4ft, are set with wide, primrose bells of silken texture, opening in summer. The spring-flowering *M. villosa* is half its height, and is as beautiful in leaf as in flower, forming rosettes thickly furred with honey-gold hairs, which makes them vulnerable to winter wet and the drip from overhanging branches. The wide, nodding, lemon flowers with amber stamens open in spring.

These plants of restrained beauty need to be accompanied by plants of equal distinction: *Hosta tokudama* 'Aureonebulosa', perhaps, with its cupped, corrugated leaves of glaucous blue hazed with soft yellow, unfurling in spring from pointed growth buds that force through the soil like shell cases, in the manner of its larger relative *H. sieboldiana*. Although, like all hostas, these do best in cool soil in shade, they should be planted away from overhanging branches, as the deep corrugations collect any fallout, and the lovely, blue-bloomed leaves look disgraceful if cluttered with scurf.

Ferns, which look completely at home in a wooded setting, could join the dicentra also, subtly associating different styles, different textures of finely cut leaf. The handsome *Dryopteris erythrosora* has pink and rufous-tinted young fronds, maturing to shining green backed with red spore capsules. *D. affinis* (*D. pseudomas*) is the golden-scaled male fern, much bigger and bolder, with unfurling croziers of bright ochre on tan-furred stems, maturing to noble, deep green fronds; even this is surpassed by the Far Eastern *D. wallichiana*, with the same vivid young fronds on dark stems, or the aristocratic *D. cycadina* (*D. hirtipes*), with smooth, symmetrical fronds of very bright green. The bold fronds of *D. goldieana* are as sharp-toned as young oak leaves in spring, fading to a pale green later. There are crested forms of the male fern and the golden-scaled male fern, for those who like that sort of thing.

HOSTAS FOR ALL

Ferns and hostas are often suggested as companions, and certainly the contrast of the broad, simple blades of the hostas in their varying colours and sizes with the green fronds of ferns is immediately satisfying, if a little obvious. In the idealized woodland we can allow plain-leaved hostas, and perhaps some of the more discreet variegations, as indeed that of *Hosta tokudama* already proposed. An unending succession of new hosta cultivars emerges yearly from the specialist nurseries on both sides of the Atlantic; only the keenest amateur can hope even to keep up with the names, let alone grow more than a selection of those that catch the eye on show stands and in nursery rows. What follows, then, together with suggestions in other chapters, represents a personal selection of old, proven cultivars, with some newer ones that seem promising. I am especially attracted by new cultivars that offer a change of scale rather than yet another variegation.

Thus, with the larger ferns, and with perennials of similar scale such as *Kirengeshoma palmata*, a bold and upstanding hosta such as 'Krossa Regal' may be planted to form its great dome of glaucous leaves, of which the paler reverse is revealed by the upward tilt of the foliage. Standing clear of the leafy mound, on 1.5m/5ft stems, are steeples of lilac flowers in late summer. Almost as tall, when well fed, is *Hosta rectifolia* 'Tall Boy', its green, heart-shaped leaves forming a plinth for the lilac-purple bells, among the finest of all hosta flowers. The old *H. ventricosa* has better foliage, smooth and shining green (which means that it does not collect rubbish from overhead trees, like *H. sieboldiana*, but sheds it cleanly), and broadly heart shaped; the violet flowers in late summer are almost as good as those of 'Tall Boy'. Having done their stint as contrasting foliage plants all summer, in their late-summer flowering they are just a little too early to coincide with the primrose-yellow, slightly lopsided shuttlecocks of *Kirengeshoma palmata*, a Japanese plant with leaves a little like a plane tree's or a poinsettia's, of soft clear green set on contrasting black stems, so that even before the flowers open this is a plant that earns its keep. It it said to dislike lime, in common with many Japanese plants; but a moderately limy soil will suit it if deep, moist and leafy, which is why I include it here rather than either among the out-and-out lime haters of acid woodland or as a candidate for a sophisticated, shady wall-border planting (soils in such borders being all too often contaminated with mortar or other limy rubbish).

Back, however, to hostas. *Hosta plantaginea grandiflora* ought to be a better companion for the kirengeshoma, as it flowers in the same season; but – even more than the kirengeshoma, which will put up some sort of show of flowers in a shady spot – it needs sun if it is to flower at all, in many areas, before autumn frosts catch it out. Its offspring 'Royal Standard' avoids this difficulty by flowering earlier, which means it, too, beats the kirengeshoma; but 'Royal Standard' is a fine thing with deeply veined, wavy-edged, green leaves topped by white, lightly scented flowers. Pity about the name, though I suppose it is better than the twee 'Honeybells', which is similar, with lilac-flushed, fragrant flowers and a tendency to grow fast and congest itself into a clump of unthrifty leaves if you do not regularly split and replant it.

Cool schemes of green and white can be made with the white-margined hostas such as *H. crispula* or *H. undulata albomarginata* ('Thomas Hogg') among *Smilacina racemosa* or Solomon's seal with ferns and white dicentras, white primroses and the splendid form of the summer snowflake (which flowers in spring) called *Leucojum aestivum* 'Gravetye Giant', leafy like a daffodil, with 60cm/24in stems topped by fat, white, green-tipped bells. A wide-faced white violet such as *Viola papilionacea* can fill any little spaces. The variegated ground elder, *Aegopodium podagraria* 'Variegatum', also fits well in such a scheme. In my experience it is not invasive, nor have I known it to revert to the plain green type which causes so much anguish to so many gardeners. It does increase, of course, to make a low carpet of cream and pale green, which you can clip – or even mow, if you have enough of it – to keep it lower still and freshen it up during summer. If, despite my assurances, you are too nervous to contemplate planting ground elder of any kind, then you could instead use as low-level ground cover the white-flowered form of *Lamium maculatum,* or the variant known as 'White Nancy', which allies to white deadnettle flowers a leaf almost wholly silvered; or, if you will permit soft yellow flowers into your white and green scheme, the silver-striated form of *L. galeobdolon* known as 'Silberteppich' or 'Silver Carpet', which seems less of a thug than the more familiar type.

FERNS FOR ELEGANCE

The ferns I prefer to add to such a group are the supremely elegant soft shield fern and its variants. *Polystichum setiferum* itself forms a pile of luxuriant, soft green fronds as much as 1.2m/4ft high, if it likes you; the plumose forms such as those in the Divisilobum group and the even more divided, moss-like Plumoso-Divisilobum group are generally shorter, but lose nothing in elegance or poise thereby. More than any other fern, except perhaps the almost metallic *Blechnum chilense*, these soft shield ferns are of so compelling a visual texture that one cannot resist stroking them. The wholly covetable 'Pulcherrimum Bevis' has dissected fronds narrowing to a flick of a tail at the tips.

The forms known collectively as the Acutilobum group, if less feathery-divided, are still beautiful in the outline of their fronds as they spiral around the crown, and have the further advantage of producing bulbils along the stem so that you can quickly build up a colony of babies. The hard shield fern, *Polystichum aculeatum*, is also most graceful and elegant, the fronds a clear, rather acid green in spring aging to deeper, polished green in summer. *P. tsus-simense* is a Far Eastern shield fern with hard-textured, clean-cut fronds of polished green. *P. braunii* and *P. polyblepharum* are sometimes listed as distinct, sometimes as synonymous; they or it are elegant evergreens, like the others of their tribe, with broad, polished fronds on black stalks.

The holly fern, *P. lonchitis* (which is not the same as the holly fern botanically known as *Cyrtomium falcatum*, or, to be more up to date, *Phanerophlebia falcata*) needs it cool and moist; unlike the shield ferns, its style is to form tough, simple, pinnate fronds of dark green, like a half-sized sword fern, *Polystichum munitum*. Just to confuse matters still further, this last, a western North American, is also known as the Christmas fern – as is *P. acrostichoides* from the eastern USA; while sword fern is a name also given to species of *Nephrolepis*, which are distinctly tender. When confronted by such vernacular obscurities, I feel that even the taxonomists' changes to familiar botanical names are easy to cope with.

SHADES OF GREEN

The sharp greens of spring come in many guises: young foliage of *Hemerocallis fulva*, new oak leaves, the bracts of spurges and the spurge-like *Smyrnium perfoliatum*. This biennial is happiest in shade, drawing the eye with its large, rounded, chartreuse-yellow bracts, of frailer texture than the spurges'. Most euphorbias grow well in dappled shade, where by choosing your species you can enjoy their acid greenery for several months, from the rather dumpy *Euphorbia polychroma* of spring and its larger, finer and longer-flowering form 'Major' – there is also a newer form with purple-flushed leaves, 'Purpurea' – through the tall and splendid *E. palustris* in late spring, and the dark-leaved, bright-bracted *E. hyberna* in summer. Once rare, *E. wallichii* is now readily available, and no wonder, for the wide, lime-green bracts last for weeks over unusually handsome foliage, dark green with maroon margins and a near-white central vein.

The spurges' sharp tones can be emphasized by hostas of like colouring. The one we all used to grow was *Hosta fortunei aurea*, very pretty in spring as the unfurling leaves pass from butter-yellow to chartreuse, but frankly dull in its green summer livery, as is *H. fortunei albopicta*, which starts life each season with bright yellow leaves margined in pale green, then fades to pale yellow as the green darkens; then, in summer, settles down to two shades of unremarkable green. Others of varying sizes are described elsewhere; some of them retain their sharp colouring all season, which makes me fear that they may in time – to borrow George Schenk's neat phrase – 'come to vulgarity by way of excellence'. Something that is good to look upon for a while may pall if it is relentlessly unchanging for months.

In other settings, the softer, bluer greens may be more appropriate. Here, too, there are plenty of hostas to choose from, to associate with the blush or cream froth of tiarellas, pink lily of the valley, dwarf pink dicentras and *Viburnum plicatum* 'Pink Beauty' perhaps. Again, even in the idealized woodland, the less assertively man-made hostas seem most appropriate, such as *Hosta fortunei hyacinthina*, a vigorous form of the green-leaved *H. fortunei*, with greyer foliage and lilac flowers held clear of the leaves. In this respect it is better than *H. sieboldiana elegans*, despite the beauty of its puckered, glaucous-bloomed, almost circular leaves, for the stubby, pale flowers of *elegans* stand hardly taller than the pile of foliage. *H. tokudama* is in effect a smaller version, with more deeply cupped leaves. 'Snowden' is a hybrid of *H. sieboldiana* with pointed, greyish leaves making a tall mound topped by white, lilac-blushed bells in late summer.

The joy of planting in allied colours is that the groups can be indefinitely extended, and seldom if ever will a plant seem out of place. There are small deadnettles to join such a group: the shell-pink *Lamium maculatum roseum*, or brighter-flowered, silver-leaved 'Beacon Silver', or the lusty 'Chequers', with leaves more like the usual badger-faced green and white, and flowers of strong pink. In summer *Anemone rivularis* opens its white flowers, which have blue anthers and sepals backed with inky blue. The best of the masterworts belongs here, too: *Astrantia maxima*, a fetching thing with old-rose flowers, the central posy surrounded by a collar of broad bracts, over three-lobed foliage like that of a Lenten rose. *A. carniolica rubra* is smaller, and has garnet-red flowers. Instead of, or as well as, the tiarellas, you could plant the hybrid × *Heucherella alba* 'Bridget Bloom', a delightful, weed-excluding plant with frothy spikes of clear pink in early summer and again later; or × *H. tiarelloides*, which flowers chiefly in late spring and has neat, ground-covering, evergreen foliage.

Earlier in the season the drumstick primula, *Primula denticulata*, in lilac and rosy-purple, or in white, bursts into flower, thriving where the soil is moist and retentive. The tall *Ranunculus aconitifolius* bears flights of white buttercups over dark green foliage for weeks in spring; *platanifolius* is a good selection, and 'Flore Pleno', with its immaculately snowy, tight rosettes, is rather shorter. It is one of several plants commonly called bachelor's buttons, and is also known as fair maids of France.

LILIES IN THE WOOD

Some lilies are appropriate to a wooded setting, though most need sun for at least part of the day; on the whole, their roots should be kept cool and shaded, and the stem-rooting kinds in particular appreciate a leafy mixture about them, provided the drainage is good also. One of the most appealing is *Lilium martagon*, typically a dusky claret-pink, but also to be had in deepest maroon-black (var. *cattaniae*), with white-furred buds (var. *pilosiusculum*) or, exquisitely, in ivory-white. The recurved, turk's-cap flowers are borne in stately spires early in the lily season. Despite its aristocratic looks, it is one of the easier lilies, coping even with dryish shade, and ready to increase by seed. It has a maize-yellow counterpart in *L. hansonii*. *L. monadelphum* (*L. szovitsianum*) is of suitably cool colouring for a wooded setting, for its nodding, widely flared bells are soft yellow, unspotted or lightly freckled with brown, and their fragrance is as good as any. Similar colouring, or a warmer tangerine, belongs to the elegant and graceful *L. canadense*, with petals less recurved than a true turk's cap, giving it a profile like a pagoda roof, with the dark anthers hanging below. The tall and easy-going *L. henryi* has turk's-cap flowers of an appealing soft orange-buff in late summer; it is content with any reasonable soil and is tough enough to withstand the virus diseases that so often attack lilies. Another that is tolerant of virus to the extent of showing few or no symptoms (and is often, in consequence, the source of infection in other less resistant lilies) is the tiger lily, *L. lancifolium* (*L. tigrinum*), with orange, dark-freckled turk's caps. A sterile triploid, it is increased by the bulbils that form freely in the leaf axils, so that the virus is never eliminated with a fresh start from seed. As well as these few, there are of course many other species, some fairly easy, some diabolically difficult to keep going in the garden; and named cultivars to count in dozens if not hundreds, some much too blatant for the woodland (the popular 'Enchantment', for one), others more or less acceptable. Dr North's hybrids are especially appealing in a range of soft colours: biscuit and maize, dawn pink and jasper red.

VI

Rhododendron Woodlands

EVEN on lime-free soil you may well want to grow some of the plants I have described for chalky woodland gardens; but your chief aspirations are likely to be towards the rhododendron, and its supporting cast of camellias, magnolias, *Pieris* and, maybe, the white-flowered trees of summer: eucryphias, styraxes and stuartias. The rhododendron is to woodland gardening as the rose to sunny gardens; except, perhaps, that rhododendron buffs are even more fanatical than rosarians. That being so, many books have been devoted to the genus alone, or to parts of it. Much of this literature induces, in the mind of the rhododendron tyro, confusion rather than clarity. The nomenclature and arrangement of the species within the genus has lately been revised so that two main schools of thought run parallel; and there is a degree of rivalry between rhodo fanciers who prefer the more understated species and primary hybrids, and those who go for the showy, floral qualities of the highly bred kinds.

As regards nomenclature, I shall use the system adopted by the Royal Horticultural Society, which is among other things the International Registration Authority for Rhododendrons. Only one point needs to be made here: following convention, I place cultivar names between single quote marks, but grex names have no quote marks. (A grex is a group of offspring of the same cross.) To add confusion, the same name may apply both to a single clone within a grex and to the grex itself: for example, Lady Chamberlain is a grex, with several named clones such as 'Exbury Lady Chamberlain' and 'Salmon Trout'; but 'Lady Chamberlain', with single quote marks, is also a clone. (A clone is the name given to a group of individuals derived originally from a single plant and maintained by vegetative propagation.)

114

As far as selection is concerned, all I can hope to consider here is a personal choice from among the hundreds of species and hybrids that are available. Unlike roses, which tend to come and go as their constitution is weakened by mass propagation or they lose resistance to one of the ills of hybrid roses, rhododendrons are generally long lived, and introductions which were new in the nineteenth century are still going strong.

<h2 style="text-align:center">THE HARDY HYBRIDS</h2>

This is especially, and to some people regrettably, true of the hardy hybrids: rhododendrons like 'Cynthia' or 'Pink Pearl' have an enduring appeal to unsophisticates but can become overbearing as one's knowledge of, and taste for, the genus develops. Personally, I would never waste good woodland space on a hardy hybrid that is tough enough to grow in the open; but the toughest have their value in cold and shady corners, so it is there that we shall meet them, in Chapter VIII. That leaves just a few which I like well enough to admit to the woodland, or to an area of garden that mimics woodland, where dappled shade and wind shelter come as part of the package, and the soil can be improved so long as the pH is suitable.

Given these ideal conditions, some of the hardy hybrids will grow into large shrubs with bold leaves and large trusses. Forget the hard, insistent magenta of 'Cynthia', and look instead at the tall trusses of large, white flowers spotted with deep crimson borne by 'Beauty of Littleworth', or the flatter trusses of 'Mrs P. D. Williams', each ivory flower marked with a greenish-sienna stain. Flowering earlier than these, 'Loder's White' is very free with its pure white flowers opening from lilac-pink buds, in large, pointed trusses. 'Sappho' is widely admired for its white flowers with boldly contrasting purple-black blotch. More subtly, 'Doctor Stocker' bears loose trusses of wide, ivory-cream bells faintly marked with chocolate.

Pale colours such as these may not satisfy everyone, but they are easier to place than the reds and purples. I know of no red-flowered, hardy-hybrid rhododendron that does not fade towards a shade with more blue in it than is quite desirable, but with that caveat there are many to choose from: 'Britannia', one of the truer reds with rather pale foliage, 'Mars', and low-growing 'Doncaster' in which the dark, somewhat glossy foliage contrasts with crimson-scarlet, black-blotched funnels, among them. Pink rhododendrons of the hardy-hybrid class also share the tendency to lean towards the blue end of the spectrum. 'Corona' is of clearer colouring than many, and the individual flowers are wide bells rather than the more usual funnel shape. 'Mrs Charles Pearson' has blush-mauve flowers fading almost to white, with sienna flare. More decidedly mauve is 'Blue Peter', with clear violet-mauve, frilled flowers with a paler centre, while 'Purple Splendour' has royal purple, black-centred flowers, needing pale yellow to bring them into prominence.

PRIMARY HYBRIDS AND OTHER DELIGHTS

Having described these few hardy hybrids, it will be much harder for me to make a selection from the more choosy, and correspondingly more beautiful, species and their hybrids; there is no hardship in rejecting a plant one cannot truly admire, but much difficulty in deciding which, from a host of deserving candidates, shall be allowed their immigration papers. At the risk of shocking purists, I suggest that primary hybrids – those of which both parents are pure species – should go to the head of the queue, before the wild species themselves. The hybrids often retain much of the grace and dignity of the species, as a result in part of conscious selection by their raisers; but hybrid vigour contributes, frequently, to an easier temperament.

One of the finest is Loderi, a cross between *Rhododendron fortunei* and *R. griffithianum*, this last a glorious but tender species whose blood runs in the veins of 'Beauty of Littleworth', 'Doctor Stocker' and others. The Loderi group grow, in time, into leggy trees displaying tan-pink, marbled bark; by this time the great perfumed, lily-like flowers are borne over our heads, so to many people the Loderis are in their prime as teenagers forming large, rounded bushes set with huge trusses of white, blush or pearl. They vary in hardiness: 'King George' is one of the easiest, and very fine with its pure white, green-flashed trumpets opening from pale pink buds. 'Venus' is deeper in bud and retains a hint of pink to the end. Nearly as good is the Angelo grex, of similar parentage, *R. fortunei* ssp. *discolor* × *R. griffithianum*. Almost anything that *R. griffithianum* touches turns out well, but Penjerrick (the other parent is *R. campylocarpum*) is unsurpassed, with loose trusses of creamy-yellow or pale pink, fragrant bells marked with crimson nectaries. Cornish Cross unites *R. griffithianum* and *R. thomsonii*; with two such parents, its bark is as beautiful as any, smooth and marbled in tan, beige and pink. The waxy bells, borne early in the season, are rose-pink.

Two groups of hybrids are especially tempting: those with the blood of *R. griersonianum* which inherit, as is too seldom the case, the pure red colouring of this Chinese rhododendron; and the yellow rhododendrons, influenced by *R. campylocarpum* and echoing its soft and delicate colouring. *R. griersonianum* itself is a very distinct species with long, tapering buds opening late in the season to flowers of clear geranium scarlet amid rather narrow leaves that are backed with buff felt. Its clear colouring with no trace of blue assorts happily with the sharper greens, as of many ferns. Fabia is perhaps its most famous offspring, a wide bush with soft orange-scarlet bells, brighter in the variety 'Tangerine' and pale orange with coppery lobes in 'Roman Pottery'. I once, quite unplanned, set Fabia near *Viburnum plicatum*, the tender coral funnels a yearly delight against the creamy globes of the viburnum.

The popular Elizabeth, a low spreading shrub with dark leaves and deep scarlet bells, is a *griersonianum* hybrid with *R. forrestii* Repens as the other parent, and so is May Day, in which the waxy vermilion funnels are held in large calyces of the same colour among felt-backed leaves. Elizabeth flowers at much the same season as the fothergillas, witch-hazel relatives that slowly form medium-sized shrubs with stubby, bottle-brush spikes of ivory stamens in spring, and fine autumn colouring of orange and scarlet or yellow as the broad leaves die off. *Fothergilla major*, the tallest species, shows yellow autumn colour; it now includes what we used to call *F. monticola*, in which the autumn colour is brighter. *F. gardenii* is a smaller shrub with abundant fragrant, white bottle-brushes in spring.

Of later red rhododendrons, Tally Ho is a very fine hybrid needing shelter, for its other parent is the tender, scarlet *Rhododendron facetum*; Matador, also half *griersonianum*, has loose trusses of deep vermilion.

The yellows with blood of *R. campylocarpum* tend to flower early in the season, so some shelter helps to protect the delicate tissues of the blooms from frost damage. The species itself is a small- to medium-sized shrub with heart-shaped leaves, glossy green above and glaucous-blue beneath, setting off the wide, tender yellow bells. Of its offspring, Penjerrick has already been described; the best forms, in soft creamy-yellow, are exquisite. Letty Edwards is a cross between *R. campylocarpum* and *R. fortunei*, forming a compact shrub with pale sulphur flowers opening from pale pink buds, while Gladys of the same parentage is a shapely bush with cream flowers faintly marked in purple. The well-known 'Goldsworth Yellow' has buds of warmer apricot opening to primrose flowers with a bronze flash. The more compact 'Dairymaid' has paler, creamy-lemon flowers marked with crimson, very freely borne. In contrast, 'Lady Bessborough' is a tall, upright shrub uniting *R. campylocarpum* and *R. fortunei discolor*, bearing apricot buds opening to ivory-cream funnels.

Other hybrids are of more complicated parentage, but still very appealing in their soft colouring: among them are Damaris with fresh lemon bells, Carita in palest lemon with a basal blotch of cerise, and the two 'Uniques' in buff or softest yellow opening from pale tangerine buds. The beautiful Hawk, 'Jervis Bay' and 'Crest' are hybrids of 'Lady Bessborough' with *R. wardii*, inheriting the clear lemon colouring of the species and the large funnels of the hybrid parent. 'Lady Bessborough' is a parent also of the Jalisco hybrids, 'Jalisco Eclipse', 'Jalisco Goshawk' and others; the straw- or primrose-yellow flowers are marked with crimson or maroon spots and streaks. There are also some most desirable yellows of different breeding, such as Mariloo, in which the lemon, green-washed flowers are set among bold foliage, and 'Roza Stevenson', with wide, citron saucers opening from deeper buds. *R. wardii* and *R. decorum*, both of which I shall try to tempt you with later, mated to produce 'Ightham Yellow', while the difficult but beautiful *R. lacteum* (one parent also of Mariloo) united with Naomi to give us Lionel's Triumph, which has clear soft yellow bells with a delicate pink flush at the margins and crimson flecks in the throat.

All these tender shades blend coolly with the slate blues and soft violet tones of *R. augustinii* and its hybrids, Blue Diamond, Blue Tit, Blue Bird, 'St Tudy', Sapphire, Bluestone, Russautinii, Augfast and others. The offspring are more compact shrubs than the parent, and their small flowers are borne with great freedom in neat, little trusses. The finest forms of *R. augustinii*, that is the nearest to true blue, are also on the whole the more tender, so the shelter of woodland is essential if they are to do well. Happily, they are easy from cuttings, so named or selected forms are readily available in commerce; 'Electra' is especially appealing in violet-blue with an acid-green flash. They are generally rather tall and leggy, and not worth another glance except when flowering, so they should be set where their gangling looks will not intrude. There are larger-flowered, off-blue rhododendrons also, closer in style to the hardy hybrid type: 'Susan' in amethyst-violet, flowering with 'Dairymaid', and pale mauve 'Blue Peter' which flowers later. Some forms of *R. campanulatum* are near to blue also, such as 'Knap Hill' and the newer 'Graham Thomas' in lavender blue. The creamy-primrose cherry 'Ukon', close in colour to some of the soft yellow rhododendrons, normally flowers at the same season as *R. campanulatum*.

THE *LAPAGERIA*-FLOWERED RHODODENDRONS

One of the loveliest of rhododendrons, *Rhododendron cinnabarinum*, is earning itself a bad name on account of its susceptibility to the fungal disease powdery mildew. If you find these *Lapageria*-flowered species and hybrids irresistible, then keep them as much in the open as is consistent with the need to give them shelter to protect the young growths and the flowers. Especially, see that they are not planted beneath the drip of other trees; the edge of a glade, in filtered shade, is what they need. A regular programme of spraying with two fungicides, alternating, once a month from late spring to autumn, should protect them and your other rhododendrons from damage; a nuisance, certainly, but worth it to ensure the safety of your cinnabarinums.

The most famous hybrid is Lady Chamberlain, which inherits the neat, oblong, glaucous-bloomed leaves of the parent, and its waxy, narrow bells of soft terracotta and coral. Different cultivars vary slightly in colour, from the pink of 'Salmon Trout' to 'Golden Queen' and the warm saffron, crimson-tipped 'Gleam'. Its counterpart in pink is Lady Rosebery, of which 'Pink Lady Rosebery' is a fine selection with waxy bells paler within than on the bloomy exterior. Lesser-known, but no less beautiful, hybrids include the Caerhays set, 'Caerhays John' with deep apricot funnels, waxy, rich orange-yellow 'Caerhays Lawrence', and warm yellow 'Caerhays Philip'; 'Conroy' in soft pink-tinged tangerine; 'Trewithen Orange' and 'George Johnstone' with tawny apricot bells; warm buff 'Bodnant Yellow'; 'Royal Flush' in two forms, pink and orange – which is actually a gentle buff-yellow with orange throat and coral shading on the exterior – and 'Comely Golden Orfe'.

And this is not the end, for when it comes to cinnabarinums I have the greatest difficulty in applying Graham Thomas's dictum: collect species, select cultivars. Clamouring for attention, then, are Biskra, a slender and free-flowering shrub with narrow funnels of soft vermilion; Alison Johnstone with amber-buff bells; Oreocinn with glaucous foliage and pale coral funnels; and Cinnkeys, which has narrow tubes, tangerine shading to lemon at the tips. This is half *R. keysii*, a strange species allied to *R. cinnabarinum* which gave Cinnkeys the other half of its name; in flower *R. keysii* recalls a fuchsia of the *splendens* type, or perhaps even a correa, far more than a rhododendron, with its clusters of narrow, vermilion, yellow-tipped tubes.

R. cinnabarinum itself is now considered to include many variants once accorded specific rank in their own right, including the Concatenans group, beautiful in their bright verdigris-blue foliage and ochre bells. *R. cinnabarinum xanthocodon* varies from waxy Naples yellow to wider bells of bloomy plum-purple. 'Vin Rosé' is wine-dark with blood-red shading within. The Blandfordiiflorum group has flowers that are mandarin red outside and yellow or even greenish within, while the magnificent Roylei group leans towards rosy-red or plum-crimson. 'Mount Everest' is wide belled, in tender apricot.

Rhododendron woodlands tend to run out of steam after midsummer, but there are a few late-flowering hybrids that keep the display going into late summer. Polar Bear is a big and muscular shrub, even a tree in time, with large, emphatic leaves and great trusses of white, lily-like trumpets full of perfume. Argosy flowers a little earlier, but still after the main rhododendron effusion; its white, fragrant trumpets are marked with a ray of crimson, in contrast to the glacier-green flash that stains Polar Bear. These and other more obscure, lily-flowered, late rhododendrons have the blood of *Rhododendron auriculatum* (a lovely species but rather temperamental) or of *R. fortunei discolor*, which is bone hardy and has large, palest blush, fragrant flowers marred only by their fragility, for the thin petals are easily bruised by wind.

Late reds may derive from the tender, pure scarlet *R. elliottii* or *R. facetum*, which has cardinal-red bells and white-backed foliage. Red Cap is compact, its other parent the squatty, black-crimson *R. didymum*; it bears its blood-red bells until the end of summer, after Romany Chal, a tall scarlet; compact Grenadier; or wide, mounded Tally Ho. Uniting *R. didymum* and *R. griersonianum*, 'Arthur Osborn' is a small shrub with crimson-scarlet funnels among narrow, tan-backed leaves; among the latest of the reds, it sometimes still bears flowers in early autumn. It may seem inconsistent to extol these late reds after being rather sniffy about red hardy hybrids; but apart from their quality of colour, untainted by the hardy hybrid leaning towards bluish crimson, there is a great difference between a red rhododendron competing at the height of the season with all the pastel tones that look so well in filtered shade, and the drama of a single bush set with blood-red bells among the greenery of summer, set off perhaps by the slim, white trunks of birches.

Pink rhododendrons are best kept away from the reds, early or late, and from the gentle yellows. As well as the insistent pinks of the hardy hybrids, there are the tender rose and mauve and shell pinks of primary hybrids such as Naomi, a *Rhododendron fortunei* hybrid inheriting some of its fragrance, its wide trumpets of pale lilac suffused with chartreuse-green in the throat. Of its variants, 'Naomi Astarte' is nearer to pink, and

'Naomi Stella Maris' is exquisite in biscuit shaded with rose-quartz and lilac. A child of *R. griersonianum* which has lost the scarlet tones of the parent is 'Vanessa Pastel', a spreading, dwarf shrub with ivory flowers flushed with shell pink and stained with cherry-red. Vanessa herself is more uniformly pink with carmine freckles in the throat. The worst thing about Winsome, another *R. griersonianum* hybrid, is its name; for the long, nodding, pink flowers are pretty and the young growths are richly copper-tinted. This must derive from its *R. williamsianum* blood, via the other parent, Humming Bird.

R. *williamsianum* itself is one of the sweetest of pink rhododendrons, a neat, flattened dome with little, heart-shaped or circular leaves, chocolate-tinted in youth, and shell-pink bells most freely borne where it is in open-skyed light, yet sheltered by slanting shade. Carmine-scarlet Humming Bird is just one of its offspring. Moonstone is paler, opening from rosy-crimson buds to ivory-primrose, inheriting the same moundy outline as its parent. With bright burnished copper young growths, Bow Bells is a compact shrub with wide bells of tender pink from cherry-red buds. Cowslip leans more in colour to the other parent, *R. wardii*, for its bells are palest primrose with, at first, the blush of youth. The frilled bells of Brocade are bright cerise in bud opening to peach. Then there is Temple Belle, which rather takes after its other parent, *R. orbiculare*, having similar, rounded, glaucous-backed leaves and bells in which the difficult magenta-pink of *R. orbiculare* is tempered by the pale tones of *R. williamsianum*.

Though a glance at any comprehensive rhododendron catalogue or work of reference will show that even this long list of hybrids is just a fraction of what there is to be grown, I am reaching the end of my tolerance, impatient to be presenting my favourite species to you. There remain a few oddments that claim my attention, such as Crossbill, which is *R. lutescens* × *R. spinuliferum*, and just what you would expect from the child of those two, being a slender shrub with buff and Naples yellow tubes flushed with apricot and decorated with the long protruding stamens of the second parent. It is enchanting with *Acer palmatum* 'Katsura', a slow-growing maple with orange-buff spring foliage touched with red, turning green in summer and vivid orange-scarlet in autumn.

Another slender hybrid rhododendron is Yellow Hammer, which bears its canary-yellow tubes in early spring and, often, again in autumn, among neat little leaves. 'Golden Horn' and 'Persimmon' have from one of their parents, *R. dichroanthum*, their warm orange-tawny colouring. Though a rather dingy little thing apt to run to mustard pickle and marmalade colours, *R. dichroanthum* has the blessed quality of imparting warmth and fire to all its offspring, unlike *R. griersonianum* which all too readily concedes its scarlet tones. (It is from *R. dichroanthum* that Fabia gets her tangerine and terracotta complexion.) Occasionally nature herself, in the wild, tries her hand at producing a hybrid that can stand against any manmade creation; 'Nereid' is one such, another child of *R. dichroanthum* united with *R. neriiflorum* to make a low, neat bush with nodding, waxy bells of apricot-pink. *R. neriiflorum* itself is delicious, varying from deep rose to crimson via a wholly desirable pure scarlet, with neat, oblong leaves that are bright glaucous-white on the reverse.

LATE-WINTER COLOUR

If it flowered during the height of the rhododendron season, no one would give 'Praecox' a second glance. But as it has the good sense to open its bright amethyst funnels in late winter, it has become very popular. Try it in a group with a good wine-purple form of *Daphne mezereum*, a patch of purple or pink *Erica carnea* or a spread of Lenten roses, *Primula* 'Wanda' and the burgeoning red buds of *Pieris japonica* 'Christmas Cheer' or 'Daisen'. If nearby there can be a tree of *Prunus* 'Okame', the purple of 'Praecox' and the daphne will be enriched and the blue-tainted pink of the cherry cleaned to a fresh, clear tone by contrast. Tessa is a smaller, later, cyclamen-pink hybrid of 'Praecox'. At much the same early spring season comes Seta, a delightful little upright shrub with narrow bells, pearl-white shading to cherry-pink at the tips. Bo-peep is half *R. lutescens* also, and bears its pale clotted-cream flowers very early on a 1.2m/4ft bush.

THE QUALITIES OF SPECIES

The risk to any early-flowering rhododendron, at least in treacherous climates like that of Britain, is of an untimely spring frost damaging the fragile blooms. Within the shelter of woodland cover, often the flowers will survive unhurt when in the open they would be singed. This does not imply that the plant itself is susceptible to damage by frost. I have written at length about the more tender rhododendrons in my book *The Milder Garden*, and will concentrate here on the species that are in themselves reasonably or fully hardy. Once you start to grow species rhododendrons, you will find that whatever their hardiness rating, with a few ironclad exceptions, you need to give them something much nearer ideal conditions than the tougher hybrids.

The geographical heartland of the genus lies in the Himalayas and western China, in areas of frequent rainfall where the slopes are often wreathed in mist, so that at all times the atmospheric humidity is high. Even in the maritime climate of Britain, the air is frequently too dry, and rain falls too sparsely and too seldom, to satisfy the rhododendrons. The more the soil can be improved with leafy humus, and the moisture of the rains of winter retained with a loose mulch of leaves and bracken fronds, the better for the rhododendrons. Within the shelter of the wood, too, drying winds are tempered so that the atmospheric humidity is conserved rather than dissipated. And in spells of severe cold, the canopy – even though now bare of leaves – offers a little protection against frost.

Having departed from my own personal preferences to give you, first, a few hardy hybrids to consider, where the floraison is all and the leaves of no merit, and then passed to more appealing hybrids some of which have beautiful foliage, or strokable marbled bark, to their credit, I want now to try to convince you that there are many species worth that little extra effort for their year-round dignity and grace. However lovely the flowers – and some are breathtaking – they last only a short time, whereas foliage and bark are with us always. If you hope never to tire of your rhododendrons, choose them for their leaves and stems first, their flowers second. After all, you can always visit one of the great rhododendron gardens at the height of the season if you want an eyeful of colour.

In rhododendrons, the appeal of foliage lies not only in its shape and size, but also, indeed especially, in the felted or woolly indumentum of silver, tan, cinnamon, umber or chocolate that backs the leaves of many species. Of these, the large-leaved species are among the most spectacular, with foliage like great paddles as much as 45cm/18in long in ideal conditions. Again, I have described these in some detail in *The Milder Garden*, so will pick out here the easier species that you can hope to succeed with outside the high humidity areas of western Scotland and equivalent climates.

THE LARGE-LEAVED RHODODENDRONS

Rhododendron hodgsonii is one of the least demanding, and its 30cm/12in leaves can stand comparison with most, with their darkly metallic upper surface and beige felting on the underside. The bark of R. *hodgsonii* is fine, too, peeling in tones of cream and cinnamon and mauve. The flowers are nothing to shout about, being often of a rather dirty pink. A selection called 'Poet's Lawn' has beautiful blooms of celadon cream tinged with appleblossom pink on the ribs: but whether it is to be obtained in commerce I doubt.

When it comes to *R. macabeanum*, life is made somewhat easier by the fact that the seedlings with the most handsome leaves, broad and bold with leathery upper surface and brightly silvered reverse, usually turn out to have the finest flowers of almost canary-yellow. In these species the flower shape is different from the flared trumpet of the familiar hybrids, being instead a squatty bell, almost parallel-sided with brief, flared lobes; the individual blooms are often marked at their base with crimson or plum-black stains where the nectaries lie, and are clustered into rounded or flat-topped trusses. Even the palest and most translucent of washed-out, creamy *macabeanum* flowers have their own primitive appeal, and there is from this species yet another lovely feature to enjoy; for as the young growths unfurl, they look like scarlet candles, the vivid bud scales peeling aside to reveal the platinum new leaves.

Another big-leaf that you may succeed with even in drier gardens, with all the help you can contrive by way of shelter, mulching and irrigation, is *R. falconeri*, which has long leaves, bright fox-red beneath, and long-lasting, creamy yellow, waxen bells in immense trusses. Its subspecies *eximium* has a deep snuff-brown indumentum that persists for almost a year on the upper surface of the leaf as well as the lower, and flowers in shades of pink. The hardiest of the large-leaved species is probably *R. rex* ssp. *fictolacteum*, with dark burnished leaves backed with deep umber-brown felt, and creamy or blush, crimson-stained bells. In the Savill Garden, thirty kilometres/twenty miles or so from London, tawny-felted rhododendrons of this kind are associated with a fine specimen of *Acer japonicum aureum*, the chartreuse-green, vine-shaped leaves of the maple seeming the more vivid for their cinnamon and sepia backdrop.

TAWNY-FELTED LEAVES

Of smaller-leaved species with felted leaf reverse, *Rhododendron bureavii* is slow and compact, but even in babyhood displays the bright fulvous backing to its deep green leaves. The flowers are unexceptionable pink bells in tight trusses. *R. roxieanum* takes long to reach flowering age, but the narrow leaves with bright tan reverse of the Oreonastes group are ample compensation. No less restrained in growth, *R. haematodes* has thick, russet felting to the reverse of the dark green leaves, and vivid scarlet bells in late spring. The related and much larger, even tree-like, *R. mallotum* bears its dark crimson trusses two months earlier; the leaves are wrinkled deep green above and rufous brown beneath. As its name implies, *R. arboreum* develops into a tree, usually with smallish leaves silvered beneath; but some forms, and especially 'Sir Charles Lemon' (which may have the blood of *R. campanulatum* in its veins) have a thick umber-brown indumentum on the reverse of the leaves. The white flowers of 'Sir Charles Lemon' are not very freely borne, but stand out against the dark leaves and mahogany stems. The flower colour of *R. arboreum* itself varies from white, blush and pink to blood-red, the small spherical trusses opening early in the year. The blood-red forms are generally the most tender. The related *R. niveum* is perfectly hardy in woodland conditions; its leaves are backed with white wool turning to fawn with age, and its tight, rounded heads are composed of grape-purple or slate-blue bells opening after those of *R. arboreum*.

THE BEAUTY OF BARK AND LEAF

Another early-flowering red is *Rhododendron barbatum*, quite hardy in itself but needing shelter to protect the glowing scarlet trusses. Even if they are damaged, you still have the lovely limbs of this leggy, tree-like rhododendron to admire, for they are clad in plum-purple bark peeling to smooth steely tones. The bark of *R. griffithianum*, already mentioned as a tender parent of many fine hybrids, is even more beautiful, rufous- and mahogany-red peeling to a bloomy surface the colour of unripe grapes. Round-leaved *R. thomsonii* has flaking bark of fawn-pink and beige and *terra rossa*; the bright glaucous jade of the young foliage sets off waxy, deep crimson bells. The soft yellow tassels of *Corylopsis glabrescens* are just right to enliven the blood-red of the rhododendron.

Although its bark is nothing special, *R. wardii* is appealing both in sea-green, oblong leaf and in flower, the wide saucers varying from creamy primrose to fresh lemon, often with a flash of garnet-red at the base. The best forms of *R. lutescens*, such as 'Exbury' or 'Bagshot Sands', are of clear primrose or lemon-yellow also, the dainty blooms borne early in the year among narrow, pointed, mahogany-bronze leaves. There is a delightful dawn pink variant also. This species belongs to the Triflora subsection, characterized by an azalea-like daintiness. *R. triflorum* itself is tall, with peeling bark and citron funnels marked with green, while *R. yunnanense*, one of the best, is very free with its pink or white, tangerine-stained funnels in late spring. I have a great fondness, too, for *R. oreotrephes*, on account of its neat, glaucous-blue foliage and clear mauve-lilac flowers.

The foliage of *R. glaucophyllum* is characterized by the vivid glaucous-white reverse and, especially, by its pungent aroma of saddlesoap; the little bells are of *rose du Barry* colouring. The species has a lemon-flowered counterpart in *R. luteiflorum*. This is about the smallest rhododendron that I am prepared to consider in my woodland context; most of the dwarf species are natives of open spaces and neither appreciate nor look right under a tree canopy, though that is not to say that they should be planted on a hot, dry slope either. Those that do need shade I propose to mention when I talk about the shady rock garden. Just two more species that *are* suited to woodland claim my attention, before some of the other shrubs of acid soil assert their right to inclusion. They are the easy, free-flowering and fragrant *R. decorum*, with large, white or palest blush funnels in loose trusses among oblong, glaucous-green leaves; and *R. irroratum*, a small tree with narrow bells of varying colour. The cultivar 'Polka Dot' is worth getting, for its white bells are thickly freckled with purple.

The Supporting Cast

If in the pages of a book rhododendrons can all too easily dominate, how much more so in the limited space of the garden. The trouble is that, however much you think you will choose rhododendrons for their foliage or their bark before their flowers, or pick the ones that flower much earlier or later than the majority, there is an underlying sameness in the genus that calls for relief. Azaleas, a distinct section of the genus *Rhododendron*, provide this in part, and I will certainly allow them a look-in later. For now, let us run through some of the genera that need similar conditions to rhododendrons and yet are different in aspect.

For a complete change of style, there are the white-flowered shrubs and small trees of summer that belong to the genera *Eucryphia*, *Styrax*, *Stuartia*, *Clethra* and, earlier-flowering at the peak of the rhododendron season, *Halesia*. The species of *Styrax* are among the prettiest of trees to assort with rhododendrons. Their deciduous foliage is light and fresh in contrast to the often heavy evergreenery of the rhodos, the branching habit —especially in *S. japonica*, which has received the briefest of notice on p. 15 – is graceful and elegant, and the flowers, little white bells hanging beneath the branches, have given the genus the pet name of snowbell. The fruits that follow are like small, velvet-coated, almond-green marbles. *S. obassia* is a more round-headed tree than the fan-like *S. japonica*, and its leaves are bolder and broader, softly felted beneath, on russet shoots with peeling bark. The little, fragrant bells are held in long sprays at midsummer, but are rather hidden by the leaves and do not last long, though you can enjoy them for another day or so as they carpet the ground beneath the branches. The blossom of *S. hemsleyana* lasts longer and opens later, and is less hidden among the leaves; the branching habit of the tree is more open. The minute-leaved *S. wilsonii* is more of a twiggy shrub than a tree, with flowers solitary or in little clusters. But without doubt *S. japonica* is the one to choose if you have room for only one snowbell tree. It flowers with amazing freedom, and when it has grown large enough for you to stand beneath – well-fed, it should easily overtop you in time – you will look up into rank upon rank of white bells at its midsummer season. So many are the flowers that if you do not feed it with an annual mulch of good leaf mould, it is likely to starve itself to death.

The related *Halesia tetraptera* (*H. carolina*), the snowdrop tree, flowers earlier and is less tolerant of shade, or, more exactly, less inclined to flower with the required abundance unless in the sun, so it will need an open position in a glade in your woodland; but the flowers do come before the leaves have expanded. *H. monticola* is a taller and more tree-like species with larger white flowers; exceptionally for the genus, var. *rosea* has shell-pink flowers. Much rarer than these is the related *Rehderodendron macrocarpum*, a small tree with white, yellow-eyed flowers in late spring, bright red, hanging, ribbed fruits, and leaves that often colour well in autumn. It is a mystery why a tree that is described as 'a magnificent species . . . equal to the best *Styrax*' in the invaluable Hillier's *Manual of Trees and Shrubs* should be so scarce.

Flowering after midsummer, the stuartias tend to make small trees with white or cream flowers borne over a long season but never making a great show. But as the leaves die, they often turn to scarlet and flame and crimson, while the bark of older trees is almost as beautiful as that of *Rhododendron* Loderi, peeling and flaking in shades of fawn and cream. All prefer woodland conditions, with their roots in cool soil that does not dry out, and a yearly mulch of leaves. The open-branched *Stuartia pseudocamellia* seems to be the most common, at least in commerce; it has the usual cupped, white flowers with a central boss of yolk-yellow stamens, rather like a small, single camellia.

Both *S. malacodendron* and *S. monodelpha* have violet or purple anthers rather than yellow; at its best, the first is beautiful, but its petals are papery, and quickly lose their shape. Like *S. malacodendron*, *S. ovata* is an American species, at its best in the form *grandiflora* with purple, not yellow, stamens in wider flowers. With *S. serrata*, we return to the Far East; here the flowers are small and flushed with red on the outside, and the autumn colour is generally very bright. The bark of *S. sinensis* is among the most colourful, and the leaves in autumn colour to rich crimson; the solitary, small flowers are fragrant. Finest of all is *S. pseudocamellia* var. *koreana*, a tree of more upright habit than most, with white flowers opening wider than the little cups of *S. pseudocamellia* itself, and the most vivid autumn colour of the genus.

TREES FOR LATE–SUMMER FLOWERS

For display, the stuartias cannot compare with the eucryphias, which chiefly flower a month or so later. Most are evergreen; the deciduous species, *Eucryphia glutinosa*, has upright but flexible branches, bowed in late summer under the weight of massed, wide, white flowers with a full, central boss of stamens. The pinnate leaves colour fiercely in autumn and last long, into early winter. It is slightly pernickety in its requirements, needing a rich, acid soil, well mulched to keep the roots cool and fed, and disliking disturbance. Double-flowered forms often appear among seedlings, which are not difficult to raise; they are far less beautiful than the single-flowered forms which resemble a snowy rose of Sharon. Of the evergreen species of *Eucryphia*, some are rather tender; these have been described in *The Milder Garden* and I will not tantalize you with them here.

Of the hardier species and hybrids, both *E.* × *intermedia* and *E.* × *nymansensis* have the blood of *E. glutinosa* and both show simple and compound leaves on the same plant. 'Nymansay' is the selection of *E.* × *nymansensis* usually encountered; it forms a rather columnar, dark-leaved tree full of honey-scented, white flower in late summer. (Why 'Nymansay'? There were two seedlings, A and B, raised in the garden at Nymans: B didn't make the grade.) 'Mount Usher' takes more after the other parent, *E. cordifolia*. Both are popular with bees.

E. × *intermedia* has glaucous backs to the leaves, deriving from its evergreen parent *E. lucida*, and very copious white, yellow-centred, fragrant flowers. The form usually found in commerce is 'Rostrevor'. *E. lucida* itself, a Tasmanian species, has almond-scented, white flowers smaller than those of *E. glutinosa* but exquisitely beautiful, with rose-tipped stamens. A pink form has been found in the wild, propagated and introduced as 'Pink Cloud'. The leaves are small and neat, dark above and glaucous-white beneath, on slender, upright branches. It can reach 20m or more (over 60ft) in the wild, but I know of no tree so ambitious in British gardens, at least.

The sorrel tree, *Oxydendrum arboreum*, has been briefly mentioned on p. 16. As a companion for rhododendrons, it is just the thing, needing the same conditions of acid, leafy soil and dappled shade, displaying its drooping sprays of white flower after all but the latest of rhododendrons have finished, and indulging in a conflagration of crimson and gold as the leaves die and fall. It is one of comparatively few woody plants to be honoured with two Awards of Merit from the Royal Horticultural Society, once for flower and once for autumn colour; and has also earned the coveted Award of Garden Merit, which is much harder to achieve as it is judged not just on display in a vase but on performance in the garden.

Clethras are mainly shrubby; the Madeiran *Clethra arborea*, which, as its name implies, reaches tree size, is only for very mild climates where frosts are rare and never severe. All of the hardier species flower in high summer, and all are fragrant. The quality of fragrance is implied in the common name of *C. alnifolia*, the sweet pepper bush, a suckering man-high shrub with spikes of white or faintest ivory-blush flowers that fill the surrounding air with perfume. They flower with more freedom in sun, but need moist soil, and perform very adequately in light shade. 'Paniculata' is generally reckoned the finest in flower, unless you succumb to the delightful 'Rosea' and 'Pink Spire', which not only have a distinctly rosy tinge to both buds and flowers, but are also superior in foliage on account of the sheeny upper surface of the leaves. In this, as in *C. acuminata*, which has fragrant, cream spikes, the dying foliage turns to lemon and ochre. The other North American species you may encounter is *C. tomentosa*, which, as its name implies, has greyish-downy foliage; otherwise it resembles a later-flowering *C. alnifolia*.

Much though I value these clethras for their fragrance, for beauty they are outclassed by the Far Eastern species, which are also scented. *C. barbinervis* is a fine thing with long spikes of flower; it is more colourful in autumn than its trans-Pacific cousins. The pure white flowers of *C. fargesii* are held in very long spikes, rivalled by the slightly tender *C. monostachya*. Beyond doubt the loveliest of the oriental clethras, though, is *C. delavayi*, a tall shrub with aspirations to treedom, needing and amply deserving a sheltered corner, where it will reward you in summer with long, flattened sprays of lily-of-the-valley flowers of the subtlest colouring, milk-white with tan anthers in grey-felted calyces that turn to pink as the petals fall, among leaves that are velvety beneath.

MAGNOLIAS

Exquisite though *Clethra delavayi* is when in flower, its charms are of the discreet kind that demand intimacy. Of the white-flowered shrubs that associate with rhododendrons and need similar conditions, and follow their main season of bloom, the most aristocratic and yet declamatory – qualities that are often mutually exclusive – are the summer-flowering magnolias, which between them fill the season from early summer to autumn. Not all are calcifuge, as I have suggested in the previous chapter; but as the chalk-tolerant *Magnolia sinensis* and *M.* × *highdownensis* are so similar to their lime-hating cousins it seems to make more sense to describe them all together.

The most decidedly calcifuge is *M. sieboldii*, valued not for having the largest or most fragrant flowers among this group of shrubby, summer-flowering magnolias, but for its long season of three or four months from late spring, when the cupped flowers are held horizontally on spreading branches among broad, glaucous-backed leaves. Turn up the face of the flower, and you will see that its waxy, white petals surround a boss of ruby-red stamens with a citron club at their centre; after the petals fall, the fruits that form are just as showy, the crimson, fleshy receptacle splitting to reveal scarlet seeds. These can be sown to raise another generation; especially with *M. sinensis* and *M. wilsonii*, this is worthwhile even if you are impatient, for in a mere five to seven years you should have flowers on your seedlings. *M. sinensis* is more tree-like than *M. sieboldii*, and the larger flowers nod more modestly, the snowy petals opening wider to reveal the rosette of crimson stamens and green central club of carpels.

Their season is shorter, lasting for six weeks or so around midsummer; vivid crimson and scarlet fruits follow. The leaves of *M. wilsonii* are narrower, and the flowers smaller. The two have united to produce *M.* × *highdownensis*, whose name indicates to anyone familiar with the garden of Sir Frederick Stern that here is a wholly lime-tolerant plant, otherwise how could it have arisen and survived in a garden made in a chalk pit? Like a more vigorous *M. sinensis* in growth, it has the same nodding, wide, fragrant flowers. The only member of the group that is scarcely worth growing, at least in small gardens, is *M. globosa*, with small flowers that stay half closed, and fast turn brown if touched by rain or even dew. The bold foliage is good, but not good enough, even in tan-backed youth, in the face of the competition from its kin.

The wholly desirable *M. hypoleuca* is another matter. It will make a tree in time, of great beauty even before it flowers, for the bold, vivid green leaves are palely glaucous beneath. The flowers open a few at a time over a long summer season, each one a confection of clotted-cream, suede petals and wine-red stamens, with a rich fruity perfume of a more immoral quality than the fresh citrus fragrance of *M. sieboldii* and *M. sinensis*. Even this is discreet compared with the swooning scent, like ripe pineapples with a hint of something still more exotic, that is carried far on the air from the creamy-fawn globes of *M.* × *wieseneri* (*M.* × *watsonii*), which is *M. hypoleuca* × *M. sieboldii*. With such parents it should be good, and indeed a mature tree, such as I was once fortunate enough to have the enjoyment of, dominates even a large garden in its summer season, simply by virtue of its perfume. That it forms a large sprawling shrub needing plenty of room seems, while the flowers last, only right as the price of such voluptuousness.

All these magnolias, and others that I have no space to describe (I refer you, if you are interested, to my *Collecting Garden Plants* and *The Milder Garden*, as well as to the specialist magnolia literature) do best in open woodland conditions, with shelter and filtered light, in a moist forest-floor soil. On no account ever dig around your magnolias, for they dislike having their fleshy roots disturbed; nor should you scrape off fallen leaves from beneath them. Better by far to add more, a cool mulch each autumn that holds the promise of sustenance and the assurance of protection. Given these ideal conditions, they grow surprisingly quickly and flower abundantly year after year.

GRACE AND DELICACY

A quality not generally associated with rhododendrons is daintiness, delights such as *Rhododendron lutescens* notwithstanding. And of the companions so far proposed, only *Styrax japonica* goes any way towards delicacy of outline, however much the different texture of deciduous leaves may relieve the worst and best of rhododendron foliage. The genus *Enkianthus*, by contrast, is in all its manifestations the epitome of grace. Twiggy, deciduous shrubs, all the species bear in late spring nodding clusters of little bells, often of the subtlest colouring and veining. *E. campanulatus* is the one to start with, for it is both easy in lime-free soil with some shade, and widely obtainable. Its upright, rather tiered growths may reach 3m/10ft in time, and the neat leaves are as vivid as any bonfire in autumn. The little, cupped flowers vary in colour from primrose to bronze, veined with terracotta; *palibinii* is a red-flowered selection and *albiflorus* is the colour of white jade. The flowers of *E. chinensis* are larger, as befits a species that aspires to reach the stature of a tree; they are sulphur yellow with jasper-red veining. For intensity of colour, *E. cernuus rubens* is unequalled; a smaller shrub, it has cardinal-red, fringed bells and autumn colour to match. The slow compact *E. perulatus* is no less brilliant in autumn, but bears abundant white bells in spring.

Another ericaceous shrub that flowers later, at midsummer and after, is *Zenobia pulverulenta*, a small shrub white-bloomed all over, stems and leaves alike. The white bells are much larger than those of any *Enkianthus*, and twice as large as the lily of the valley they resemble in all but fragrance; but Zenobia's amplitude of flower detracts not at all from her elegance.

Just as dainty as these is the one remaining species of *Corylopsis* that I promised you. *C. pauciflora* positively demands an acid soil, unlike its kin which prefer it but submit willingly enough to a higher pH. A slow, slender-branched shrub, it has the smallest leaves of the genus, unfurling in shades of coral-pink and very susceptible to a late frost at this time, so overhead shelter is needed for protection; especially as the bright sunlight of an early heatwave can be almost as damaging to the tender new tissues. Before the leaves come the flowers, fewer to a tassel but individually larger than any other species, scented of cowslips, and of clear pale yellow, just a shade more definite than that of a wild primrose.

Some azaleas are as pretty in flower as flights of butterflies, and a few are deliciously fragrant with a far-reaching perfume. None does this better than the common *Rhododendron luteum*, the honeysuckle azalea, which happens also to be one of the most attractive, with rounded heads of clear citron-yellow flowers borne on a bush which may reach as much as 3m/10ft high and wide. In autumn it earns its keep again, the dying leaves a Byzantine blend of orange, cinnabar and plum-purple. It flowers at about the same time as the earliest of the hybrid deciduous azaleas, the lovely Mollis group, which unite the fragrant, tangerine or coral-red *R. japonicum* and the rather tender, yellow-flowered *R. molle*. In spacious woodland gardens, the Mollis azaleas can be planted among white cherries or birches, with bluebells and Welsh poppies and forget-me-nots; they are most beautiful when the yellows – from lemon to saffron – are allowed to dominate, with just a few of the brilliant mandarin- and terracotta-reds if these are to your taste.

These pure and lovely colours must be kept well away from most rhododendrons; almost all pink and red rhododendrons have too much blue in their colouring, and almost all the near-blues have too much pink, to be seen in the company of these azaleas, while most of the yellows are so gentle that the vivid azaleas make them seem pallid. But the nearly true blue of the *Anemone nemorosa* forms described in an earlier chapter blends delightfully with the yellow and soft flame azaleas, near which you might set a cut-leaved *Acer palmatum* in green or coppery-purple.

There are, of course, pink azaleas as well as all the hot colours. The early azalea season is graced by *Rhododendron albrechtii*, a smaller shrub than the common yellow azalea, with deep rose-pink flowers; and by *R. schlippenbachii*, a taller shrub with flights of shell-pink to rose, fragrant flowers. Many people complain about the name of this lovely thing; but I find a certain satisfaction in enunciating these syllables, and why should poor Baron Schlippenbach not be honoured? A week or two later than these Far Eastern species, it is the turn of *R. vaseyi*, a North American azalea with shell-pink, red-freckled flowers. Like the Baron's azalea, this one offers another treat to the eye in autumn, competing with the honeysuckle azalea in dying leaf. Even before *R. albrechtii*, the first peach-pink funnels of *R. pentaphyllum* may open. All deciduous azaleas are at their best in woodsy soil with leaf-litter or bracken mould for a mulch, in dappled shade; *R. pentaphyllum* is rather temperamental, and you should give it as near ideal azalea conditions as you can. The leaves, held in whorls of five at the ends of the branches, go in for the usual azalea pyrotechnics in autumn. Pink azaleas, whether deciduous like these or evergreen, look well among the white stems of birches, with the snowy blossom of *Amelanchier canadensis* above, and a mossy floor at their feet. In areas of high atmospheric humidity and low pollution, they may become bearded with a silvery-grey lichen that adds its own subtlety to the colour scheme.

LATER AZALEAS

As the azalea season advances, so it is the turn of the Knaphill and Exbury hybrids, in which other species have played a part. One of these is *Rhododendron calendulaceum*; its name means marigold-like, which suggests the brilliance of its saffron to fiery scarlet flowers, opening in the late spring. The colours of the Knap Hill azaleas all reside in the yellow to pure red half of the spectrum, with pure, but never bluish, pinks. With azaleas, as with rhododendrons, I have to leave out far more than I can include: but it would be a shame to omit 'Harvest Moon', on account of its gentle straw yellow colouring, or the subtle buff and apricot-cream 'Lapwing'. Specialist growers list dozens of cultivars, or you can choose the colours you like best from the garden-centre sales beds.

Last of the main hybrid groups to flower, in early summer, are the Ghents; they come late enough to avoid the last of the spring frosts in colder gardens, and generally miss the searing east winds of spring that can be so damaging in Britain and parts of Europe. As *R. luteum* enters into their parentage, they are often fragrant, with long-tubed, honeysuckle-like flowers; but they are also influenced by *R. calendulaceum*, and by other species such as the tree-like *R. arborescens*, which has heliotrope-scented white funnels opening at midsummer to fill the warm evening air with fragrance. From among the many Ghents that have been raised, I want to mention just a few. 'Narcissiflora' is an old hybrid, dating from before 1871, and full of charm with its soft yellow, fragrant hose-in-hose flowers. Another which is every bit as sweetly scented is 'Daviesii', its dainty trumpets white with a yellow flare. It retains much of the grace of a species, and indeed is a simple hybrid between R. *molle* and the swamp honeysuckle, R. *viscosum*, which has white, spice-scented flowers. For a real eyeful of colour the vivid flame-scarlet 'Coccineum Speciosum', over 150 years old but still going strong, remains unbeatable, and its near contemporary 'Gloria Mundi' (no false modesty when these old cultivars were named) is almost as good in bright orange with a yellow flare. One of the latest of all azaleas is the North American R. *prunifolium*, a tall shrub with large funnels of vivid orange-scarlet.

If you prefer pastel shades to a riotous assembly, R. *occidentale* and its hybrids are there to join 'Daviesii' and the late-flowering R. *viscosum*. The wide funnels of R. *occidentale* range from creamy-white to shell-pink, with a basal stain of primrose or apricot; they are fragrant, and open at midsummer among the glossy foliage, which in autumn adds to the conflagration of dying leaves we expect from azaleas. A new, late-flowering, hybrid azalea that promises well is 'Summer Fragrance', with small, white flowers bearing a clear yellow flash on the upper lobe, scattered abundantly over the bush, which has light green foliage, so that the distant effect is exceptionally fresh and pretty. The scent, which no doubt derives in part at least from its R. *luteum* blood, is as good as the name suggests, sweet and far-reaching.

BRIGHTNESS CAN BE BORING

There is a fine line to be drawn between plant groups that belong to the idealized woodland and the garden proper, and each one of us will trace it differently. The groups that I find acceptable, such as those I have proposed, might be added to by someone who likes more varied colour even in the woodland. Thus the late Michael Haworth-Booth, who was single-mindedly dedicated to what he called 'flower power', the brighter the better so long as it was not purplish-pink, and hardly recognized leaves at all. He proposed assorting the pale azalea 'Harvest Moon' with *Rhododendron* 'Purple Splendour'; that seems to me to be too self-conscious a mix for even the most sophisticated woodland. So, too, Sybil Emberton's three-colour schemes, as it might be salmon-orange azalea 'Queen Emma' with R. 'Goldsworth Yellow' and near-blue 'Susan'. To me, these and similar combinations belong in a border of shrubs, rather than an idyllic woodland. It is partly a question of familiarity, too. What can seem exciting when you first see it, on a visit to someone else's garden perhaps, may become unbearably banal if you try to copy it and end up actually having to live with it.

Evergreen azaleas lend themselves exceptionally well to bright, and ultimately boring, combinations. They are the bedding plants of the acid woodland garden, low and humpy in the main, absolutely smothered in flower in their season, moveable and colourful. But they have other less acknowledged qualities also, not least the sombre tapestry of muted colours, claret and mahogany and bottle-green, of their winter foliage. First to flower, in early to mid spring, are the Kurume types, most of them small in flower and in leaf; on the whole, where there is sufficient moisture, they prefer to grow out in the open. A parent of the group, *R. obtusum*, bears flowers in shades of crimson to rose red; the splendid 'Amoenum' derives from this. Here is a shrub with a spreading, tiered habit, ultimately quite tall (I know of one at least 2.4m/8ft tall) with hose-in-hose flowers of the assertive magenta. This quarrelsome colour needs the right setting, and indeed I like to give it nothing but plenty of green – greens tending to blue, not to the sharp chartreuse of young oak foliage – and perhaps white or palest primrose. The Kurume 'Hinode-giri' is almost as bright in crimson, and 'Hinomayo' is a pretty, clear pink.

Azaleas with the blood of *R. kaempferi* lean towards coral and blood-red as well as to pink and rose-madder, and few of them are whole-heartedly evergreen. This tendency to shed their leaves comes from *R. kaempferi* itself, which flowers later than the Kurumes and varies from pale terracotta to coral and orange-scarlet. It has two good late-flowering selections in 'Mikado', clear salmon, and 'Daimio' which has flowers of brighter coral-red. Early or late, the colours of the kaempferi azaleas are easily bleached by the sun; dappled shade keeps the colour fresh, and the green of ferns and moss is all that is needed by way of contrast.

There are other groups of evergreen azaleas, some of them with much larger, even gross flowers. Although its flowers are not small, 'Palestrina' escapes the charge of grossness; it is of unsullied paper-white with just a touch of lime-green, lovely with clear pinks. The later-flowering 'Mucronatum' is a pretty shrub with dark, hairy leaves and fragrant, white funnels in late spring. There were several plants of this scattered through a garden I once had the care of, some of them in gloomy corners where too closely planted trees had interlaced into a dense canopy; there the little azalea gleamed in the dark, seemingly none the worse for never seeing the light of day.

Despite my puritanical observation about associating kaempferi azaleas with nothing but green, just one paragraph ago, I have to admit that a group I saw and greatly admired, so many years ago I cannot remember where, set the terracotta 'Orange Beauty' with *Acer palmatum* 'Dissectum Atropurpureum', *Enkianthus campanulatus*, and *Pieris* 'Forest Flame'. The colours were harmonious, the outlines complementary of mushroomy maple, spreading azalea, and tiered, airy enkianthus with the dark evergreen foliage, flaring in spring into scarlet, of the pieris. Nor are the flowers of 'Forest Flame' to be despised, for the shrub bears large, drooping sprays of little, white pitchers like tiny lilies of the valley, opening among the vivid spring foliage that slowly fades through pale coral to cream before adopting the sober green of maturity. 'Firecrest' is at least as good, with foliage passing from coral through peach and lemon to green.

Although, given a moist, leafy soil, all pierises flower most freely in the sun, the colourful spring foliage is very soft and quickly damaged by frost, wind or sunscorch, so it needs filtered, overhead shade for protection. This is even more true of *P. formosa forrestii* and its named selections, for this originates in Burma and Yunnan and is not so hardy as 'Forest Flame'. However, where suited it can be magnificent, with large, broad sprays of lightly scented, purer white flowers among spring foliage of brilliant scarlet. The best-known clone, and still in many ways the best, is 'Wakehurst', which has shorter, broader leaves of sealing wax red in spring, fading through shrimp and primrose to light green and sometimes giving a fainter repeat performance in late summer.

It looks very fine in company with snake-bark maples such as *Acer capillipes*, which has green and snuff-brown, white-striped bark and coral-red young branchlets to echo the scarlet of 'Wakehurst'. Other selections of var. *forrestii* such as 'Jermyns' and 'Charles Michael' are slowly becoming more widely available, but both are less winter-hardy. The first especially is worth growing for its waterfall outline and the tawny-port colouring of the inflorescence all winter, this cosy colouring retained in the calyx in contrast to the white urn-shaped flowers. 'Rowallane' departs from the usual grenadier-scarlet to display butter-yellow young growths, retaining their colour until late summer. Another of this colouring, more likely to be available in commerce, is 'Bert Chandler', a compact and rather small shrub. You could, of course, pair these with 'Wakehurst', but it might be more subtle to give 'Bert Chandler' a setting of dark, rather bluish greens where it could glow quietly, undimmed by more assertive companions.

When I first began gardening, there were few *Pieris* available: 'Wakehurst' and 'Forest Flame', the rather dull *P. floribunda*, *P. taiwanensis* and a handful of cultivars of *P. japonica*. But this species, which is now considered to include *P. taiwanensis*, has of late given us a surge of new cultivars, including the pink and red-flowered kinds which have partly shifted attention away from those with bright spring foliage, with which a mere white-flowered cultivar could scarcely compete. There are times when I deplore all this fascination with colour; it detracts from other good qualities of plants both in the garden and in the books we read. In the days of black-and-white photography, our attention was focused on form and outline, on light and shadow; before that even, when word pictures had to suffice, we recalled fragrance and texture and could evoke subtlety as well as stridency. Nowadays, television and lavishly illustrated books with a paucity of text bombard our retinas with saturated tones of red and yellow and purple and sugar pink; repose is sacrificed to freneticism. I stand up for white-flowered pierises, but will admit that some of the pinks are pretty too.

Pieris japonica seldom bothers with spring pyrotechnics; with a few exceptions, such as 'Scarlett O'Hara', a burnished coppery-bronze is as far as it goes. The type has white flowers, larger and more waxy than those of *P. formosa forrestii*, and opening earlier. Of newer whites, 'Dorothy Wyckoff' has warm brown buds in winter on a rather tall, slender shrub, and 'Purity' is exceptionally free with its upright spikes on a compact 1m/3¼ft dome. 'White Cascade' is valued for its exceptionally long flower sprays, and 'Grayswood' for its bronzed young growths and long, gracefully arching sprays opening from tawny buds.

'Blush' was the first of the pinks and is still one of the best, with deep pink flowers and neat, small, dark green leaves. 'Pink Delight' has quickly become popular, despite its trite name, for its deep pink bells in drooping sprays on stronger, less open growth than 'Blush'. Both 'Daisen' and 'Christmas Cheer' have received a brief mention as agreeably clashing companions for *Rhododendron* 'Praecox'; their burgundy buds open to a pleasing mid pink. Deepest of the pinks is 'Flamingo', with richly coloured buds opening to a curious shade of wine-red – not the purplish red which is usually implied, but something nearer to an honest red wine diluted with a little water, such as the Fleurie at four francs the bottle which we used to mix with Evian at luncheon on weekdays. *Pieris japonica* also has a regrettable tendency to produce variegated cultivars, such as the old 'Variegata' and newer 'White Rim', each with fairly unassertive cream margins tending to distort the leaf outline. In spring the young growths are touched with pink or bronze.

CONDITIONS FOR KALMIAS

Like *Pieris*, the midsummer-flowering *Kalmia latifolia* flowers more freely in full sun, but quickly suffers from dryness at the root unless the soil is of that elusive kind that is always moist in the growing season. The best compromise will usually be a position with light overhead shade, where surrounding trees help to keep the soil leafy and the atmospheric humidity high.

A kalmia that is not crowded among other shrubs, but growing freely in a little clearing, forms a large, rounded shrub with dark glossy foliage, comely all year. At midsummer it should be well furnished with clusters of pink flowers, each one looking in bud like the sugar-icing twirls that topped the tiny biscuits we ate as children, and opening to a little saucer with a dark speck in the pocket where each of the stamens is held. Like the pierises, *Kalmia latifolia* has of late become available in many different named cultivars, of which 'Ostbo Red' is a good deep crimson-pink, surpassing the older 'Clementine Churchill'; but the clear candy-pink of the type is so pretty that I hardly see the point of richer colouring. Where space is limited, and a shrub that could reach 2.4m/8ft or more will be too big, var. *myrtifolia* could be chosen instead, for it grows slowly to no more than 90cm/36in. Of much the same height is *K. angustifolia*, usually offered in the form *rubra*; it slowly forms a little thicket of slender stems set with rather narrow leaves and clusters of smaller, rosy-red flowers over a longer season.

THE QUIETER SHRUBS OF THE WOODLAND

Although it suckers mildly, *Kalmia angustifolia* can hardly be considered ground cover. The related leucothoës – we are still in the great family Ericaceae – are genuine weed-excluders, and beautiful, too, forming dense and luxuriant clumps. I would not admit to the woodland the immensely popular *Leucothoë fontanesiana* 'Rainbow', on account of its colouring, the leaves marbled with cream, pink and yellow on green; this seems to me to belong with other man-made creations, though I suppose you might use it as a link between the dignified inhabitants of the idealized woodland – nature's own species and the results of man's best endeavours to emulate them – and the more overtly artificial parts of the garden where such jazzy manifestations can be tolerated.

The plain green *L. fontanesiana* has long-pointed, gleaming foliage, burnished to copper in winter, on elegant, arching stems; clusters of little, white pitchers hang all along the stems in spring. The less familiar, shorter-growing *L. davisiae* opens its white flowers, held in upright spikes, about a month later, while later still comes the delightful *L. keiskei*, barely half the height – knee high, say, as against hip high or more for *L. fontanesiana* – and more restrained in its thicket-forming tendencies. The neat, glossy dark green, pointed leaves are set on reddish, zig-zag stems, a leaf at every zig or zag; the flowers, opening after midsummer, are the expected white urns, but larger. It differs also from the first two in insisting on soil that remains permanently moist (not wet); its larger brethren are surprisingly tolerant of summer drought once settled.

The most unusual leucothoë is *L. grayana*, which has non-suckering mahogany-red stems bearing leaves that turn to purple and bronze in autumn before falling – for unlike the others it is not evergreen. The flowers that open in high summer are pale green, on one-sided spikes. The whole tribe of leucothoës is shade-loving, among the best shrubs to furnish the woodland floor, and beautiful where allowed to run to the edge of a mossy clearing or path, or mingling with other low shrubs of clear-cut pattern such as *Mahonia nervosa*.

If quiet shrubs like these appeal to you, then the menziesias are for you, even if you boggle at the alternative pronunciations: do you say menzeezya or mingizzia? The second will do you no good with most interlocutors but the first lays you open to criticism from Scotsmen and students of the vagaries of British family names. On balance, I think menzeezya has it. A small shrub, *Menziesia ciliicalyx* is enchanting in flower, the clusters of *Daboecia*-like, waxy urns of cream, soft mauve or muted purple nodding from slim branches set with ciliate leaves; var. *purpurea* has slightly larger flowers of brighter mulberry-purple.

The other species you may come across is more reticent: *M. ferruginea* has little, pinkish, tubular flowers at the same late spring season. Both shed their leaves in autumn, without fanfare. So, too, *Lyonia ligustrina*, a smallish shrub with *Pieris*-like, white flowers in sprays, in high summer. By contrast *L. lucida* is evergreen; the polished leaves are borne on angled stems, and the white or blush flowers open in late spring. The stagger bush, *L. mariana*, resembles *Gaultheria shallon*, the salal, but is deciduous.

BRIGHT 'BERRIES'

A more modest spreader than the rampant salal, *Gaultheria procumbens*, or wintergreen, is one of the best, low, non-aggressive weed-excluders for acid soil, tolerating drought as will few ericaceous shrubs, and forming a dense carpet. The little white barrel-shaped flowers are not showy, but the scarlet fruits that follow make a bright picture of complementary colour with the shining, dark green leaves, both berries and leaves smelling of oil of wintergreen. Apart from the tiny gaultherias that I will describe when I come to the shady rock garden – though you could of course plant them in your woodland if you are willing to watch over them – the prettiest are those with turquoise or white fruits.

Anyone who gardens on acid soil will before long encounter the name of Frank Kingdon Ward, a collector of amazing endurance who had an eye for a plant that would translate to gardens. *G. wardii* is no exception, a bristly shrub with leathery, deeply veined leaves, white pitcher-shaped flowers, and porcelain-blue fruits. The name of *G. fragrantissima* refers to the flowers, but it is the cobalt-blue fruits that catch the eye. It is taller than *G. hookeri*, a dense, small shrub with arching stems and flower clusters followed by turquoise fruits. The colour of the berries of *G. semi-infera* is more variable, commonly a deeper indigo-blue. Most showy in flower as well as fruit is *G. forrestii*, with waxy, white, fragrant urns on spreading growths, followed by ultramarine fruits.

Although white fruits might sound less appealing than the uncommon pure blue of these species, the gaultherias with white 'berries' are pretty shrubs also. *G. hispida* is from Australia and Tasmania, one of a handful of antipodean species, some of which will crop up later in the shady rock garden.

In sheer exuberance of fruit, the pernettyas outclass the gaultherias. They are low shrubs, suckering into dense clumps of neat, evergreen foliage, flowering abundantly and set, in autumn and winter, with showy fruits. The most familiar species is *Pernettya mucronata*, with dark green leaves tipped with a sharp point (or mucro) and clusters of marble-sized fruits in sealing wax red, cherry, mother of pearl, lilac, blush, candy-pink, mulberry and white, an opaque and declamatory white that remains long unspoiled by frost's brown fingers and unravaged by birds. Although they fruit more freely when grown in the sun, I have had wonderful displays from a group of pernettyas on a north-facing bank shadowed by trees; to be sure of fruits, though, you must plant a male among your berrying females. The males especially tend to have burgundy-red shoots, so they are not wholly colourless beside their fecund ladies.

The names of the fruiting clones often suggest their colour, from the old-style 'Lilacina' and 'Rosea' to the more modern 'Pink Pearl', 'Cherry Ripe', 'Signal', 'Mulberry Wine', and a cluster of 'White' this and thats. Be warned, some of the reds are near enough to scarlet to quarrel with the lavender-pinks and magenta-purples, or to cancel, almost, the pretty blush and pearly pinks. The fruits of the bigeneric hybrid × *Gaulnettya wisleyensis* are not so bright, being of deep blackish-maroon, sometimes called oxblood-red, but the dried, not the fresh substance. The name 'Wisley Pearl', the original of the cross, refers to the abundant creamy-white bells, not to the fruits; 'Pink Pixie' has blush bells on pink stalks.

FRUITS TO EAT

With the genus *Vaccinium*, we return to a group of shrubs more usually characterized by restraint than exuberance, though some are as flamboyant as any New England maple in autumn livery. Few are brighter than the highbush blueberry, *V. corymbosum*, which will fruit enough to be worthwhile even in a part-shady position; but it must have moisture, even a near-bog. However, a soil too rich in nitrogen urges it to run to leaf at the expense of flower and fruit. A deep mulch of fresh sawdust (15cm/6in is not too much) both helps to conserve moisture and draws nitrogen from the soil as it breaks down, and I have had superb crops from blueberries of named varieties (with non-charismatic names like 'Herbert' and 'Berkeley') treated thus after planting in a sandy but moist soil, beneath trees where the sun reached them for less than half the day. And this in grey-skied England, where the sun's intensity is only an echo of the rays that shine upon continental gardens.

The blueberries look splendid at all stages among the heavy ever-greenery of rhododendrons, with little white urn flowers in spring, all those bloomy indigo fruits in late summer, and dying leaves in all the shades of scarlet. But you will have to arrange to net the shrubs, unless you are willing to let the birds have all the blueberries; it is easier, therefore, to group, rather than scatter, 'Herbert' and his colleagues.

The European and Asian bilberry, whortleberry or whinberry is a dwarf, suckering, evergreen shrublet more suited to open spaces, but the Caucasian whortleberry, *V. arctostaphylos*, is larger, of spreading habit with large, veined leaves that turn to plum-purple in autumn and are reluctantly shed at midwinter. The showy clusters of flowers, waxy white or ruby bells, are borne in summer and autumn, and the fruits are shiny – not bloomy – black spheres.

The Madeiran whortleberry, *V. padifolium* (surprisingly hardy considering its native land) is taller again, and takes dappled shade very well. It is one of those half-hearted evergreens that hangs on to its leaves until well into winter, then drops them without fuss or any hint of fiery colour to leave a rather stiff, upright outline of branches. The flowers, which open at midsummer, are dainty, green bells with a brown eye. Another semi-evergreen that has no business to be frost resistant, for it comes from the Azores, is *V. cylindraceum*, a tall shrub of great beauty when bearing its dense clusters of tubular flowers, currant-red in bud opening, during late summer, to citron-green tinged with terracotta and followed by sloe-black fruits that are cylindrical, not the usual globes.

The genus goes in for surprises, for *V. floribundum* (*V. mortinia*) grows in Ecuador, near the equator, yet the frosts of southern England and the northern Atlantic coasts of France leave it undisturbed. It is an exceptionally pretty, evergreen shrub with small, dark leaves, maroon and coppery-red when young, dense racemes of pink, barrel flowers at midsummer, and red, edible berries. A similar effect of neat, dark foliage in elegantly patterned sprays belongs to the taller *V. ovatum*, brighter burnished copper in young leaf and white or pink in flower; the red fruits ripen to black. The light that filters through the overhead canopy catches the polished, upper surface of the leaves as they darken to the deep green of maturity.

The little wintergreen has its counterpart among the vacciniums in *V. vitis-idaea*, the unglamorously named cowberry of northern woods and moorlands. The box-like, evergreen leaves are burnished in winter, and the tiny, blush bells are followed by red fruits: 'Koralle' is an especially good selection. There are also a couple of species which, though very low-growing, hardly more than a film of foliage on the ground, are too widespreading to be considered as rock garden shrubs. *V. oxycoccos* is the cranberry, and *V. macrocarpon* the American cranberry; both can reach a metre across or more as the slender stems root down in the moist, leafy soil they relish, and both bear edible, tart red fruits. In both, too, the minute, pink flowers have reflexed petals, giving them an outline quite different from the usual little urns or pitchers of the genus.

The most beautiful of the spreading or suckering species, though (excluding the tinies, which I intend to save for a later chapter), is *V. glaucoalbum*. On stems sometimes man-high, though often lower, are borne large, oval leaves, grey-green above and intensely glaucous-white beneath, forming a self-contained harmony of colour with the pale pink flowers that are held among blue-silvery, rose-flushed bracts in early summer. Its companions should be as understated as itself – ferns, mosses, unfussy dark green foliage of shrubs that flower at another season – so that nothing gaudy can detract from its subtle appeal.

CAMELLIAS FOR WOODLAND GARDENS

Though the glossy foliage of *Camellia japonica* is quite handsome, nobody grows camellias of any kind for their foliage: the *raison d'être* of a camellia is its flowers. The formal doubles with their almost artificial appearance, the looser doubles with a hint of stamens at the centre, and the full-centred, anemone-form and paeony-form camellias have no place in the woodland, and even the semi-doubles seem to me to belong in the garden, linking perhaps the manicured plantings with the wilder areas. Few of the many cultivars of *C. japonica*, then, rate a mention here. Scarlet 'Jupiter', a single with occasionally an extra petal or two and always a bright boss of yellow stamens, is acceptable: 'Adolphe Audusson' is not, for the semi-double flowers are too large to be in proportion. The striped and splashed cultivars most certainly have no place in the woodland, but shapely singles such as 'White Swan' and soft pink 'Furoan' are very welcome.

In the woodland context, I like to plant species and primary hybrids of camellias just as of rhododendrons. The lovely *C. saluenensis* has beautifully shaped, clear pink flowers very freely borne in late winter and early spring; the forms that open their flowers wide are generally admired, but I have a weakness for the narrow, almost funnel-shaped outline. More important than the form of the flower is the presentation; in the best seedlings the blooms are held in graceful sprays, in others they are half hidden. A hybrid of this species is 'Donation', immensely popular in part because even a small, rooted cutting will flower in its pot; to my eye it has too many petals for the woodland. It belongs to the group of hybrid camellias of which *C. japonica* is the other parent, collectively known as *C. × williamsii*. The original of them all, and still the most beautiful, is 'J. C. Williams', a clear pink single; 'St Ewe' is a little deeper in colour, with cupped petals. Most of the williamsii camellias have the estimable habit of cleanly shedding their fading blooms, unlike the japonicas which often cling to a shameful glob of browning tissue, the more offensive the more petals there are. Another charming hybrid of *C. saluenensis* is 'Cornish Snow', bearing an abundance of small, pure white flowers. The other parent is *C. cuspidata*, which almost constitutes an exception to my observations about camellia foliage, for the young growths are a deep coppery-black; the small flowers are creamy-white.

AUTUMN COLOUR AND WINTER FLOWER

Although many viburnums are plants of chalk soils and are grown mainly for their flowers, there are two handsome species which insist upon an acid soil and are valued above all for their autumn foliage: *Viburnun furcatum* and *V. lantanoides* (*V. alnifolium*). They are closely related and quite similar, the first an oriental plant, the second from North America; both have attractive flower heads like a white lacecap hydrangea, opening in late spring. The leaves of both are bold and rounded, and both take on rich, deep colours of claret and burgundy and blood-red in the fall, when the red fruits are ripening to black. Both can grow taller than head high, but the Japanese species has a much more upright habit. To these we might add a third, *V. cassinoides*, which is barely lime-tolerant, and a pleasant thing with its bronzed young foliage, creamy flowers at midsummer and fruits that age from red through indigo to black among crimson autumn leaves.

The witch hazels are usually chosen for their winter flowers, but they also make their mark in autumn. They earned their vernacular name from their hazel-like foliage, and from their use as water-divining rods. It was the North American *Hamamelis virginiana* that was first so nicknamed; it remains the source of commercial witch hazel that we used to dab on bumps and bruises as children and later, as adolescents, on our enlarged pores in the hope that its astringent qualities would spirit away the spots that burgeoned before a party. As a garden plant, it is inferior to the other North American species, *H. vernalis*, which produces its tiny but abundant, heavy-smelling, pale copper flowers in winter. 'Sandra' is a selection of this species which has leaves suffused with plum and claret-purple when unfurling, retaining a slight infusion of purple on the reverse and blazing with orange and scarlet in autumn.

The old *H. mollis*, the Chinese witch hazel, is valued for the fragrance of its yellow flowers that seem to be composed of twists of little ribbons, opening undaunted by frost during the winter months. 'Coombe Wood' is the name given to the original introduction, of spreading habit, with large flowers and a strong, sweet perfume; it is not offered by name as frequently as it should be. 'Goldcrest' is later-flowering, and deeper yellow in colour, with a suffusion of wine-red at the base of the petals; 'Brevipetala' has shorter petals but the rich orange-yellow flowers are thickly clustered on the branches. The beautiful 'Pallida' is of uncertain origin; it has large, pale lemon flowers all along the branches, and a delicious fragrance.

The Japanese witch hazel, *H. japonica*, is smaller and less downy in leaf than its Chinese counterpart, but colours to the same rich yellows in autumn; the petals are more twisted and crimpled, the scent often fainter, or slightly pungent. Variety *arborea* is virtually a tree when mature, with horizontal branching that gives it a very individual outline; 'Zuccariniana' is a rather upright shrub, with pale sulphur flowers opening very late, in early spring.

The Chinese and the Japanese species unite in *H.* × *intermedia* to produce some of the most exciting cultivars, including the red witch hazels. Some of these are nearer to a washy, tawny orange than to red, and their colour is easily lost in the garden; furthermore, they mostly have no trace of scent. However, the autumn foliage borrows the same shades of orange and cinnabar that infuse the flowers. In this respect 'Jelena' is as good as any, and the coppery flowers are large. 'Ruby Glow' is deeper tawny-red, though far from ruby; 'Diane' is deeper still in oxblood-red. Though it cannot quite compete in colour, my choice out of the reds would be 'Magic Fire' ('Feuerzauber'), for it has large copper-orange, red-flushed flowers with a distinct, sweet and spicy perfume: the only scented red, I believe, though you may not find this mentioned in catalogues. Of yellows in this hybrid group, 'Primavera' is a fine near-lemon with crimson heart, and 'Moonlight' a beautiful pale citron not unlike the colour of 'Pallida'. 'Arnold Promise' has short-petalled but well-filled flowers of pure yellow, with a strange and faintly disagreeable perfume, so that I should rank it behind 'Sunburst', of which the long, barely twisted petals are of the same clear colouring.

My original intention was to include the witch hazels in the preceding chapter; for they are not, I believe, truly calcifuge. What they dislike is a dry soil in sun; given part or dappled shade and sufficient humus in the soil, they will do well enough on limy soils, or so I am reliably informed by gardeners who grow them. My own gardens have all been on acid soils, so I cannot comment from personal experience.

In the case of embothriums, however, I can. They are said to be sunlovers, but I have successfully grown several specimens in shade. Provenance may have a good deal to do with this; many of my plants were seed-raised, the seed collected from plants growing at forest margins away from the sun. Of course, so long as they have the moist, leafy, lime-free soil they need, they flower most freely with their heads in the sun, as they might if they were growing in a woodland clearing.

In light shade, so long as they are kept away from the blue-toned rhododendrons, it is often easier to contrive emollient companions for the flowers of *Embothrium coccineum*. Each little, honeysuckle-like floret is vivid vermilion-scarlet, a colour that quarrels fiercely with pink, almost any other red, and the whole range of purples, violets and blues, but can be soothed by cream or clear yellow, and is happier among sharp greens leaning towards yellow than near the blue-toned greens. The finest form is still the one referred to, from its original location, as 'Norquinco Valley', for it is both hardy and very free flowering, the branches wearing clusters of scarlet strung along their length. If so vivid a red is too much

for you, take heart: we may hope before too long to be able to buy
yellow-flowered embothriums, easier to place with their bright but clear
colouring.

Little Plants, Lilies and Blue Poppies

Among all these shrubs of acid soils, we need some lowly plants.
Although rhododendrons, especially, are happiest when their root ball is
simply covered with a loose, moisture-holding mulch of leaves, the
spaces between them can be furnished with creeping things. In Chapters
II and IV I have suggested several seductive small plants for acid soils,
such as the clintonias, and *Cornus canadensis*. Then there is *Galax urceolata*
(*G. aphylla*), which in cool, lime-free soil slowly forms clumps of
polished, rounded, evergreen leaves, bronzed and crimson-tinted in
winter, especially where touched by the sun. The flowers are minute and
white, borne in slim spikes in summer. It is related to the shortias, which
are much too choice and fussy, in most gardens, even to include here.

As well as the carpeting gaultherias and vacciniums, there are such
generous ground-covering, creeping shrublets as *Arctostaphylos uva-ursi*
and the even more far-reaching *A. nevadensis*; they can safely be used
between larger shrubs, and are especially valuable on light, acid sands.
Both form dense, low carpets of shining, dark green leaves; the flowers,
typically ericaceous, are tiny bells, white in the North American species
and blush pink in the European bearberry; in both, the flowers are
followed by red fruits.

LILIES AND LILY-RELATIVES

Between your shrubs, too, places can be made for lilies, *Meconopsis*, the
taller ferns, and clumps of the plants already described as suitable for cool
shade or for the woodland on limy soils, such as trilliums and Solomon's
seals, willow gentians and erythroniums. The king of the lilies is
Cardiocrinum giganteum, a massive plant reaching high above our heads, its
thick stalk set with big, heart-shaped leaves that diminish in size from the
base upwards. Above this tapering plinth hang, in summer, the long,
elegant trumpets of alabaster-white with wine-red at their hearts. Var.
yunnanense differs in being shorter – a head taller than a tall man at most –
and in its dark stems, bronzed young foliage, and trumpets held at an
angle nearer to the horizontal to display the rich claret at their throats.

To feed this exuberance of leaf and flower, a rich, leafy soil that is well drained yet never dries out is needed. Miss Jekyll, who gardened on the hungry, acid sands of Surrey, succeeded with the giant lily by digging deep pits in her woodland garden, and throwing into them quantities of garden waste so that they became great compost pits. The rich, dark humus that resulted was topped with soil and some of the original sand, and the cardiocrinum bulbs planted so that their roots could reach down into the cool goodness below, while their snouts remained level with the soil surface. After flowering, each bulb perishes, leaving offsets which need to build strength from the rich nourishment beneath them before they can reach flowering size in turn. The fading trumpets give way to handsome seed heads, from which many little bulbs can be raised and, with patience, grown to maturity to give you the potential for a sweep of cardiocrinums through your woodland.

Most other lilies need more sun than the shade-loving cardiocrinums, though many will give a good account of themselves in broken shade. Few insist on acid soils; of those that do, the heavily perfumed *Lilium speciosum* is very beautiful, with wide turk's caps of white more or less heavily spotted and stained with crimson: but it is perhaps a little too opulent for the woodland. So, too, is *L. auratum*, with wide, white stars, each segment rayed with soft yellow and flecked with blood-red. One of the most covetable of all species for acid soil among shrubs is *L. duchartrei*, a dainty turk's-cap lily with white flowers flecked and stained with maroon.

Close relatives of the lily, *Nomocharis* species are elegant and beautiful, but distinctly tricky unless they have just the conditions that suit them, of a leafy and well-drained soil with no lime, shelter from wind, and a cool, moisture-charged atmosphere. The name means 'grace of the meadows', but the meadows in question are high, Himalayan pastures. Even the south of England is too hot and dry for them, unless in the most ideal of woodland settings. That, of course, will not stop addicts struggling with them, raising them from seed, setting the bulbs in specially contrived, cool soil mixtures, and even erecting windscreens to protect the wide, starry blooms from intrusive breezes. The genus is given to promiscuity, if so crude a word is permissible for such aristocratic plants; but the result is that seedlings (effectively the only means of increase) may or may not be true, though they can only be beautiful. The colour range is not wide, varying from white through shades of pink to plum and purple; it is how those colours are combined, in flecks and stipples and dots on a paler ground, that enchants. *N. pardanthina* attests in its name to the spotting of maroon or purple at the centre of the blush to mid pink, translucent flower, of which the inner petals are fringed; *N. farreri* is similar. Heavier spotting and fringing characterize *N. mairei*. To judge from its avail-ability in commerce in Britain, *N. aperta* may be an easier species; the wide saucers are pale rose with purple spotting at the heart.

The notholirions are just as temperamental, needing coolth, moisture yet impeccable drainage, and mild winters where the leaves, which emerge in late autumn, will not be damaged. The flowers are more bell-shaped than those of *Nomocharis*, and range in colour from shades of lilac to wine-red, the petals sometimes tipped with green. The only one I have ever attempted is *Notholirion bulbiferum*, in lavender and green; others that are offered are *N. macrophyllum* and *N. thomsonianum*, which is fragrant. After flowering, the main bulb dies and the tiny bulblets that survive should be nurtured to maturity.

THE HIMALAYAN POPPIES

By comparison, many species of *Meconopsis* are quite undemanding. The most familiar is *M. betonicifolia*, discovered over 100 years ago but not introduced to cultivation in the West until 1924, when it became instantly popular for its clear sky-blue colouring, at its best without any trace of pink. Easy from seed and not difficult to increase by division, it needs a moist, lime-free soil, in a cool position with shelter from drying winds. If it has a failing, it is a tendency to behave like a biennial; I believe that if it is discouraged from flowering until it has made more than one rosette, it may be more truly perennial. The crumpled, silken petals open from fur-hazed buds from the top downwards in early summer, their azure colouring enhanced by yellow stamens; there is also a white form, only less valued because the pure blue of the type is such a rare colour in the garden.

Flowering before the Himalayan blue poppy, the noble *M. grandis* has larger flowers of pure ultramarine in the most coveted forms, but sullied with purple in others. It is a good perennial, quickly forming clumps of furry leaves, so that named clones such as George Sherriff's GS600, with wide, nodding flowers of purest tint, can be divided to remain true to name. Where suited, in rich, moist soil, it may be as much as 1.5m/5ft tall. Most meconopsis are promiscuous, and this is no exception; so that hybrids between *M. grandis* and *M. betonicifolia* must have arisen in more than one garden. Known as *M.* × *sheldonii*, they are tall and stately blue poppies of equable temperament, increased by division. 'Slieve Donard' and the Crewdson Hybrids are both of the finest, most vivid blue; 'Branklyn' is not so pure in colour but much larger in flower, which you may or may not regard as a good thing. For different reasons, some people disdain *M.* × *sarsonii*, for it has ivory, not blue, flowers of great beauty and refinement.

Some meconopsis are biennial or monocarpic: that is, they may take more than two seasons to reach flowering capacity but, having once flowered, they set seed and die. Of these the most magnificent is *M. integrifolia*, which bears huge, clear yellow flowers of the usual crumpled-silk texture, from 15cm/6in to as much as 30cm/12in across, decorated with a large, central boss of stamens. The nodding saucers of *M. regia* are scarcely less fine, their colouring a softer primrose-yellow; but the glory of this species is the foliage. While building up strength to flower, it forms huge rosettes, as much as 90cm/36in across, of blond-haired leaves, soft as a kitten's fur to the touch; this may prove its downfall in gardens, for the fur traps winter rain and may induce rot. A cold and steady winter suits it better than the stop-go, wet-dry regime of the British climate.

Much more reliable is *M. napaulensis*, which comes in a range of colours, wine-red, purple and dusky pink (in my gardens *M. napaulensis* has never given me the white or light blue colouring promised by some authors), with rather small flowers held on stems up to 1.8m/6ft tall. The rosette of deeply cut leaves, though much less fine than *M. regia*'s, is handsome enough and less apt to suffer in wet weather. *M. horridula* is fairly dependable also, and its blue flowers, many borne on each 45cm/18in stem, are the only part of the plant free of spines.

VII

Warm Shade

WARM shade, in a cool temperate garden, is one of the most precious habitats you can contrive. Here you will be able to grow plants that demand shelter from winds which both desiccate and chill, that thrive where atmospheric humidity is high and reasonably constant, and that survive only where they are protected from damaging frosts. Shrubs of the temperate rain forest margins, perennials of the Himalayan foothills, tree ferns of the antipodes even, may find a congenial home in warm shade. Warmer still, and you can experiment with tropical jungle-dwellers, which may at least be able to live outside in a shaded courtyard during summer, to be kept frost-free inside in winter. But the delights of gardens in Florida, southern California, Karachi and such places, where jacarandas and flamboyants shade caladiums, ferns, begonias, anthuriums and the like: these are for climates much warmer than I am writing about, so that warm shade in this context must be taken as roughly equivalent to the coolness that tropic-dwellers dream of at the height of the torrid, summer heat. Looking to the other extreme, gardeners in parts of North America where the winters are very cold (though the summers may be hot) may regard as warm shade a place where they can succeed with evergreens that British gardeners take for granted: *Choisya ternata*. say, and even evergreen azaleas.

There is at least a begonia that even gardeners in cool temperate areas can grow outside without a tremor. *Begonia evansiana* (*B. grandis*) is quite able to withstand several degrees of frost, for it sensibly disappears below ground in winter, bobbing up again in spring to unfurl its typically lopsided leaves of almost succulent texture, burgundy-tinted on the reverse. The crystalline flowers are blush, opening from deeper-tinted buds; or white. I had most success with this begonia in a shady grove of

150

myrtles by a stream, as part of an interweaving planting where leaves were at least as important as flowers. The narrow, light green, sword leaves of *Arthropodium cirrhatum* contrast with the begonia's, and the only common attribute is their light-reflecting surfaces; the white flowers, with orange and lilac central pointel, are borne in open sprays on thin 90cm/36in stems in early summer.

Plants that flower very early in the year may need a sheltered corner to protect their blooms from frost. In the case of *Bergenia ciliata*, the rootstock is perfectly hardy, but the great, rounded, furry leaves and the blush flowers in contrasting reddish calyces may both be damaged by spring frosts. *Helleborus lividus* is a more tender plant, exquisite in its greyish, marbled foliage and fragrant, bowl-shaped flowers in sheaves overtopping the leaves in late winter. The colour of the flowers varies from jade to dove-grey flushed with old rose. After they are over, the lovely leaves remain to form part of a soft-toned grouping of grey and glaucous leaves, unexpected in a shady corner, which includes the hardy fern *Athyrium niponicum pictum*. When I first acquired *Senecio candicans*, I assumed it needed sun and drainage, so silvery-felted are the wide, seductively tilted leaves; but I soon learned that it is a plant of moisture and half shade, where the slight loss of silvery-whiteness shows all the more clearly the faint white deckle edge of the leaf. The last component of the group is *Astelia chathamica* 'Silver Spear', with broad sword leaves, grey-green above and steely-white beneath, forming a bold, evergreen rosette. The little blooms of tan or green colouring are inconsequential, but may be followed by orange fruits.

Like many gardeners who have to do their own weeding and who find the hoe too destructive of desirable self-sown seedlings, I abhor bare soil around my plants and seek always to cover it with leaves, whether green and growing or as an autumnal mulch ready to form leaf mould where it lies. Around the astelias and hellebores, *Viola hederacea*, the chinless violet of the antipodes, spreads its low carpet over which the white and lilac flowers hover on 8cm/3in stems. Nearer the greener foliage of dianellas, the violet gives way to *Parochetus communis*, a busy little creeper with shamrock leaves and perky, gentian-blue pea flowers to foreshadow the lapis lazuli of the *Dianella* berries.

SWORD LEAVES

Where suited, in moist, preferably lime-free, leafy soil, the strong sword leaves of dianellas form dense, weed-excluding clumps over which airy sprays of pale blue, yellow-anthered flowers are pleasant but not one tenth as exciting as the oblong, shining, ultramarine fruits that follow. One of the most readily available is *Dianella tasmanica*, a tall plant – up to 1.2m/4ft in flower and fruit; *D. caerulea* and *D. revoluta* are smaller, but no less striking in fruit. There is a pleasant variegated form of *D. caerulea* (or perhaps of *D. intermedia*), its leaves discreetly margined and striped with cream.

In the same bed grows the cane-stemmed, crested *Iris wattii*, with the similar *I. confusa*. The first is larger, and its clear green fans of sword leaves are borne on a distinct, bamboo-like stem. Both have branching flower stems topped with glacier-white or faint lilac, frilled flowers, with deeper lavender markings and the typical Evansia orange crest. They are much more lush and grand than the familiar *I. japonica*, which will grow almost everywhere. In the cosy warmth of a sheltered, shaded corner I would allow *I. japonica* 'Variegata', ('Aphrodite') which, like other variegated irises, has clean, vertical stripings of ivory and cream on green. Hybrids between *I. japonica* and the more tender Evansias are beginning to creep into commerce: 'Bourne Graceful' and 'Bourne Elegant' are names to look out for. They are beautiful, but not more so than their parents. I have never seen, let alone tried, the roof iris, *I. tectorum*, in a shady place, but as the other crested irises do so well it would surely be worth the experiment for its clear lilac or white, lavender-crested flowers with frilled falls. Again, there is a variegated form.

The calanthes are near-hardy Asian orchids of elegance and charm that grow best in part shade and shelter, in a rich and leafy but well-drained soil. *Calanthe discolor* is an easy Japanese species with broadly oblong, pleated leaves rising from fat roots; the flowers open in spring or early summer, in a range of colours varying from olive to rust, maroon and chocolate, always with a white or blush lip. Each flower is 2cm (just under an inch) wide, and several are borne on each 30cm/12in stem. *C. discolor flava* used to be known as *C. bicolor*; Paul Christian the bulb grower informs us that it is 'probably a stabilized hybrid of Miocene origins when *CC. discolor* and *sieboldii* [*striata*] crossed in the wild'. I love that statement; it puts *Homo sapiens* in his place as a late-coming upstart. The Miocene plant, then, is also somewhat variable, differing from *C. discolor* itself in the broad, soft primrose lip and sepals in shades of tan, terracotta and sienna-brown. *C. striata*, the other putative parent, comes in shades of yellow with a wide, paler lip. The taller, elegant and easy *C. tricarinata* has airy sprays at midsummer of broad, creamy-green flowers with a frilly, maroon and red lip. Later flowering still, *C. reflexa* grows much like *C. discolor* but has longer flowers, white or pale lilac with blackberry-mousse lip, borne in late summer and even into autumn.

ARUM LILIES

The leaves of the white arum lily, *Zantedeschia aethiopica*, are scarcely less handsome than the flowers, broad spearheads of glossy green. But it is thrilling to see the great white spathes, with the typical aroid spadix like a yellow candle at their hearts, unfurling on tall stems, as much as 1.2m/4ft high when the plants are set in the mud of a stream or pool. A form known as 'Crowborough' is both hardy and more tolerant of dry conditions, while the half-sized 'Little Gem' is also tough and resistant. 'White Sail' falls somewhere between the two in size, and unfurls its spathe more widely. Then there is 'Green Goddess', in which the white spathe is suffused with leaf green except in the throat, so that it disappears into the general leafage when seen from a distance. Warmer conditions are needed for *Z. elliottiana*, which is similar in size to 'Little Gem', with white-flecked leaves and spathes of canary-yellow. The soft pink *Z. rehmannii* is a little tender also, and its spathes expand less widely, in keeping with the narrow leaves.

Most exciting of all are the new, coloured hybrids with the blood of these and of *Z. angustiloba* (*Z. pentlandii*), which has a deep purple throat. In 'Black Magic', the spathe is citron- to primrose-yellow, with darkest maroon in the throat, while 'Golden Affair' is pure yellow and 'Aztec Gold' is suffused with orange. Taking after the pink parent in colour, though retaining the wider spathe, are 'Dusky Pink', 'Bridal Blush', 'Pacific Pink' and the magnolia-purple 'Majestic Red', a good plant badly named. There is now so wide a vocabulary of colour words that I can see no justification for resorting to sixteenth-century usage, when anything pink (a word not then used for the colour) was called red. Light shade only is needed for these; though I get plenty of flower on my white arums growing on shady streamsides.

FERNS FOR SHELTERED CORNERS

Warm shade suits several ferns, allowing them to reach an apotheosis of feathery or clean-cut fronds. The holly fern, *Cyrtomium falcatum*, has bold, polished, leathery fronds with broad, toothed segments, at their most luxuriant in the form 'Rochfordianum'. *C. fortunei* has narrower pinnae, giving it greater elegance but less magnificence. (Some authorities now place *Cyrtomium* in *Phanerophlebia*.) The young fronds of *Blechnum chilense* are copper-tinted, the broad, arching adult fronds rich green and of hard texture, so that when you run your hand up the frond each of the finger-wide pinnae makes itself felt as a separate tactile incident. (*B. chilense* may or may not be the correct name for the robust fern I have described; *B. tabulare*, a more familiar name, is said to be similar but smaller. The epithet *tabulare* is sometimess qualified by the phrase 'of gardens' – which is a way of opting out of controversy between taxonomists, some of whom assert that the smaller plant is actually *B. magellanicum*, and that the true *B. tabulare* has narrower pinnae. To add still more confusion, I once was given, as *B. capense*, a most elegant blechnum with narrow pinnae.)

Though recognizably ferns, none of these has the finely dissected fronds that are usually associated with the group and encourage one to use the epithet 'ferny' for any plant with much divided leaves. *Woodwardia radicans*, though, comes nearer to the popular image, with gracefully arching fronds of clear green, up to 1.8m/6ft long in the warm, moist, leafy shelter that best suits this fern. At the tip of each frond is a bud that will root to make more, if you hold it down with a stone.

The biggest of the ferns that can be attempted in cool temperate gardens is *Dicksonia antarctica*, a tree fern. At first, a young dicksonia looks like an ordinary fern of extra magnificence; but as the years pass, the root fibres gradually accumulate above ground, so that in time the huge, thrice-divided fronds spring from what looks like a shaggy, dark brown trunk.

It is said that when your tree ferns grow too tall, you can cut them down and replant the top; I have never had the nerve to do this, and anyway it is a thrill to walk beneath the fronds and look up to the light through their green filigree. Constant moisture at the root and in the air is essential to the tree ferns, together with shelter from drying winds; if these imperatives are satisfied, it will not matter if filtered sunlight strikes the fronds at times during the day. In autumn the fronds turn brown; in spring, as the new, young croziers unfurl, the old fronds collapse. Do not tidily remove them, but leave them to shelter the trunk during the winter ahead, or even tie them loosely to it.

FRAGRANT RHODODENDRONS

The smaller ferns fit well into the shady corners of a sheltered courtyard. Here, too, the fragrant, slightly tender rhododendrons typified by 'Fragrantissimum' do well; they need, of course, an acid soil, but will thrive in a container, given suitable compost and attention to watering with non-calcareous water. Indeed, even if the occasional dousing with tap water is inevitable, a corrective dose of Sequestrene or Epsom salts should ensure that no damage is done. These rhododendrons, members of the Maddenia subsection, have lily-like flowers, delectably perfumed, and almost invariably white or blush. 'Fragrantissimum' is, of course, a hybrid, but none the worse for that, with flowers in clusters of four, each one a wide, white funnel flushed with pink on the exterior and washed with green at its heart, filling the surrounding air with fragrance in spring. The foliage, though not to be compared with the magnificent large-leaved hybrids, is pleasant in its dark, polished and corrugated green.

A less familiar hybrid is 'Tyermannii', with enormous flowers, the legacy of the exquisite *Rhododendron nuttallii*, which has great, drooping, pale sulphur trumpets of waxen texture. *R.johnstoneanum* is one of the easier members of this group, with fragrant, ivory or clotted-cream trumpets stained with wine at the base; sometimes it disgraces itself by producing double flowers, as in 'Double Diamond', where the distinction of the simple, lily-trumpet outline is lost among the extra petals. 'Countess of Haddington' has flowers almost as large as the rather weakly *R. dalhousieae*, in pearly-white flushed with pink on a shrub of good rounded habit; while the wholly covetable *R. dalhousieae rhabdotum*, which is slow, rare and tender, has lily-like trumpets of the purest line, milkwhite with a crimson flush heightening the ribs. 'Ashcombe' is of this style also, a form of *R. veitchianum* Cubittii group, with ivory trumpets opening from tawny-pink buds. The blood of another subsection, Edgeworthia, meets the Maddenia bloodline to create 'Lady Alice Fitzwilliam' and 'Princess Alice', two old hybrids that, though rather leggy, have such fine, white trumpets opening from dawn-pink buds, and so eloquent a fragrance, that they survive to delight us to this day.

SCENTED OR OPULENT CAMELLIAS

Among the camellias, the sasanquas are the gardener's equivalent of the Maddenia rhododendrons: fragrant in flower, and a little tender. They have the blessed habit of flowering in autumn and winter, when they are apt to receive one's undivided attention; for it must be said that if they flowered with the tender rhododendrons, they would take second place. There are fewer of them to choose from than of the rhododendrons, and of those, one stands out for its ease of cultivation and relative hardiness.

'Narumi-gata' has slightly cupped, white, sweetly scented flowers as wide as the palm of one's hand, the petals faintly pink at their tips, opening from pink buds. The leaves are narrower, and the growth more slender than the buxom and glossy japonicas. The other cultivars, which may be pink or crimson as well as white, are said to need plenty of sun;

but my own experience is that if they are baked, the foliage looks parched and impoverished, scarcely an adequate setting for the cupped blooms.

We come back to that vexed question of light levels in different areas; in most English gardens, the recommendation to plant in full sun must be heeded. Some camellia experts say that any plant said to be 'Narumi-gata' which flowers freely in light shade must be *Camellia oleifera* and not the *C. sasanqua* cultivar; but I still believe, on account of the size of its flowers and the distinct though faint pink flush to the margins of the petals, that the plant I had by that name, which did extremely well in thin woodland, was 'Narumi-gata'.

One of the brightest of *sasanqua* cultivars is 'Crimson King', with single red, scentless flowers. 'Rosea Plena' is, as its name suggests, a double-flowered pink; 'Variegata' has blush to white flowers, and leaves margined with white. A few others are available from one or two specialist sources.

The hybrids of *C. reticulata* flower in early spring, and although they lack the sweet scent of the sasanquas they are large and colourful in flower; indeed, some of the most voluptuous cultivars are almost blowsy. They are large shrubs, needing sheltered positions, though the plant first introduced to the west, a semi-double, rose-pink garden form known as 'Captain Rawes', is remarkably hardly although its sumptuous flowers suggest conservatories, and corsages for ample bosoms. As well as their opulent, often frilled flowers, cultivars of *C. reticulata* have distinctive foliage, hard and leathery with a conspicuous network of veins. 'Inspiration' and 'Salutation' are hybrids with *C. saluenensis*; both have large, semi-double, pink flowers, paler in 'Salutation'. Others may have much more sumptuous flowers; the only one of which I have personal experience is 'Howard Asper'. Somehow I could never reconcile the masculine name with the flouncing, indeed almost blowsy, femininity of the huge, pink bloom. 'Leonard Messel' is scarcely less ample, and its paeony-form flowers are an attractive peach-pink. The lax habit of 'Francie L.' makes it especially suitable for training on a wall, preferably not of brick, on which its semi-double, deep rose flowers do not look their best.

Climbers for Warm Shade

On the warm, shady wall behind your fragrant rhododendrons and camellias, you might succeed with *Ficus pumila*, a little, clinging, climbing, evergreen fig, most appealing in the form 'Minima', with tiny, heart-shaped, dark green leaves. It shares with ivy the peculiarity of two forms of growth, climbing and shrubby; in the juvenile, climbing stage, if the climate is warm enough for it, it will completely mask a shady wall, even one that is dark all day.

With a little more light, even in slightly cooler conditions, you could expect to succeed with *Berberidopsis corallina*, provided your soil is neutral or acid; you will of course have added to it as much crumbly, moisture-retaining humus as you can spare, for the soil at the foot of a wall is often dry and impoverished. This Chilean evergreen climber has dark, holly-like foliage, though without holly's ferocious spines, to set off its hanging, red-stalked trails of small, crimson bells that open from buds like drops of blood all through summer and autumn. Also from Chile, *Mitraria coccinea* is the easiest of three woody gesneriads (belonging, that is, to the same family as those popular houseplants known as gloxinias) that you could grow in this sheltered corner. A scrambler or ground-spreader after the manner of ivy, though without aerial roots, the mitraria has small, neat, evergreen leaves of no particular distinction, and bears its bellied trumpets of bright orange scarlet in summer and autumn. The form to seek out is the one from Lake Puye.

It is much more of an achievement to make a success of *Asteranthera ovata*, although in the wild both this and *Sarmienta repens* reach the tops of tall trees, attaching themselves like ivy by aerial roots. The asteranthera has rounded, bristly leaves, thin-textured and susceptible to a dry atmosphere; in the shrubby phase each pair of leaves is set alternately right-angled along the stem, but in the climbing state they flatten into one plane – which, when you think about it, is inevitable if every other pair of leaves is not to get squashed against the plant's chosen support. The flowers are thrilling, lipped tubes of rich, crushed raspberry with deeper veinings and white in the throat, opening from midsummer on. In its native land it forms carpets beneath *Desfontainea spinosa*, a holly-like shrub (though with opposite, not alternate, leaves) that bears most unholly-like, tubular flowers of bright scarlet with rounded, yellow lobes. An especially fine form of desfontainea with richer red flowers is named 'Harold Comber' in honour of its collector.

The third of the shrubby gesneriads that you might attempt, if you can get it (for so far as I am aware it is not available in commerce, in Britain at least), is the aforementioned *Sarmienta repens*, a plant that like the asteranthera prefers to climb over mossy rocks and tree trunks. The rounded leaves are semi-succulent, so that the plant can cope with a short spell of drought; yet it is by no means easy to grow, let alone to persuade to produce its bulging, carmine flowers, in Britain.

Although it looks so exotic, the twining, evergreen *Lapageria rosea*, another Chilean climber, is much easier to grow than the gesneriads. The thin, stiff shoots are set with leathery, dark green leaves of attenuated, heart-shaped outline, but it is the long, waxy bells, of high-shouldered, narrowly flaring outline, that enthral. The typical colouring is crimson-pink, but there is also a white form, as perfect as though carved from the finest votive candles, and the large-flowered 'Nash Court', in softer pink flecked with rose. So long as you obtain fresh seed, lapagerias are not hard to raise in this way, and occasionally another fine variety is given a cultivar name, though I cannot enthuse about 'Flesh Pink' as a name for so elegant a plant, however delightful the pale colouring.

In a sheltered corner you also could try to establish *Philesia magellanica*, which, though fairly hardy, bitterly resents dryness, whether at the root or in the atmosphere; yet if too deeply shaded, in an attempt to give it the moist stillness it appreciates, will scarcely flower. Though pleasant enough in its very dark green, narrow, white-backed leaves, it is a plant grown above all for its flowers; wide waxy, hanging bells of crimson pink recalling those of the related lapageria. The hybrid between the two, × *Philageria veitchii*, is just as covetable, with waxy, rich pink bells in late summer. If suited, *Philesia* and its hybrid will gradually spread into a thicket of stems suckering through leafy humus, or can be encouraged to climb moss-covered rocks or tree trunks.

Also related to the lapageria, and also needing sheltered shade, *Luzuriaga radicans* is a more modest plant, its thin, wiry shoots filtering through the leaf litter or climbing to waist height on a mossy rock or stump. The flowers are borne only on climbing plants, and need a close look, for they are little, white stars with a prominent yellow central cone of stamens, nothing like the voluptuously elegant bells of the lapagerias; the fruits that should follow are orange.

Light shade only, with shelter, is the recipe for success with *Dicentra macracapnos*, a Himalayan bleeding heart of climbing or scrambling habit, which will spread over the ground if you do not give it a neighbouring shrub to infiltrate. Like its Californian cousin *D. chrysantha*, a species which is more decidedly sun-loving, the Himalayan has clear yellow flowers, of the usual hanging, locket shape, lasting for a long season in summer, and typical divided foliage.

The Luxury of Foliage

From modesty to magnificence. *Gevuina avellana* is one of the most splendid foliage plants that can be grown in warm, sheltered and shady places; it is hardy in the coastal gardens of Cornwall and Devon and in the woodland gardens of Ireland, but that represents the limit of its climatic tolerance in Britain; though I suspect that in a very sheltered town garden in London, say, provided the soil were made suitably neutral to acid and leafy-moist, it would be worth attempting, especially if we are to have more of these very mild winters. At first glance it might be taken for a mahonia of unusually lush texture; but then you see that the leaves lack the fierce spines, and are not merely pinnate, but also bipinnate, with the leaflets varying from thumbnail to postcard size, of dark gleaming green, at first furred with tawny velvet, which remains on the stem and petioles. The ivory-white flowers, if your gevuina should ever get to that stage, are of intricate, spidery construction and gathered into narrowly cylindrical spikes, and the fruits that follow are as red as cherries, but have an edible nut inside. But the finest foliage belongs to plants that are not flowering, and gevuinas respond well to hard pruning; which is as well, for even the most incompetent flower arranger would be tempted by such magnificent fronds.

It may be unkind to tantalize you with the Chilean hazel (a name the gevuina owes to its edible nuts, for otherwise it is singularly inappropriate for a shrub in the Protea family). But the proteaceous *Lomatia ferruginea* is scarcely less handsome, and both hardier and easier to obtain, doing well in a sheltered and lightly shaded position in neutral to acid, leafy soil. Its much divided leaves recall some fine, bold fern, and like the gevuina's they uncurl from tawny, velvet-coated croziers; the flowers are clusters of burnt orange and buff claws.

Other lomatias are of more modest stature, and hardier, but still worth a sheltered corner. *L. tinctoria* has elegant, slender foliage, the leaves varying from entire to twice or even thrice pinnate, and heliotrope-scented, cream flowers on pale pink stalks, opening in summer from green buds. The primrose-yellow flowers of *L. myricoides* are even more fragrant, and the leaves are long and slender, with toothed margins. It is always difficult, when discussing plants to be grown near the limits of their climatic tolerance, to suggest sizes, but I have seen *L. ferruginea* well over 3m/10ft tall, while *L. myricoides* might be half that, and *L. tinctoria* is a low shrub spreading by suckers into a dense thicket.

COLOURED LEAVES

The camellia relative *Cleyera fortunei*, a shrub that can grow large where the soil and climate suit, is valued for its lustrous, pointed leaves that are marbled with grey at the centre, with broad cream margins flushed with rose. There is a variegated form of another tea-family shrub for warm, shady places, *Ternstroemia gymnanthera* – but it may not be in commerce at present. The plain green form is well worth attempting, though, for the sake of its thick, blunt, evergreen leaves with a glossy finish, clustered at the ends of stout, fox-red branches; and it is unlikely to outgrow its space in most gardens.

In *Pseudowintera colorata*, the leaf shape is an unexceptionable oval; it is solely the colouring that allures. If you can contrive to grow the shrub in moist, leafy soil in sheltered shade of the kind that is open to the sky, it will develop metallic tones of old-gold above and bloomy steel-blue beneath, with flecks and stains of wine-red and margins of blackberry-purple. Again, though I have seen it as much as 4.5m/15ft tall and bulky to match, it is slow growing and, if it should ever get too large, flower arrangers will queue for a spray or two of foliage of such unique colouring.

The pseudowintera is related to *Drimys lanceolata* (now *Tasmannia aromatica*), a perky, evergreen shrub of more conventional colouring with myrtle-like leaves on dark red petioles, the young growths cinnamon red; the white flowers in spring are borne on separate male and female plants, and if you have both, the ladies bear a good crop of black fruits. The much larger *Drimys winteri* (which varies from shrubby manifestations to full treehood) has bolder leaves, in the best forms bright glaucous-white beneath, and fragrant, creamy flowers in loose heads in spring. It needs the same conditions, loose and leafy soil about its roots, shelter and overhead light; with due attention to the soil, this makes it a good candidate for a wall facing away from the sun, in a sheltered corner where it can expand to make a splendid furnishing of evergreen foliage.

BOLD FOLIAGE

But if your wall is large enough, then it must be allowed to host *Magnolia delavayi*, a noble Himalayan with great leaves like a rubber plant's, dark with sea-green bloom. The flowers are chalices of clotted-cream suede, with a swooning fragrance; they are somewhat hidden by the leaves, and prefer to open towards evening, the petals falling by morning. Imagine returning from the office to inhale the fragrance of these velvety bowls; it makes one feel, for a moment, endowed with untold wealth.

The rubber plant itself is, of course, a familiar houseplant in cold regions, but too tropical a creature to attempt outside in temperate zones. Good glossy leafage of almost tropical quality belongs also to the forms of *Pseudopanax lessonii*, an ivy relative to which antipodean nurserymen have lately turned their attentions. A branching shrub growing to 3m/ 10ft or more in its native haunts, it has stout branches with polished, boldly three- to five-parted leaves clustered at the extremities, after the style of the Araliaceae. 'Adiantifolius' is a fine selection with rich green, gleaming foliage; 'Gold Splash' is certain to appeal to those who like variegations, for it has a central streak of lime-yellow. A quite different houseplant, that will grow outside in even deep shade, is *Aspidistra elatior*, the very same that is consigned to the most difficult corners of the house and survives, though it does not exactly thrive on, almost total neglect. In decent, nourished soil, sheltered from the wind, it is a splendid thing with shiny, evergreen leaves of broad, lancehead shape in a clump. Do not look for flowers, for though this is a lily relative, now kicked sideways into Convallariaceae, which is where lily of the valley belongs, the aspidistra does things unromantically by producing stemless, brown flowers pollinated by slugs.

VIII

Shade as a Problem

I hope I have by now convinced you that in the shaded garden you can grow plants of infinite variety and subtlety when compared with many of the conventional border plants and annuals, the 'garden-centre top 100' shrubs and popular bedding plants. But I cannot turn my back on those gardeners who have to cope with dry, rooty shade or cold draughty corners where the sun seldom reaches. To them, talk of cool, leafy soil or warm, sheltered shade is not much use. They want to know what to do when their garden is overshadowed by greedy trees that they can do nothing about because of a tree preservation order, or whether there is anything that will help to cut the wind that slices in from Siberia around the corner to the back door.

Dry, Dense Shade

Please do not think that I am trying to evade responsibility before I even begin, if I say that the best response to an area of dense, dry shade may be to do virtually nothing. A spreading, mature yew tree or holm oak, for example, will make a canopy so dense that, except at the very margins, not even a blade of grass will grow beneath it. It is a waste of time to try. Better to enjoy the beauty of the tree itself, perhaps – if it is large enough – flinging a white *Clematis montana* or a fragrant synstylae rose over it, and simply to cover the floor beneath the canopy with a scattering of chipped bark or of sand, or with nothing at all. This minimalist approach leaves you free to concentrate on the parts of the garden where plants will grow without all the time looking at the point of death. Montbretia, it is true, will grow under a holm oak, but it will be sparse and patchy from the

162

leaves and scurf dropped on it by the tree, and in the dim light it will not flower.

Where it is worth making an effort, though, is beneath a tree which, though greedy and dense-canopied, still lets in enough light while leafless, or is tall-trunked enough, to encourage a bit of weed growth. Here, the advice about doing all you can to enrich the soil before planting needs to be qualified; you will have to accept that the tree will gratefully absorb much of what you add, leaving the nutrient levels much as before, though the texture of the soil may be improved. So you either have undernourished plants, or you fertilize each year, and hope that the underplantings will take advantage of what they can before the tree muscles in.

The most difficult trees to cope with are horse chestnut, beech, lime, sycamore, plane, and to a lesser extent Norway and sugar maples, many pines . . . trees, in short, that cast a dense shade when mature and have hefty roots as well. You may be able to help a little by limbing up the tree (work of this kind on trees blighted by TPOs, tree preservation orders, may often be justified on the grounds of good husbandry), so letting in more light; but there is little you can do about the roots. At least no great harm is likely to result if you inadvertently, or even advertently, hack at the roots in order to make space for your underplantings. Trees such as birch, though they have far-ranging feeding roots making a network near the surface, are nowhere near so threatening, and oaks are deep rooting, while ash is a fairly friendly tree, shady in summer when full of leaf but letting in all the light of spring.

If a densely leafy, greedy tree occupies only part of your estate, leaving you space to garden in the rest as you choose, then here, too, you may decide that a restful expanse of nothing much is better than some struggling ground cover. Here, modern herbicides come to our rescue. Paraquat, dangerous stuff though it is (lethal, indeed, to humans when swallowed, so take every precaution when using it), will kill off any green, growing thing that it touches, with the exception of moss, which seems instead positively to thrive. And moss usually grows of its own accord beneath deciduous trees, though few of us could aspire to the pale and hummocky carpet of velvety *Leucobryum glaucum* that grew beneath beeches in the Savill Garden at Windsor. Above the moss rise the trunks of your trees, uncluttered, in the same way as a fine specimen tree rises unencumbered from a smooth lawn.

Whatever I may say about moss or a covering of chipped bark or raked sand beneath your tree, you may still retort that you want plants, proper plants with leaves and even flowers. Very well. Let us look first at foliage.

The challenge is to find leaves that will look good in their season and not disgrace you at any time. The supreme candidates are *Pachysandra terminalis* and *Euphorbia amygdaloides* var. *robbiae*. In writing about the first, I am conscious of bias; quite simply, I dislike the poor plant. But so discriminating a gardener as Graham Thomas says that pachysandra 'ranks with the very best, most luxuriant and satisfactory of evergreen covers'. It positively needs shade if it is not to look slightly chlorotic, and furthermore must have a neutral or acid soil if it is to retain its fresh and healthy greenness, and is a slow spreader except in light soils. The leaves are more or less diamond shaped with toothed edges, and the little, scented, whitish flowers are borne in small spikes in spring. Because I do not much like it I have never actually planted it (but have grown it, for it was in a garden I took over), but I was almost converted on seeing squares of it, generous squares interspersed with equal-sized expanses of cobbles and paving, in front of a hotel in Washington, where it was shaded by trees and fully living up to its reputation as a tough and tolerant carpeter. It is much used throughout the United States wherever the climate allows.

The euphorbia is another matter, so good-looking a plant that it has actually found its way into earlier chapters. In well-nourished soils, indeed, it increases so fast that you may come to dislike it as I dislike the pachysandra; but in dry, difficult shade it grows like nothing else, making a spread of darkest green, polished leaves in rosettes topped, in spring, by plumes of acid-green bracts on 60cm/24in stems. Like all spurge inflorescences these last long, but when they start to look disreputable you should cut them right out at ground level, as you do with the bigger, shrubby spurges from the Mediterranean area. This is not only for immediate cosmetic effect; it also keeps the plant dense. There is no point in growing a fine plant in place of the weeds, if you then allow it to get thin and patchy so the weeds can get in again.

Gaultheria shallon is the salal, the friend of gardeners with too much acid soil to cope with, for it is a busy spreader, making a man-high thicket in moist, shady woods in its native western North America, but closer and more compact at the forest margins or in drier soils. You can hack it back as much as you like, for it is a very forgiving shrub: but it does want space. The rounded leaves are glossy, the little, blush-pink bells are held in sprays in summer, and indigo-purple, edible fruits follow. If you have an overgrown woodland, with places where no light penetrates, then the salal will furnish them, even in the perpetual night of a grove of tall rhododendrons, just as willingly as Mrs Robb's spurge will cope with dark, rooty corners in limy soil.

Most daphnes like sun and a perpetually moist yet well-drained soil, a combination that is difficult to achieve, but *Daphne laureola* is an unassuming evergreen that grows in European and British woodlands, with shining leaves disposed a little like a spurge's (its vernacular name is the spurge laurel) and flowers resembling *D. pontica*'s, clusters of lime-green half hidden among the leaves in early spring, when much of their sweet fragrance goes wasted on the cold air.

BRITISH EVERGREENS AND SOME IMMIGRANTS

Ivies, of course, grow in nature often in quite dark corners, and the Irish ivy, *Hedera helix* 'Hibernica', is almost as vigorous as the salal, though flatter, with big, shiny leaves making a carpet 30cm/12in high. The stems seem little inclined to run up vertical supports, so your tree trunks should remain unwreathed. Its hybrid with *Fatsia japonica*, which bears the logical but absurd-sounding name × *Fatshedera lizei*, is just as tolerant of dense shade, and very handsome with its large, ivy-like leaves of polished green, on sprawling stems mounding up to knee height and spreading to 1.2m/4ft or more across. The flowers are ivy umbels of pale green, in autumn. Other than the Irish ivy, most forms of *H. helix* are too pretty, in the diversity of their leaf outlines, to waste in impossible places.

Ivy calls to mind the Christmas carol about the holly and the ivy; and common holly is surprisingly tolerant of dark, dry places. Common box, too, is a tolerant evergreen, with masses of small, dark green leaves. And to complete the set of British evergreens, if you want shrubby ground cover beneath your trees, then the spreading form of yew, *Taxus baccata* 'Repandens', does as well in deep shade as in sun. It grows slowly, stays dense, and is of the same black-green as the common yew. Unfortunately, the 'golden' forms such as 'Summergold' lose their bright colouring in dark places.

I would never have imagined that *Thujopsis dolobrata* 'Laetevirens' ('Nana') would do well in dry, rooty shade, but in the Botanic Garden at Geneva it grows right beneath the canopy of a large pine, where it makes a wide, tabletop bush of rather pale colouring, for the wide needles are white backed. The Pfitzer juniper, *Juniperus* × *media* 'Pfitzeriana', is another conifer that will grow beneath trees, even under beeches, making a large-scale, high ground cover of green with a faintly blue cast. Since it will grow equally cheerfully in sun, it is a good plant where space permits to use as a link between the dark places beneath your trees and the sunny parts of the garden.

The same goes for *Choisya ternata*, and for the spotted laurels, which will put up with almost as much neglect in the garden as aspidistras in the house, but are all the better for a bit of jollying along. If you are going to plant a spotted *Aucuba japonica*, let it be the spottiest of all, not the familiar 'Variegata' with its half-hearted measling of yellow flecks. 'Crotonifolia' does the job far more boldly, with great blotches of colour on leaves of generous proportions. It is a male; 'Gold Dust' is a female with bright freckles, if you aspire to fruits as well as foliage. The plain green forms have received due acknowledgement already; while cream-margined 'Sulphurea', though bold and handsome in leaf, is inclined to revert to plain green in shade.

To return to British native plants, *Iris foetidissima* (which like ivy, yew and box is also European) pays for its adaptability by being dumped in horrible corners; for it does cope remarkably well with dry shade. I grew up with a pair of clumps that had been planted on the sunless side of a privet hedge, than which there is nothing greedier and more able to induce a dustbath dryness around itself; the iris flowered, not that you would really notice it for the type has dingy flowers of beige veined with dirty mauve, and then set seed, the pods bursting to show off their vivid orange seeds. At this stage they were cut and brought indoors, to gather dust during the winter in a vase of 'drieds' with honesty, Chinese lanterns and mustard-yellow achilleas. There is a superior form of *I. foetidissima* called *citrina* on account of its clear lemon, veined flowers; the seed pods are better too. 'Variegata', which is mentioned elsewhere in these pages, does nothing in the way of flower or seeds, but the cream-striped leaves are livelier than plain dark green. I have also seen a wonderful clear citron, unmarked flower, the falls fading to sorbet paleness, from a plant collected on the Pico de Europa in northern Spain; another rarity is the white-fruited form. But I mention them here not as candidates for difficult corners – they are too special – but to keep all the variants together in my text.

The butcher's broom, *Ruscus aculeatus*, seems just as willing as the ordinary *Iris foetidissima* to cope with difficult places; but as it stands cold and draughts as well, I shall describe it later in this chapter.

BENEATH TALL TREES

In cold gardens the libertias are cherished in warm corners for their brilliant white, three-cornered flowers in early summer. But in milder areas *Libertia formosa* grows freely even in deep shade under pines, flowering no less abundantly than in the sun, setting a huge crop of orange-brown seeds, and making impenetrable ground cover, before which even brambles retreat, as its firm-textured, dark green sword leaves spread into dense, evergreen clumps. In colder areas, you could forego the bright white flowers and grow instead *Luzula sylvatica*, the woodrush, which makes a dense cover of evergreen blades even in the most unpropitious conditions. Some ferns will do surprisingly well in dry, rooty shade, especially if you give them a good start. Once they are established, sporelings may crop up to extend your fernery. The male fern, the polypody and the hart's tongue are the most tolerant, and so long as the soil is acid the hard fern, *Blechnum spicant*, will do well too.

Most people know how willingly honesty grows in any shady corner. The perennial honesty, *Lunaria rediviva*, is no less obliging, and its pale mauve-white spring flowers gleam in the dark. The papery seedpods that follow are like the familiar 'honesty money', but elliptical instead of rounded. Later, in early summer, come the clove-scented flowers of sweet rocket, *Hesperis matronalis*, in white or lilac, like single, tall stocks. The sweet rocket seeds itself generously and will cope with dry soils. But if anyone ever offers you a plant of the double sweet rocket, cherish it in the very best conditions you can contrive, for it is a rarity with a most uncertain temperament.

If your dense and dry shade is the product of deciduous trees, and only presents a problem in summer, then there are bulbs and small perennials that would be worth planting. Most of them have been described in earlier chapters: *Anemone apennina*, lily of the valley, bluebells, *Omphalodes cappadocica*, snowdrops, *Crocus tomasinianus*, Solomon's seal, *Arum italicum marmoratum*, *Colchicum autumnale*, *Cyclamen hederifolium*. With the exception of the last two, these are plants that hasten to flower early in the year; by the time the overhead canopy is in full, light-excluding leaf, they have done their stint for the year and have either retired below ground or, if still leafy, exist happily enough with little light. If these do well enough, try adding others: *Colchicum speciosum* 'Album' to gleam in the darkness, *Crocus speciosus* for its near-blue candleflames which almost fluoresce among fallen autumn leaves, the Lent lily (*Narcissus pseudonarcissus*) for spring and *Ornithogalum nutans* for early summer, contrasted with the black-green fingered leaves of *Helleborus foetidus* or the shiny sheaves of *Danaë racemosa*. Re-read the chapters on cool shade and on woodland, and resolve to be adventurous.

Cold and Shady Places

If the first concern, when you tackle a dry and rooty bit of shade, is to get something growing that looks better than starved weeds, in cold and dark places the aim is often to plant something that will take the edge off the wind. You will, of course, understand that almost anything you plant in the teeth of a chilly wind in a shady spot would look better with more shelter, or more light, or both. Inevitably, this section of the book takes on a slightly *faute de mieux* air.

In the search for a plant to fill a difficult corner, gardeners hope for a hardy evergreen with bright flowers. Amazingly, provided your soil is acid and leafy, and can be kept moist by natural or artificial means, just such a creature exists, in the shape of the toughest, hardy-hybrid rhododendrons. The hardy hybrids are distinguished by their big, bold and often bright trusses of flower, and by foliage that is as boring as a laurel's: worse, indeed, for it lacks the polished surface that reflects the smallest glint of sunlight. But, as the label hardy hybrid suggests, they are tough and undemanding, and some will even cope with full exposure. Do not suppose, however, that it is true of all; the designation 'HH' in the catalogue is not a guarantee of survival in impossible conditions. But there are those that seem able to put up with anything except lime in the soil.

The hybrids of *Rhododendron caucasicum*, indeed, are better grown 'hard', where they remain more compact and dense than in shelter. The old hybrid 'Jacksonii' is one of the toughest, a broad dome of a bush, slow growing and seldom very tall. The flowers, funnels of rose-pink with maroon freckles, are borne in well-formed trusses in spring. 'Caucasicum Pictum' is very close in style to the species itself, with clear red-flecked, blush-pink trusses. Another that is so tough it used to be much planted in the smoky industrial north is the cross between *R. caucasicum* and *R. ponticum* known as 'Cunningham's White', with lilac-tinted buds opening to white flowers with a tan flare, held in loose trusses.

R. ponticum itself, of course, is virtually unkillable; it will grow in exposed places, and in dark corners – even under beech trees – so that even its poor colour and territorial inclinations may be forgiven. The off-mauve colouring is at its best in the evening light. I wonder what has happened to the beautiful white *ponticum* hybrid which Michael Haworth-Booth promoted as 'Tondelayo', the neglected jungle beauty; it had an elegant truss of pure white flowers with a tangerine flare. The related *R. catawbiense* is another tough shrub, making a dense thicket with time as the stems layer down; the bell-shaped flowers vary in colour from lilac to pink or white and are held in a generous truss opening in early summer. The two united to produce 'Fastuosum Flore Pleno', a big, hardy shrub with rather frilled, doubled flowers of a pleasant shade of lilac-mauve. 'Madame Masson' is of the same parentage, and was also raised in the first half of the nineteenth century; the lilac buds open to white flowers with an acid-green flare.

Whether your soil is acid or not, the need to improve it in all ways available to you applies still more to the cold and shaded areas of your garden. Then such standby evergreens as *Lonicera pileata*, *Mahonia aquifolium* and *Euonymus fortunei* will do their best for you, instead of looking pinched and starved. As a municipal landscape plant, *Lonicera pileata* earns little more than contempt, for it is altogether too reliable for its own good; in shade, allowed free rein to spread into ferny sprays of neat, evergreen foliage, enlivened in spring as the new growths stand out brightly against the sombre, older leaves, it is quite another thing. Although they are not showy, I even love its little translucent violet-mauve fruits, so much more subtle than the scarlet baubles of pyracantha or *Cotoneaster horizontalis*. Any little scrap of the shrubby lonicera will root, and the spreading stems layer themselves as they go, mounding up to 90cm/36in or so.

The forms of *Euonymus fortunei* are hardly less willing to root and grow, and several are very bright, not in flower (like ivy, in the climbing phase they do not produce flowers at all) but in leaf colour. Cultivars such as 'Emerald Gaiety', in white and green, and 'Emerald 'n' Gold' sell on sight. They look better in shade; in full sun and starved soil the yellow-variegated kinds can seem rather hectic, as their green and gamboge tones are flushed with pink. The white-splashed cultivars bring a welcome gleam of light to shady places. If there is support for their creeping stems, they will turn into climbers, when they may reach 2–3m/7–10ft in height. 'Silver Queen' is especially pretty in green margined with cream.

The Oregon grape, *Mahonia aquifolium*, is scarcely less easy going, quickly making thickets of pinnate, prickly leaves set in early spring with blunt clusters of yellow flowers and later with blue-black fruits. A lower but even denser thicket, free of prickles, is formed by *Cornus stolonifera* 'Kelseyi', which looks almost like a lowly bamboo in its close-set slender stems. If you want prickles, as a deterrent to shortcuts, then you should plant butcher's broom, *Ruscus aculeatus*. This will bear fruits only if male and female, or the hermaphrodite form, are grown; the sharply spiny 'leaves' are in fact cladodes, modified stems, upon which the tiny, insignificant flowers are borne and are followed, on female plants, by bright scarlet berries. A brake of the close-packed, upright stems of butcher's broom, though only 90cm/36in high at most, is an impassable barrier to anything larger than a mouse.

Some people find the larger yews too churchyardy for the garden. They are most tolerant and hardy trees, as befits any evergreen which survived the ice age to remain as a genuine British native. Try to look at them dispassionately, admiring the differing forms of the upright Irish yew, slim in youth and endearingly obese in middle age, or the graceful, half-weeping 'Dovastoniana', the Westfelton yew. Tree-like yews are good candidates for upward pruning, for they have beautiful trunks, which can be enhanced by scrubbing to remove the outer flaking layers, revealing the mahogany-red inner bark.

SHRUBS THAT LOSE THEIR LEAVES

When it comes to deciduous shrubs, you have to remember that in winter their bare stems will offer no protection against the wind. It makes sense to choose those that offer some colour, as compensation. The dogwoods, forms of *Cornus alba* and *C. stolonifera*, will not show their brightest stem colouring out of the sun; but they are tough, and even without the enlivening rays of the sun, red and greenish-yellow stems are better to look at in winter than brown or grey. *C. alba* 'Sibirica' is not the strongest grower, but its stems are a brighter scarlet than any other; 'Elegantissima' and 'Spaethii', with their white and yellow variegations respectively, might be preferred in summer even though in winter their bare shoots are a less cheering crimson. A newer cultivar, 'Winter Flame', has plain green leaves, but they colour to orange and amber in autumn, and the bare stems in winter are bright tangerine, as jazzy as the orange-stemmed willows of Chapter III.

Although by contrast it is distinctly sombre, I have a fondness for 'Kesselringii', which has almost black stems; it looks especially well mingling with the yellow-green of *C. stolonifera* 'Flaviramea', a much more vigorously sideways spreading plant that makes a suckering and rooting thicket. Whichever you choose, cut the stems hard back each spring (or only half of them every spring, if chopping back the lot seems too ruthless) to keep the shrub as neat as can be and full of young wood for the best winter stems. Almost any soil and situation suits these resilient dogwoods. *Kerria japonica* is no less hardy, and in winter its slender stems are bright green. Rather than the usual pompon double, I recommend 'Guinea Gold', with large, single flowers of clear yellow. There is a variegated form, 'Picta', rather a weak grower, with white-margined leaves and squinny, yellow, single flowers.

In winter, the forms of *Hydrangea paniculata* look like a bundle of dead sticks; but, unlike the forms of *H. macrophylla*, they are bone hardy. The popular 'Grandiflora' responds to hard pruning in spring by producing wands tipped by massive, cone-shaped heads of white flowers, fading to pink; left to its own devices, it produces more but smaller heads on a shrub that builds up a twiggy framework. Although this is the form that you will find everywhere, the list of suppliers offering the forms with sterile and fertile florets intermingled, the *paniculata* equivalent of the lacecaps, suggests that their greater grace and elegance is winning hearts. Furthermore, by choosing your varieties, you can stretch the season of flower to four months, from midsummer to autumn. 'Praecox', 'Floribunda' and 'Tardiva', in that order of flowering, make fine, large shrubs set with frothy cones of cream and ivory if unpruned. The wild form is more airy still: 'Kuyshu' is a long-flowering selection with lacy flowers raised from wild-collected seed. All have an easy temper as regards soil, and predictable colouring – at most, they blush becomingly as the flower heads age, and 'Praecox' ages to green without a suggestion of pink. This can be worth bearing in mind when you plan colour schemes using white hydrangeas, just as with white dogwoods, which also tend to go pink with age; the leaning to pink disqualifies them from any groupings in which yellow or orange features.

Several viburnums share with the hydrangeas a tendency to develop from the mixed or lacecap flowerhead of sterile and fertile florets towards a more showy inflorescence composed only of sterile florets. The guelder rose, *Viburnum opulus*, in this way becomes the snowball tree, *V. opulus* 'Roseum' (formerly, and less confusingly, 'Sterile'). A large and energetic shrub, it is comfortingly able to cope with difficult conditions, flowering almost anywhere. At first the snowballs are apple-green, fading to ice-green then ivory; as there are no fertile florets you will not get the showy, translucent fruits of red or yellow that follow the lacecap forms, but even in shade the shrub should give you a hint of autumn colour as the leaves fall. If you decide to go for the lacecap-flower style, 'Notcutt's Variety' is a selection chosen for its larger flowers and red fruits, and 'Xanthocarpum' is the one with amber-yellow berries. In 'Aureum', the name refers to the lime-yellow leaves, not to the fruits. 'Compactum' is stockier, but still quite a bulky shrub in time; it flowers and fruits abundantly. You might be disappointed by 'Nanum', however; the smallest of them all, it hardly ever flowers, though it does colour up in autumn.

IX

Shady Rock Gardens

IT is unlikely that anyone would actually set out to make a rock garden in a shaded spot; but there must be many gardens where an existing rock garden, made in a once-open site, has become more or less shaded as trees grow or neighbouring buildings are erected. So long as the trees are not actually overhanging the rocks, dripping on them when it rains and smothering the plants with fallen leaves each autumn, there are plenty of plants that will grow and thrive. Then, of course, there are the plants of the peat garden, many of which need cool conditions away from direct sunlight.

A conventional rock garden, with limestone or sandstone rocks and a gritty planting mixture between them, can just as well be made on an open slope facing away from the sun as not, and in hotter, drier districts the plants may do better there than if they were baked each day. The big rock slope at Wisley is an example; it faces north, yet all the plants usually described as sun-loving do very well. But here I shall assume a little more shade than this; for at Wisley there are no buildings to cast a shadow, and, except at the margins, no trees, so much of the slope is beneath the open sky and you have no feeling of being in a shady garden as you walk through it.

In such a rock garden, even on the shadier side of each outcrop, you should succeed with *Saxifraga oppositifolia* and the adorable *Primula marginata*, a limestone cliff-dweller with rosettes of mealy, saw-toothed, silver-edged leaves and flowers varying from pale lavender to near-blue and violet. In lime-free soil the gentian blue *Lithodora diffusa* and its selections 'Heavenly Blue', 'Grace Ward' and 'Cambridge Blue' flower almost as freely facing away from the sun as into it. And this must lead me to the true gentians, and to the leafy, cool soil that suits them and other plants for the shady rock garden.

172

THE ROCK GARDEN ON ACID SOIL

Many people, determined to grow *Gentiana sino-ornata*, cassiopes or shortias, are prepared to go to the trouble of constructing a special bed, if the natural soil of their garden is rich in calcium. I do not propose to go into detail about such constructions; suffice it to say that whatever method you choose, you must ensure that lime from the natural soil cannot taint the leafy, acid mixture you create. That means, for example, that if you make your lime-free bed on a slope, it should be at the top and not the bottom, so that lime-rich water cannot seep down from above. You should do all you can to make sure that you are not dependent upon hard piped water when – as will certainly happen – the natural rainfall is not enough to supply the plants with all the moisture they need. If your supply of stored rainwater should run out in times of drought, though, it will be better to resort to the tap than to let your plants go dry at the root; for almost all are very susceptible to lack of moisture. You can, after all, give them a dose of Sequestrene and a foliar feed in such an emergency, to counteract the effects of what the water company supplies.

This is not the place to embark on a study of the plants that can be grown in the peat garden, even if I felt it appropriate to suggest you constructed such a thing when we must all do what we can to stop using peat. Maybe it does mean forgoing those cosy, dark brown blocks run through and through with the roots of plants that have responded to years of careful nurture. But now that the peat bogs are so seriously depleted, responsible gardeners and growers are seeking alternatives, such as coconut fibre, from which coir peat is made. Let us not forget, too, that until quite recently no one used peat; our forbears made their potting soils with sieved loam, grit and leaf mould, and enriched their gardens with farmyard or stable manure, while more and more people are discovering how much goodness can be returned to the soil by means of the compost heap.

In some areas bracken mould can be collected from among the fallen fronds of this most cosmopolitan and invasive of ferns; it is a wonderful tonic for calcifuge plants. I have grown a great many so-called peat garden plants by setting them in leafy mixtures retained, on a slope, by sandstone, or in old stone troughs, or raised beds with railway sleeper sides, over which plants can trail and tumble even if they cannot root. Raised beds and stone troughs also have the advantage of being accessible, for weeding and planting, and closer to the eye, for admiration.

There is hardly a plant that does not merit closer attention than we habitually give it, revealing a beauty quite other than the first impression – usually one of colour – that we receive. Take, for example, those gentians. Certainly, *Gentiana sino-ornata* makes, if suited, a sheet of fine green needle-leaves vanishing, in autumn, beneath brilliant blue trumpets. Look at the way the bud is scrolled tight, so that the pale citron ribs, outlined in ultramarine, give way to the azure tip of the unfurling petals. Within the flower the pale ribs are echoed in faint blue receding at the centre to ivory and rimmed by the flaring lobes of molten blue. It would seem scarcely possible to improve upon such a flower, yet there exist selected forms, including the ivory, green-washed *alba* and its exquisite selection 'Mary Lyle', deep blue 'Brin Form' which shows scrambling tendencies if you set it near a shrublet, and 'Angel Wings' in ultramarine feathered with white.

The elusive *G. farreri* is even lovelier, its blue more ethereal, touched with turquoise, around a lime and ivory throat. *G. veitchiorum*, with royal-blue flowers, belongs to this group also and has, with *G. farreri* and *G. sino-ornata*, given rise to several hybrids. One is aptly named: 'Kingfisher' in electric-blue; the rest you have to take on trust, with such names as × *macaulayi* (like an early-flowering 'Kingfisher'), paler 'Wells's Variety', 'Christine Jean' with a touch of violet in her colouring, verdigris-blue 'Carolii', × *stevenagensis* and its ultramarine and primrose selection 'Bernardii', and 'Inverleith' with very large, azure trumpets.

None of these autumn-flowering gentians is difficult given a lime-free soil, moist but free-draining, and a cool position but open to the sky; the shade of distant trees or buildings suits them well. The summer-flowering gentians exemplified by *G. septemfida* do not insist upon lime-free soil and I will come to them later. If you relish a challenge, there are some thoroughly tricky customers that will only grow for you, if at all, in a shady position in cool, humus-rich, lime-free soil. Thus the mayflower, *Epigaea repens*. The name is said to date from the time of the Pilgrim Fathers who crossed the Atlantic in a ship named the Mayflower; for this is a North American creeping shrublet that bears its fragrant, white, urn-shaped flowers, white or blush opening from rose-pink buds, in spring. Though very difficult in Britain, it is easy enough in its native continent to use as ground cover among shrubs, the rough, leathery green leaves forming a close carpet. *E. asiatica* is its Japanese equivalent, not quite so recalcitrant, with pink flowers; there used to be a hybrid between the two called 'Aurora' but whether it is still grown I know not.

From the Black Sea area comes *E. gaultherioides*, formerly *Orphanidesia gaultherioides*, by which designation it more nearly fulfilled the dictum that the longer the name, the more difficult the plant. It is the leaves that are 'gaultheria-like', leathery of texture and subglossy on the upper surface, set on prostrate, spreading, hairy stems; the flowers are little, open saucers of tender dawn-pink. All three species actually prefer a leafy canopy over their heads, as it might be of some small rhododendron.

The shortias (which includes the former genus *Schizocodon*) are related to *Galax aphylla*, but unlike that accommodating plant they are easy neither to establish nor to increase. That, of course, only makes them more desirable in the eyes of some. They need a lime-free, humus-rich soil and a shaded position protected from cold winds but not, unlike the epigaeas, directly overshadowed by the leafy branches of a taller shrub. The North American species, *Shortia galacifolia*, has evergreen, rounded, scalloped leaves, burnished or even crimson in winter and bright polished green in summer; the frilled, funnel-shaped, nodding flowers open in spring, white flushing with pink as they age.

As with *Epigaea*, the genus occurs also in Japan; *Shortia uniflora* is a slow and slender creeper with prominently toothed, evergreen leaves and large, soft pink flowers held singly on 10cm/4in stems in late spring. 'Grandiflora' is the name given to a form with extra-large, frilled flowers up to 4cm/1½in wide. Most enchanting of all is *S. soldanelloides* (*Schizocodon soldanelloides*), a Japanese species forming mats of woody stems set with rounded, toothed, glossy leaves, bronzed in winter. The flowers are open, fringed bells, recalling those of *Soldanella* except in colour, rosy-pink at the heart and fading to white at the margins. Var. *ilicifolia* has leaves toothed like holly, though not so fierce; *minima* is a tiny form.

SHRUBLETS OF THE HEATH FAMILY

In the great heath family are many shrublets that can join these calcifuge plants. The smaller gaultherias are among the most charming, with fruits of snow-white or turquoise: among them, *Gaultheria trichophylla* with tiny leaves, pink flowers and blue fruits, *G. cuneata* with white fruits that smell of antiseptic among bronzed, net-veined, glossy leaves, and creeping *G. itoana* with white fruits scattered over the bright green mats of foliage. *G. miqueliana* has polished foliage and white or pink fruits; like *G. cuneata*, it is a spreader, its underground shoots pushing through the leafy soil. This is how the tiny *Vaccinium praestans* proceeds, to form a patch of little leaves that colour brightly in autumn; the white or blush barrel flowers in ones and twos are followed by bright shiny red, sweet-tasting berries.

The little pernettyas are no less appealing. The tiniest is *Pernettya tasmanica*, its thread-like stems set with minute leaves, the fruits that ripen in autumn normally red but also known in white and yellow. *P. prostrata pentlandii* looks rather like a miniature of the familiar *P. mucronata*, with very large, lilac-purple fruits, while a species I received as *P. buxifolia* had enormous, palest lavender berries on short, arching stems.

The little bog rosemary, *Andromeda polifolia*, is grown for its pretty flowers, pink urns held in clusters at the shoot tips in early summer, contrasting with the waxy sea-green foliage. 'Compacta' is a neat little miniature, while the Japanese cultivar 'Nikko' forms low hummocks of blue-grey foliage topped by large rose-pink bells. The phyllodoces are dainty shrubs closer in appearance to the heaths. *Phyllodoce caerulea*, an arctic-alpine species, sounds as though it should have blue flowers, but they are in fact mauve to purple; perhaps if expectations of a purer colour were not created in our minds by the name, the poor plant would be more valued for what it is. *P. breweri*, surprisingly, comes from California, and differs from the other species in its open, saucer-shaped flowers of rosy-purple, in place of the usual *Erica*-like urns borne by the fetching chartreuse or soft yellow *P. aleutica* and its subspecies *glanduliflora*, or by the pale or bricky-pink *P. empetriformis*, which forms mats of glossy bright green foliage. The last two have crossed to give *P.* × *intermedia*, a vigorous hybrid with puckered flowers of rose-pink or purple, as in 'Fred Stoker', or the damson-purple 'Drummondii'. The pet of the genus, though, is *P. nipponica*, neat and upright with white or blush bells in late spring.

If you like kalmias, you are sure to be seduced by the miniature *Kalmiopsis leachiana*, a pet of a shrublet no more than 30cm/12in high, with neat, little, dark leaves and rich pink cups in racemes in spring. The first introductions were rather tricky, but later discoveries, including those in the Umpqua River Valley of Oregon, seem more amenable given open sky above but unfailing coolth and moisture at foot to save the shallow roots from perishing. Named forms of slightly differing shades of pink are 'Glendoick' and 'Le Piniec'.

The genus has crossed with *Phyllodoce* to add to the small collection of bigeneric hybrids: × *Phylliopsis hillieri* is much what you would expect from a cross between the kalmiopsis and *Phyllodoce breweri*, which you will recall has open-cupped flowers not the usual urns. Either of the named forms, 'Pinocchio' or the scarcer 'Coppelia', is worth acquiring. *P. empetriformis* has crossed with *Rhodothamnus chamaecistus* (which departs from the usual ericaceous tendency to dislike lime, and also needs sun) to produce × *Phyllothamnus erectus*, slightly taller at up to 40cm/16in, its stiff, upright stems set with linear, green leaves and little, rosy funnels in spring.

Shade is needed for the fastidious cassiopes only in so far as they, too, must have cool conditions with a moist atmosphere; if these can be combined with an open, sunny position so much the better. But we all know that except in areas where there is less sun and more mist and rain than humans enjoy, this is hard to achieve; so a position away from the sun it must be, yet with open sky above. I am not sure if my slight dislike of the genus is because I have never been very successful with it, or if I have failed because I do not like cassiopes enough to strive to give them what they want. Either way, I am unlikely to do them justice here, so I will merely mention that they have whipcord-like stems clad with tiny, imbricated leaves; and clustered or solitary white urns in spring. According to Hillier's *Manual of Trees & Shrubs*, the hybrid 'Edinburgh' is 'perhaps the most accommodating of a pernickety genus'. Let that, then, be your starting point if you want to have a go for the first time with the genus; if you already grow cassiopes to perfection you will not need me and my descriptions anyway, so I need not do violence to my aim to write only about what I know.

When it comes to *Leiophyllum buxifolium*, I am once again on familiar ground. This ericaceous shrublet has small, rather glossy leaves on hummocky growths, tipped with clusters of white flowers opening in late spring from rosy-pink buds. It is an accommodating little thing, preferring a cool, moist soil in light shade. Though there are other desirable shrublets in the family Ericaceae, I am inclined to leave it at that – except, of course, for the dwarf rhododendrons, which can hardly be ignored – as on the whole they prefer more open conditions, even full sun, so long as they can be kept cool and moist at the root.

DWARF RHODODENDRONS

The little rhododendrons themselves can be most successfully grown according to Captain Collingwood Ingram's recipe: a completely open-sky, though not sunny, position away from tree drip, a bed of acid soil well laced with lime-free sharp sand and acid leaf-mould, and a stone, preferably a sandstone slab, close to the stem of each plant on the sunny side. Furthermore, for at least a week after transplanting, the little rhodos should be covered with a large pot or shaded cloche, to reduce water loss through transpiration. Any suitable branchlets can be pegged down into a gritty, leafsoil mixture; if necessary, tie the tips upright to a little cane until they have firmed up. Even if you do not want to detach the layers once rooted, they will make the plant more stable, and help to keep it from getting leggy.

There are so many small rhododendrons, both species and hybrids, that I can only give a selection here, trying to exclude any that grow to more than 45cm/18in or so, however desirable they may be. The season opens with *Rhododendron moupinense*, a little bush with box-like leaves and coral-pink buds opening to large, fragrant flowers, white or blush with red freckles. The amusing little *R. pemakoense* is a low, suckering shrublet with disproportionately large, pale mallow-pink flowers in early spring. If you garden in an area where spring frosts are common, the flowers of these early-season species may be spoiled by a cold snap; in which case, the later-flowering species may be a safer choice.

There is quite a little gaggle of them with rosy or plum-purple flowers. In *R. calostrotum* 'Gigha' the wide, claret-red saucers are contrasted with glaucous-grey foliage; a self-contained colour scheme is just as precious among tiny plants as it is among the larger occupants of the border, so this little shrub earns extra marks. The species has, the taxonomists decree, swallowed up the tiny, hummocky *R. keleticum*, which has plum-purple saucers over close-packed, pointed leaves; and *R. radicans*, a creeping shrublet with glossy, bright green leaves and crimson-purple, flat-faced blooms. The little mat-forming *R. saluenense* has deep crimson-purple flowers with wide-flaring lobes. Another almost portmanteau species is *R. campylogynum*, with waxy thimbles varying from rosy-purple to maroon, over shining green leaves. One of its smallest manifestations is the Myrtilloides group, with smaller, plum-crimson bells.

Not everyone cares for purple and claret-coloured flowers, but the 'blue' rhododendrons are always admired. Tiny species suitable for the rock garden include *R. impeditum*, a dense shrublet with tiny, sea-green leaves (or slate-blue in 'Blue Steel') and violet flowers very freely borne; and *R. scintillans* (now included in *R. polycladum*), of which the FCC form has deep violet, almost royal-blue flowers on rather slender growth with tiny leaves. *R. fastigiatum* in paler lavender is ultimately rather tall at 60cm/24in or more, as is *R. intricatum* with olive-green leaves and lavender-blue flowers. The many hybrids, Blue Tit and others, already mentioned, tend to grow to 90cm/36in or more with time, but as rhododendrons are very portable you could grow them in the rock garden until they become too large, and then move them on elsewhere.

To grow with these little indigo- and smoky-blue rhododendrons, there are some clear pale yellow species. *R. hanceanum* has a dwarf form, Nanum, with bronze-green foliage and clear yellow funnels; *R. sargentianum* has more tubular flowers of lemon or ivory over small, aromatic leaves. In time, *R. lepidostylum* may grow to 60cm/24in or more; but it is so endearing, with its bristly, bright glaucous-blue leaves and pale citron funnels, that it must always find a place in a cool, shaded rock garden.

Among dwarf hybrid rhododendrons, there are several enchanting yellows, such as 'Curlew', 'Chikor' and 'Princess Anne'. It is from the hybrids, too, that I would choose a dwarf scarlet, for in several of these the blood of *R. forrestii* Repens is allied with a species more willing to flower in captivity. Carmen has blood-red, waxen bells, and 'Creeping Jenny' bears large, deep scarlet flowers on prostrate growth. 'Little Ben' is a low-spreading shrublet with bright scarlet, waxy bells, rather like a smaller version of the popular Elizabeth which is too large for our purposes. Although the evergreen azaleas are not shrubs for the rock garden, there is a little species in the Azalea section that is quite irresistible, *R. nakaharae*, now available in several forms running to brick and terracotta shades, flowering very late in the season.

A calcifuge shrublet that flowers all summer and spreads investigative roots through cool soil to make a mat no more than a hand's-span high, *Polygala chamaebuxus grandiflora* is a milkwort with small, box-like leaves and flowers of saffron and claret constructed somewhat like a pea flower, with a keel and wings. *P. vayredae* is smaller still, with narrower leaves and flowers of carmine-purple just tipped with yellow on the keel.

LITTLE PLANTS FOR LEAFY SOILS

Midsummer is the season for the twin flower, *Linnaea borealis*, which grows in the wild in woodsy soils among pines, trailing its long, slender, reddish stems across the soft carpet of needles and rooting here and there. The tiny leaves are in scale with the dainty, blush bells; var. *americana*, as you might expect, is larger, with bronzed leaves and pink bells with a faint almond scent.

There is a tiny lobelia that mimics the twin flower: *Lobelia linnaeoides* creeps flat along the ground, the tiny, rounded leaves varying from dark green to a curious metallic bronze, below pale pink flowers on thread-like stems. From coniferous woodlands in Japan comes *Pteridophyllum racemosum*, no less dainty a plant, with little tufts of fern-like leaves and small, white flowers in sprays, in summer. *Tanakaea radicans* is a Japanese saxifrage relative, with running stems that like to scuttle through leafy, sandy, lime-free soil; the leathery, heart-shaped leaves are evergreen, setting off sprays of ivory flowers in early summer. Quite unrelated, *Luetkea pectinata* is a little, creeping shrublet that mimics, with its dissected leaves, a mossy saxifrage; the white flowers in late spring are borne in spikelets.

The prostrate *Calceolaria tenella* is no more than a film of green over the surface of moist soil or mossy stones; the tiny, pouched, yellow flowers are held on 8cm/3in stems in summer. Provided it is never allowed to dry out, and can seek out new soil to refresh itself, it is not a difficult plant despite its frail appearance. Most people find *C. darwinii* and *C. fothergillii* much more difficult to keep, though they look more robust, with their little tufts of dark green leaves and larger, solitary pouches, of tawny-yellow marked with a white bar as though waiting for a neat hand to inscribe their names. The hybrid 'Walter Shrimpton' is of this style also. The yellow-flowered *C. biflora* is a better perennial with twin flowers, *C. falklandica* makes green, cushiony growth topped by bright yellow pouches, and *C. polyrrhiza* is a tentative creeper with solitary, yellow, maroon-spotted flowers. These little slipperworts are like the big-bellied, blotchy-faced, greenhouse calceolarias only in as much as a fairytale princess is like the bloated madame of a brothel.

Earlier in this book I promised you a word about the exquisite but capricious *Corydalis cashmeriana*. If there is a recipe for success at all, it certainly includes a cool soil, preferably free of lime, and protection from birds, which may scratch the tempting, loose soil surface and in so doing disturb the tiny tubers just below. If their fleshy roots once dry out, they are unlikely ever to recover. But when it does succeed (and enough nurserymen offer it to encourage us to think it cannot be that difficult; recent introductions are said to be more amenable) it will hold its little clusters of long-spurred sky-blue flowers over tufts of ferny, sea-green leaves. If you long for the glacier blue of *C. cashmeriana* but cannot please it, try *C. ambigua*, which seems easy to satisfy and is just as fetching in its electric- to turquoise-blue colouring, though it occasionally disgraces itself with a purplish flush. A native of shady Japanese woods, it clearly needs deep, leafy soil. Almost as covetable as these ethereal blues is the warm bricky pink of 'G. P. Baker', a form of the easygoing *C. solida* but by no means so dependable.

It might seem curious to find a genus related to the campanulas among the plants for acid soil; but the species of *Cyananthus* are only marginally lime-tolerant, needing that elusive balance of constant moisture with free drainage. Given such an ideal, they prefer an open position, but they will do very well in light shade, finding compensation for occasional spells of dryness at the root. 'Cyananthus' means blue flower, and though they cannot quite compete in purity of tone with the gentians, and are better kept apart from them, they are very appealing, with wide saucers opening in late summer over mats of fresh green. *C. lobatus* is the most familiar, its stems radiating from a thick, central root, each stem upturned at the tip and set with a single, large, royal-blue flower with the propellor outline more familiar in periwinkles. There is a pretty albino, a form with midnight-blue flowers, imaginatively dubbed 'Dark Seedling', and powder-blue 'Sherriff's Variety'. As its name tells us, *C. microphyllus* has smaller leaves, uncut and not lobed, on radiating stems forming a green pat rimmed with starry, violet-blue flowers.

A plant from the Rockies, *Boykinia jamesii*, is apt to be shy-flowering in captivity, and is most likely to reward you with its large, cherry-pink flowers in early summer if you grow it in a cool crevice, in poor, lime-free soil; not the easiest of recipes, given that for most of the time we endeavour to create acidic mixtures that are leafy, well-nourished and never dry. The leaves of the little Coloradan native, rounded and toothed, take on rich autumn colours.

I have found that similar conditions suit the lewisias, another North American genus, provided that behind the cool and gritty mixture (which will preferably, but not essentially, be free of lime) there is some dark and crumbly leaf mould, ideally from oak trees, for the roots to reach into. They are happiest growing in a crevice where the fleshy leaf rosette, vertically flattened against the rocks, can shed winter rain; a dry wall facing away from the sun also suits them well. As there is not space in just one chapter on rock plants to go into the details of the genus, I can admit that the lewisias with which I am most successful are grown from seed of a mongrel strain of *Lewisia cotyledon* in which colours occur from ochre to magenta, via all the sunset and terracotta shades. If fresh seed is sown you can very quickly have pan after pan of babies, which fast plump up for planting out. Purists might shudder; but anyone who likes a bit of fun can have a wall-full of lewisias in no time, as bright as any bedding annuals.

For Alkaline Soils

Much more to the taste of the rock-gardening sophisticate are the hardy gesneriads, *Haberlea* and *Ramonda*. Both will thrive where they never see the sun, in cool crevices where their roots reach back into leafy but free-draining soil – whether limy or not is immaterial. *Ramonda myconi* is a Pyrenean species, forming flat rosettes of dark green, crinkled leaves, over which the rounded, wide-petalled flowers of lavender-blue with yellow centres are borne in short sprays in late spring. There is a pink form, *rosea*, and an exquisite white. The Bulgarian *R. nathaliae* is similar, but the leaves are glossy, and edged with dark hairs. *R. serbica*, another

Balkan species, has smaller, more cupped flowers. The haberleas, which are exclusively eastern European, are very similar, with flowers of less regular shape over leaves with toothed margins. *Haberlea rhodopensis* has flowers of soft lilac with white in the throat; or all white with an apple-green throat in 'Virginalis'. The resoundingly named *H. ferdinandi-coburgi* has larger, more open-mouthed, lilac flowers freckled with sulphur in the throat.

By comparison with these, *Erinus alpinus* is a jokey little plant with tufts of crinkly leaves and stems no longer than your little finger, topped, in spring, by heads of starry flowers, usually lilac or pinkish-mauve, sometimes (as in 'Dr Hähnle') crimson-purple, or, enchantingly, pure white. It looks like a sun lover, but grows very well in shade, and will seed itself into the cracks of a shady wall, pressing its little rosettes and vertical flowering stems flat against the bricks or stone.

Most of the dicentras are too large except for the most expansive rock garden, but *Dicentra cuccularia* is a tiny species for a cool and shady spot, with tufts of finely cut leaves and flights of white, lemon-tipped flowers in early summer on 10cm/4in stems. After flowering it dies away, so you should mark it carefully lest you fall with glee upon an apparently empty space, later in the year, and plant something on top of this miniature Dutchman's breeches. It is in scale with the diminutive *Iris cristata*, which bears its orange-crested, lavender-blue flowers over a tangle of thin rhizomes and small, pointed sword leaves. The albino form is even more fetching in lemon and white. *I. lacustris* is smaller still, its flowers held on stems barely 3cm/1in tall. At 25cm/10in, *I. gracilipes* is a giant by comparison, its branching stems bearing flattish, lilac flowers with a bold tangerine crest.

BULBS FOR THE ROCK GARDEN IN SHADE

Bulbs for the rock garden should be in scale with these miniatures. The tiny trilliums, which would be lost among their more vigorous cousins, can be kept under close observation in a leafy pocket of the rock garden. *Trillium rivale* flowers early, its short stems topped by deep green leaves and flowers varying from white to blush, freckled at the centre with maroon. Later it is the turn of *T. undulatum*, the painted trillium, so called on account of the bold, angled stripe of crimson at the base of each pink petal. The emerging leaves are bronzed, fading to dark green as the flowers open. The prairie trillium, *T. recurvatum*, is less exciting, but compensatingly easier to grow, with mottled, burnished leaves and flowers of curious toad-like colouring, murrey suffused with tan and citron. The snow trillium, *T. nivale*, is tiny, and its pure white flowers appear very early, so it is a bit of a gamble in the open.

The true *Narcissus cyclamineus* can be curiously elusive, nursery stock often wrongly named unless you buy from a specialist. The real thing is quite unmistakable, with its narrow, canary-yellow trumpet and fully reflexed perianth, on 8cm/3in stems. It can take plenty of soil moisture so long as the drainage is unimpaired, and prefers a leafy soil in light shade. I have also found the hoop petticoat daffodils, *N. bulbocodium*, perfectly happy in light shade, even surviving years of neglect on a mossy bank. There are several forms, some easier than others, such as the richly coloured *conspicuus* and pale lemon *citrinus*. *N. minor* is a miniature version, 10cm/4in tall, of the lent lily, *N. pseudonarcissus*, with buttercup-yellow trumpet and lemon or sulphur perianth, and just as happy as the larger species in light shade. Other small daffodils I have succeeded with in shady positions include *N. triandrus triandrus*, the angel's tears, and the soft lemon *triandrus* hybrid 'Hawera'.

Most crocuses are sun-lovers, but the uncommon *Crocus cvijicii* is said to prefer a cool place away from the sun, and a soil that does not dry out in summer; it has rich yellow flowers and, I am told, a distinct fragrance of freesias. Remember that mice like crocus corms as much as small children like chocolates, and be prepared to encase your *cvijicii* corms in a protective cage of fine-mesh wire netting. *C. scharojanii* is the only yellow crocus flowering in autumn, and is none too easy; it needs cool, leafy soil and should not be allowed to dry out. This will also satisfy *Iris winogradowii*, which is related to the reticulatas and makes them seem coarse, so enchanting are its short-stemmed, lemon-primrose flowers with narrow, sulphur flare and faint brown freckles. 'Katherine Hodgkin' is its hybrid with the deep blue *I. histrioides* 'Major'; the result is a flower so subtle in colour that it is hardly a colour at all, the standards palest seagreen veined with verdigris and the falls freckled and flecked with chocolate on a ground of sulphur lined with slate-blue and crested in yellow.

A MIXED BAG

Trollius pumilus earns few points for subtlety, but plenty for ease of cultivation and cheerful demeanour. A smaller version of the moisture-loving globe flowers, it opens its yellow cups in early summer on 15cm/6in stems over deep green, divided leaves. A little carpeting plant that is unlikely ever to cause you a moment's worry is *Houstonia caerulea*, which bears an abundance of four-petalled, porcelain-blue flowers in spring over glossy leaves. 'Fred Millard' is a selection with deeper blue flowers, and there is a pretty white form. It might be a little over-exuberant for *Polygonatum hookeri*, a tiny species which seems to have nothing in common with the familiar Solomon's seals; it forms a close mat of rhizomes with tiny, lilac-pink flowers tucked away in the leaf axils. If you look closely, you will see that the flowers are tubular in shape, but all that appear are the starry lobes, peering up at you from the leafy carpet in spring. The tiny fern *Blechnum penna-marina* is a slow but steady spreader making a close mat of leathery, dark bronze-green, divided leaves. The maidenhair, *Adiantum pedatum subpumilum* (more familiar as *aleuticum*), is a perfect little miniature, deciduous unlike the blechnum, and irresistible in its compact neatness of black stems closely set with blue-green pinnules. In this green corner it would be tempting to add *Daphne laureola philippi*, a dwarf form of the evergreen spurge laurel with blunt, polished leaves and yellow-green flowers in spring. In early spring, too, the creamy flower spikes of *Polygonum tenuicaule* (*Persicaria tenuicaulis*) are borne over gently creeping, leafy mats.

Spring is the season of the soldanellas, enchanting alpine plants with rounded leaves and nodding, fringed flowers of lavender or purple-blue. One of the easiest is *Soldanella villosa*, as softly furred as its name suggests, with violet flowers, on taller stems than the diminutive, deeply fringed *S. alpina*. Somewhere between the two in size is *S. montana*, with wider flaring, fringed bells. 'Montana', in this case, means the European Alps; *S. pindicola* is one of the Balkan species, with flowers of rosy-lilac, and heart-shaped leaves. Two species, I believe, have given us albino forms: *S. carpatica* and the tiny *S. minima*. Give them all a gritty, leafy mixture in a cool position, and watch for slugs, which plunder the flower buds in winter to leave you with a violated, empty rosette in spring.

PRIMULAS

Although they look superficially very different, the soldanellas are in the same family as primulas. And in the great genus *Primula*, there are many species that need cool, leafy, moist soil and lightly shaded conditions. Some are easy, some are anything but; I will try to avoid tantalizing you too often with primulas that will succeed only in conditions that few of us can emulate. Most people would consider the Petiolares primulas rather tricky, and certainly they need a moist atmosphere, with protection from drying winds and drought. Growers in the higher latitudes are often more successful than those of us who find our climate drawing ever nearer to the continental model; thus, for example, Scotland is more to the taste of the Petiolarids than southern England. But at least one grower in the south has been quite successful, planting his Petiolarids in damp hollows in mature woodland, where the high canopy holds the moisture in the air and the soil is black and crumbly from generations of leaf fall. As with the more familiar primroses, regular division is essential to keep the plants in good health.

One of the easiest of the Petiolarids is *Primula gracilipes* which makes dense rosettes of pale green, toothed leaves, with at the heart of each rosette a tight posy of lavender-pink, yellow-eyed flowers in early spring. Another relatively docile species is *P. edgeworthii*, which in winter is a congested rosette of leaves around the crowded clusters of flower buds, the whole thing heavily dusted with meal; in spring the buds open to soft mauve or white, sulphur-eyed flowers. Far more beautiful are the allied *P. whitei* and *P. bhutanica*, which form egg-like winter resting buds, more distinct than the tight dormant bud of *P. gracilipes*. In early spring the rosette of mealy, serrated leaves expands, encircling a cluster of ice-blue, white-eyed flowers. The taxonomists have juggled with these two species, at first considering them distinct, then lumping them together; the consensus now seems to be that they are two, not one, with *P. bhutanica* much the finer. So appealing a plant would have to be as easy and as invasive as a dandelion before one could begin to disdain it.

The challenge posed by *P. reidii* may be even greater. This is one of the Soldanelloides section, none of which is easy; but the subspecies *williamsii* is quite widely offered by nurserymen, which always suggests that the amateur should have a go. The compact rosettes of hairy leaves (which detest wet when tucked up into dormant buds for the winter) are topped by 10cm/4in stems ending in a head of several nodding, wide bells, of lavender-blue with ivory hearts, endowed with a delicate, sweet fragrance. There is a pure white form of heart-stopping charm. The allied *P. nutans*, which we must now call by the ugly name of *P. flaccida* – no longer 'nodding' but now simply 'limp' – tends to die after flowering, so you must save and sow seed. The rather upstanding, narrow leaves surround scented, pale violet flowers in a little pyramidal cluster on white-dusted, 30cm/12in stems. It is at its most fetching at the halfway stage, when the upper flowers are still in dark bud, and the lower have expanded to wide-flaring bells.

The Nivalid primulas are the third of the tricky groups of which some are worth attempting. *P. chionantha*, which means snow-flowered, has scented flowers, white with a yellow eye. They are carried in clusters, one topping the 30cm/12in stem and another just below, almost candelabra-fashion, above strong, upright leaves of narrow outline, mealy beneath.

Like *P. flaccida*, it tends to be monocarpic, but usually sets good seed. The same is true of *P. capitata*, which has its own section; the violet flowers are held in dense, rounded heads over a starry rosette of white-backed leaves. It recalls a drumstick primula, but flowers at the other end of the season, during late summer and early autumn. White to violet is the colour range of *P. ioessa*, a diminutive Sikkimensis primula with a delicious fragrance, its bell-shaped flowers hanging on slender stalks. It is by no means so finicky as the Nivalids, Petiolarids and Soldanelloides primulas, and leads me to some easier species for the rock garden.

A cool and leafy soil is a fair substitute for the moist, northern meadows where *P. farinosa*, the bird's eye primrose, is found. The botanical name refers to the mealy powdering of the neat, leafy rosettes; the little mauve-pink, yellow-eyed flowers are held on 10cm/4in stems. A more robust version of this from eastern Europe is *P. frondosa*, with brighter rose-pink, white-eyed flowers. The miniature of this group is *P. clarkei* from Kashmir, a tiny, bright-eyed primula which needs frequent division. The near-unpronounceable *P. warshenewskiana* has triumphed over its name to be readily available; it is easily increased by division of the spreading stoloniferous growth, and offers the expected bright pink, yellow-eyed flowers, borne on 5cm/2in stems over mats of pale green leaves in spring. In the same section, *P. yargongensis* adds fragrance to late spring with its mauve-pink flowers on taller stems, up to 20cm/8in, amid lax rosettes of narrow, lettuce-green leaves. *P. involucrata* is virtually the same thing in white; this species is now deemed to have swallowed up *P. yargongensis*. The easiest of all, provided it has constant moisture – a boggy soil suits it perfectly well – is *P. rosea*, which makes itself known very early in the year, colouring up even as it emerges from its below-ground winter dormancy and gradually expanding to a fat little plant with red young leaves fading to bronzed green around the central cluster of shocking-pink flowers. The selection 'Micia Visser de Geer', which used to be known more concisely as 'Delight', is brighter still, a shout of defiance at the lingering cold of early spring.

Somewhat arbitrarily perhaps, I propose to deal with the named forms of primrose, single and double, in the chapter on town and courtyard gardens. They are, of course, often grown in cottage and country gardens, but the essentially man-made character of the doubles, especially, seems to me to disqualify them from the rock garden, and – like the little double daisies that are also quintessentially cottage garden plants – they are garden toys that need the cossetting and constant attention they are more likely to receive if you garden in a small space.

Like *Primula flaccida*, the related *Omphalogramma* species are easier to grow in high-latitude areas where the atmosphere is cool and moisture-charged, than in southern England, where even the weather is beginning to realize that the EEC is an inescapable reality, and has started to jump straight from grey winters to hot, dry weather more like a proper summer than an English spring. A cool, limy soil, with plenty of humus and enough grit to ensure impeccable drainage, in a position facing away from the sun, offers the best chance of success with the easiest of the genus, *O. vinciflorum*. Over rosettes of hairy leaves, the large, solitary, tubular flowers are rich violet in early summer.

FROM MIDSUMMER ON

Apart from *Primula capitata*, there is nothing much among these soldanellas and primulas to see except the little leaf rosettes, after spring has fully yielded to summer. At midsummer it is the turn of *Phlox adsurgens*, which forms a tumble of stems bearing large, clear coral-pink flowers with a darker stripe to each petal; 'Wagon Wheel' is a selection with the petals cut into narrow segments. Cool, leafy soil in light shade also suits *P.* 'Chattahoochee', rather tall perhaps at 30cm/12in, but captivating with its loose clusters of rounded, slate-blue, crimson-eyed flowers. There are two fine selections of *P. stolonifera*, 'Ariane' with white flowers over apple-green foliage, and 'Blue Ridge' with azure, orange-eyed flowers; both grow to around 15cm/6in and may spread quite widely in leafy soil.

Something much smaller and choicer is *Oxalis enneaphylla*, a native of peaty crevices in the chilly and rainswept southernmost parts of South America. The folded leaves of ice-grey are a cool setting for the huge, crystalline white or blush cups that open at midsummer. Its hybrid 'Ione Hecker', with pale mauve, veined flowers, is no less appealing. *O. magellanica*, which is self-evidently from the same corner of the world as *O. enneaphylla*, is more of a carpeter for cool soils, with mats of diminutive bronze-green shamrock leaves and little, snow-white flowers. Do not be tempted by the appalling *O. corniculata*, however pretty you may find it with its mahogany foliage and lemon-yellow flowers; it will repay you by getting into everything, with a special penchant for seeding into the crown of something extra precious and smothering it to death.

The little oxalis is not the only good thing to come from the South American continent. *Ourisia microphylla* is a small Andean creeping plant, none too easy to please so that some growers keep it in the alpine house; the slender stems are set with whipcord leaves and, when the plant is happy, it bears an abundance of large, rose-pink, tubular flowers in summer. Other, larger members of the genus (which crosses into New Zealand and Tasmania) have already been proposed for the woodland garden; but *O. caespitosa* is quite neat enough for the more restrained setting of the shaded rock garden, with prostrate stems bearing white flowers; var. *gracilis* is smaller still, very dainty.

There are many instances of closely related plants growing in both South America and Australasia. The Chilean *Hypsela reniformis*, however, plays the game differently, by looking remarkably like *Selliera radicans* from across the Pacific, which is in a different (though not distantly related) family. Both are low, carpeting plants for cool places, with rounded, bright green leaves; the *Hypsela* has small, pale pink, crimson-flashed flowers (or white in 'Greencourt White') while the *Selliera* is white-flowered. Its close relative *Goodenia repens* is in the same mould, its tiny, creeping stems set with bronzed, paddle-shaped leaves among which appear the stemless white flowers like miniature lobelias. The pratias actually *are* miniature lobelias, in effect, being closely related within the same family. *Pratia pedunculata* is the easiest to obtain, and typical of the genus, with little, creeping, rooting stems bearing rounded leaves topped by lavender-blue flowers in spring. *P. angulata* is commonly white-flowered, but the selection 'Tim Rees' is a rich violet-blue. There are several others, all in shades of white, lavender or clear violet.

The little antipodean and south American gunneras, which look utterly unlike their giant waterside relative, are carpeting plants of great character. *Gunnera magellanica* is the easiest and most territorial, with rounded, pleated leaves and short spikes of flower, usually of greenish tint. *G. prorepens* is more colourful, with chocolate- and burgundy-tinted foliage, and minute flowers of crimson and cream followed by succulent red fruits in a grape hyacinth-like spike. In *G. hamiltonii* the leaves are what count, for they are dusky brown in colour, of leathery texture, and pointed at the tips, forming neat, geometric rosettes slowly multiplying in a cool and sheltered corner.

It is time for a change from all these little carpeting plants. *Hosta venusta* is one of the smallest of the genus, with tiny, dark green, arrow-head leaves forming a diminutive clump, and little spikes of violet-purple trumpets in late summer. The later-flowering *H. tardiflora* is no bigger, with thick, glossy leaves and spikelets of lilac flowers. Another small species is *H. minor*, with good late flowers of sulky violet. So long as you have no objection to coloured foliage in the rock garden, 'Hydon Sunset' would be a good choice among the lime-yellow hostas, for its leaves, of broad lance shape, are no longer than one's thumb. 'Hadspen Heron' is one of the tiny blue-leaved hostas, and 'Ginko Craig' is a small lance-leaved cultivar with the green blades edged in white.

Their foliage of simple, firm outline contrasts with the finely divided leaves of *Thalictrum kiusianum*, as delicate as a maidenhair fern, topped by fuzzy heads of tiny, madder-purple flowers during summer and early autumn. Although most sedums are plants of drained soil and sun, *Sedum pulchellum* breaks with tradition, for it grows lush and green in cool, moist places, the fleshy leaves topped by starfish sprays of bright pink flowers in summer.

The celmisias are not shade lovers as such, but a cool, leafy and gritty soil and a moist atmosphere suit them; light shade can help to protect them from dry air. The lance-shaped or tufted leaves of several species are silver-felted, and their daisy flowers are white, bringing an unexpected note to the shaded rock garden. The easiest of them all, *Celmisia bellidioides*, forms creeping mats of dark green leaves, glossy not white-felted, and flowers in spring and summer. *C. ramulosa* is half woody, a low mound of grey-green; *C. coriacea* is much bigger, with long, silvered lance leaves, white woolly beneath, and woolly 30cm/12in stems bearing the large, pure white, yellow-eyed daisies in early summer. I have grown several others, sometimes raised from seed and not necessarily rightly named; but I have never grown a celmisia I did not like.

Easy Cover for Large Rock Gardens

It may be all very nice to read about small and exquisite plants for shaded, cool crevices or leafy soil, but what if your problem is a more conventional rock garden that has become overshadowed, where you simply want to grow easygoing plants that will fill the gaps, trail over the rocks, keep the weeds at bay and look respectable all year and colourful in their due seasons? There are such plants, of course, some of which are to be found among the conventional rock plants and alpines of your local garden centre. The mossy saxifrages, for example, are easy, spreading plants for cool soils, limy or not, with fresh green rosettes of foliage all year, spangled with pink, white or red flowers in early summer. You can buy on sight, or go for named varieties such as 'Bob Hawkins', with white flowers over cream and green rosettes; 'Ballawley Guardsman' with crimson-scarlet flowers; the very splendid red 'Triumph'; miniature carmine 'Elf'; pink 'Dartington Double'; white 'Pearly King' or the bold 'James Bremner'; or the creamy-yellow 'Flowers of Sulphur'. 'Cloth of Gold' is a form of *Saxifraga moschata*, one of the parents of this mixed-blood group, with lime-yellow foliage and white flowers; it is very slow. All you need do with these is divide the mats every few years, in autumn, before they begin to go bald at the centre.

The London Pride saxifrages are just as accommodating, with their rosettes of rounded, dark green leaves and sprays of pink flowers in early summer. *S.* × *urbium* is the name that covers variants on the theme, such as *primuloides* 'Elliott's Variety', a delightful miniature with clouds of rich pink flowers on 15cm/6in stems, and then there are the rather horrid, yellow-measled *S. umbrosa* 'Aureopunctata and 'Variegata'. *S.* × *primulaize* is a size smaller again, with narrower leaves and salmon-pink flowers. A saxifrage of a different stamp is *S. sibthorpii*, virtually an annual, which will seed itself in cool corners, decorating them with yellow flowers.

Most of the small geraniums flower best when grown in sunny positions, but *Geranium dalmaticum* seems equally at home in the shade, where it forms a neat, bumpy mat of shining, rounded leaves, crimson-tinted in autumn, topped by rose-pink flowers in summer. The little English form of G. *sanguineum*, which used to be called *lancastriense* and is now *striatum*, is more of a spreader, with hairy, deeply cut leaves and pale pink, crimson-veined flowers over a long season.

The pink theme carries on into autumn with *Polygonum vaccinifolium* (*Persicaria vaccinifolia*) a trailing knotweed with slender stems, neat, pointed leaves, and countless pink spikelets in late summer for many weeks. It is far prettier than the popular forms of *P. affine*, valuable though these are with their mats of narrow leaves turning to brown in winter (often cited as a feature, but to me they look rather dead), and upright stocky spikes of pink or crimson from summer to autumn. 'Darjeeling Red' is deeper in colour than the rose-pink, larger-flowered 'Donald Lowndes'; but the one I like best is 'Superbum', its pokers opening blush-white and aging through pink to crimson so that there is a play of colours across the little patch of flowers. 'Dimity' is either the same, or very like.

Ivy-leaved toadflax is a common weed of shady walls; it has a pretty albino form, less vigorous, with apple-green leaves and little white, lemon-eyed snapdragon flowers in summer. Look for it in catalogues under *Cymbalaria muralis* 'Nana Alba'. *C. pallida* grows flatter and wider, with rounded leaves and larger pale lilac flowers. Much more vigorous than these are the two campanulas with impossible names. *Campanula poscharskyana* is a rampageous spreader, making a mat of long, tangled stems smothered for weeks in starry, powder-blue flowers; it has a pretty mauve form called 'Lilacina'. 'E. H. Frost' is more restrained, and very charming with larger, creamy stars tinged with blue; 'Stella' is a good clear lilac-blue. Also suited to polite company is *C. portenschlagiana*, which has deeper lavender-blue bells in clusters at midsummer, over leafy weed–smothering mats; var. *bavarica* has slightly larger flowers.

With its greyish, softly sticky leaves, *Asarina procumbens* looks as though it should grow in sun, but it does equally well in light shade, producing a long succession of creamy-yellow snapdragons on trailing stems. A brighter yellow belongs to the strawberry flowers of *Waldsteinia ternata*, which makes a carpet of trifoliate, dark green leaves sprinkled with flowers in spring. In summer there follow the sprays of yellow stars belonging to fleshy-leaved *Chiastophyllum oppositifolium*. Spring through to summer is the season of the horned pansies, *Viola cornuta*, which form a carpet of rooting stems and will hoist themselves into neighbouring shrubs in a friendly but not smothering way. The type has lilac-blue pansy flowers, and there is a pretty albino and the paler *lilacina*, while 'Belmont Blue' is pale azure. Hybrid violas that are as easy, and small enough in flower not to look out of place, include 'Haslemere' in a strange shade of muted lilac-pink, bright 'Huntercombe Purple' and deep purple 'Martin'. The bicolour, chocolate and canary 'Jackanapes' needs a bit more keeping, in my experience, and may die out in time if you do not regularly take cuttings. But 'Moonlight' is more persistent, and one of the prettiest in pale primrose.

The easiest of all gentians, *Gentiana septemfida*, will grow in any soil and in light shade or sun, making tufts of leafy stems each crowned by a cluster of tubular flowers, their mid to deep blue just off the pure tones of *G. sino-ornata*, in summer. *G. lagodechiana* is similar, with one or two flowers per stem, while × *hascombensis* is a hybrid between the two. What you get from the nurseryman may or may not be the true thing, but I have never had a bad plant under any of these three names.

FILLING BETWEEN THE ROCKS

If you do not want to obscure the rocks, but simply fill the spaces between them, the little, creeping mint *Mentha requienii* will do the job nicely in a cool spot. A mere film of green over the soil, with minute mauve flowers, it has a peppermint aroma more pungent than one would think could possibly belong to such a tiny plant. *Arenaria balearica* makes a green carpet scarcely deeper-piled than the little mint, spangled with tiny, white stars in spring. The cotulas are grown more for their close mats of tiny, ferny leaves than for their little, creamy button-flowers. *Cotula squalida* (now *Leptinella squalida*) has triumphed over its unfortunate name on account of its willingness to spread into a flat, bronzed mat in shady places, while *Leptinella potentillina* (*C. potentilloides*) is green. The only one I have grown that I valued for its flowers was *L. atrata luteola*, with wine-red and cream heads over taupe foliage, very fetching but undeniably a touch more finicky than the others.

Some little shrubs will give solidity to the rock garden, especially if they retain their leaves in winter. The popular coloured forms of *Euonymus fortunei* are too big, however tempting they may seem as bright infants in the nursery rows; but the tiny 'Kewensis', with creeping slender stems, is more restrained, a dainty thing with leaves the size of a capital O. Even more than this, *Cotoneaster pyrenaicus* (*C. congestus nanus*) makes dense, tiny-leaved, evergreen cover, as the little woody stems creep slowly but inexorably forward over any rocky obstacle, and, in the absence of a rock, hump themselves up into hummocky, hard mounds. The small, white flowers lie flat on the dark green carpet and may be followed by red fruits.

Solidity comes, too, from the leathery, rounded leaves of *Bergenia stracheyi*, a half-sized version of the big ground-covering kinds, with pink or white flowers on short stems in spring. Like its larger brethren, it grows equally well in sun or shade, and will fill a vertical crevice or grow on the flat, whatever you ask of it. Even the smallest of the ivies will spread too far for most rock gardens, but there are amusing little shrubby forms of *Hedera helix* called 'Conglomerata' and 'Congesta', which have erect stems closely set with tiny leaves in two ranks; 'Congesta' has more triangular, cupped leaves than 'Conglomerata' which is nearer to the conventional lobed outline.

X

The Shady Border

Perhaps this chapter should have a heading in the plural, for I shall write about several shady borders I have known or made or attempted to improve. They have in common, apart from the fact of being shaded, that they belong where the surrounding garden style is semi-formal or formal, with beds and borders of fairly conventional mixed plantings near the dwelling house. Though some of the plants may be the same, the style of these borders is therefore far removed from the woodland plantings we have discussed earlier. Nor does any suffer from the handicaps of extreme dryness, very dense shade, or exposure to wind without compensating sunlight. They are, in short, the kind of border that anyone might have in a garden facing away from the sun, or beneath a tall wall that casts its shadow for much of the day, or even within high hedges. I shall assume that the soil, whatever its fundamental nature, is generously treated, with compost or manure to improve its texture and add nourishment for the plants growing there. This may be a large assumption, but there is no escaping the fact that virtually any plant is the better for some feeding, and many of the summer-flowering plants that we choose for shady borders are as greedy as any. There is little satisfaction to be had from wan, undernourished Japanese anemones, phlox, rudbeckias and the like.

A Border on Clay Beneath a Wall

In the gardens where I grew up, one in England and one in Switzerland, there are just such borders. The English garden is in the south, on a rather ungrateful alkaline clay which is slow to warm in spring and lies cold in

193

winter, especially beneath the tall brick wall which separates it from its grander neighbours in the 'big house'. Years of compost-making and use of the grand neighbours' stable manure has improved the soil, and the long border beneath the wall has long been virtually self-sustaining with only the help of an annual mulch.

It is separated by a rolled gravel path from a small formal garden, entirely in shades of green with grass and clipped box hedges – at least, they should be box, but for expediency when the garden was made fifty or sixty years ago *Lonicera nitida* was used, and has proved surprisingly satisfactory, kept at 60cm/24in or so – punctuated by balls and obelisks of clipped yew. The border below the wall was conceived in shades of green, cream, white and yellow, to add light without contrast to the sober formality alongside.

On the wall itself a pyracantha foams with creamy blossom in late spring and sets a good crop of amber fruits in autumn. Two climbing roses, 'Madame Alfred Carrière' and the exquisitely fragrant, pale 'Golden Showers', last long in flower. All winter the ground at their feet is clothed in the evergreen foliage of *Hypericum calycinum*, *Euphorbia amygdaloides* var. *robbiae* and white periwinkle. The rose of Sharon can be a menace in some soils, but here it has spread only slowly, and against its ability to exclude weeds its territorial ambitions are little inconvenience. It is clipped hard back in spring and quickly refreshes itself with fresh green growths as the backdrop to its large, canary-yellow flowers filled with a brush of stamens. The euphorbia, too, behaves well in clay and contributes its dark rosettes of leaf and, in spring, acid-green spires. If, here and there, the spurge, the rose of Sharon and the periwinkle run into each other, no harm is done.

From this unifying carpet arise incidents of flower and leaf to mark the seasons. In the darkest corner of the border, Solomon's seal arches over a carpet of ferns and self-sown primroses, only the pale wildling and its white cousins allowed to remain, in spring. In early summer come the lily-like flowers of *Hemerocallis lilio-asphodelus* (*H. flava*), the day lily that, were I limited to just one, I would choose for its delicious fragrance. The primrose-yellow foxglove, *Digitalis grandiflora*, is short enough to come forward to the front of the border where its freckled, faintly whiskered bells can be admired close to. *Nepeta govaniana* has flowers of similar colour borne in airy, open sprays over pale green leaves; it is quite unlike its lilac-flowered cousins in aspect and in tastes, for it thrives in cool shade. Summer is the season, too, for the monkshoods with primrose- or creamy-yellow flowers. *Aconitum lycoctonum vulparia* (*A. orientale*, *A. vulparia*) is the one chosen for this border, for its long spikes of hooded flowers.

Iris orientalis, which I first knew more descriptively as *I. ochroleuca*, the white and yellow iris, opens its grand white *fleur de lis* blooms, touched with yellow on the falls, on 1.2m/4ft stems in high summer. *I. monnieri* is similar in clear yellow, with slightly shorter flowering stems over the same stiff sword leaves. These are contrasted with the velvety leaves of *Alchemilla mollis*, like fans unfurled almost to full circle, beautiful when pearled with raindrops or dew and the ideal underpinning for the clouds of starry, lime-yellow flowers. Over glossy, dark green blades the spiky green heads of *Cyperus eragrostis* and hanging tassels of *Carex pendula* frame a clump of *Astilboides tabularis*, its pale green leaves as big and round as dinner plates.

Lesser incidents in this border of bold drifts include white drumstick primulas (*Primula denticulata*) in spring, a white *Tricyrtis* – the newish 'White Towers' – in autumn, and white *Bergenia* 'Silberlicht' by a lusty clump of the male fern against the watertank which concludes this border, at the point where the path leads to the kitchen garden.

An Enclosed and Shaded Garden

It was perhaps the success of this border, never spectacular but always quietly satisfying, that inspired me to make an entire garden in cream and pale yellow and white, when I was faced with a small plot shaded by tall holly and Lawson's cypress hedges, planted by someone with a mania for seclusion. The hedges had been kept clipped, and galvanized iron sheets sunk into the ground when they were first planted prevented their roots from spreading too far, so here was a relatively simple situation of open-sky shadow. Apart from a fairly kempt lawn, there was nothing in the garden other than some hopelessly leggy bushes of *Hebe salicifolia*, which I ripped out to make space for a wide bed to one side.

Planting began with some young *Cornus alba* 'Elegantissima', set in a curving sweep. This is not one of the finest for winter bark, and in any event specimens grown in shade do not show as much colour as those in full sun; but its cream-splashed foliage provided just the note I wanted against the sombre holly. A smaller group of *Philadelphus coronarius* 'Bowles's Variety' echoed the white variegations; all the forms of the old mock orange do well in part shade, and the creamy blooms in summer fill the still air in this enclosed garden with rich perfume.

Two bold groups of variegated shrubs seemed enough; the rest must be green, with a leavening of pale almond greens and acid lime tones among the darker leaves. Linking the two variegated groups, then: *Berberis sargentiana*, chosen for its long, evergreen leaves and clear yellow, honey-scented flowers in spring; *Choisya ternata* with glossy, fingered, dark green leaves and fragrant white stars in late spring; and *Viburnum* × *burkwoodii*, which gives a long succession from winter to late spring of daphne-scented, rounded clusters, pink in bud opening to white. The glossy leaves of this dome-shaped shrub remain, more or less, all winter. Another evergreen shrub that, in time, makes a rounded mass, is *Mahonia japonica*, bold of leaf all year and full of arching, yellow sprays, each little flower a bell fragrant of lily of the valley, in winter.

Determined to include as many scented flowers as possible, to take advantage of the tranquil atmosphere in this enclosed garden, I planted *Skimmia japonica* 'Fragrans'; in spring the buds open to panicles of white flowers even more strongly suggestive of lily of the valley than the mahonia. The sarcococcas open their insignificant flowers in winter; they are whitish, and warmly honey scented, among elegant, glossy, ever-green foliage. I chose *S. hookeriana* var. *digyna*, and did not regret my choice; the narrow foliage is elegant, with petioles and stems maroon-flushed. Both the skimmia and the sarcococca are low growing, and were set near the front of the border to swell forward, in time, into firm mounds of foliage. Also designed to form a dome of foliage to the front of the border, in fresh apple-green this time, was *Hebe rakaiensis* (still often called *H. subalpina*).

The backbone and part of the plinth of the border in place, I decided it was time to choose the perennials that would contribute much of the spring and summer flower. Bergenias are content in shade and their bold, paddle-shaped leaves make a firm foundation for more flimsy ingredients, so a drift of 'Silberlicht' went in near the sarcococca. There are, of course, plenty of good bergenias other than white 'Silberlicht', and I shall mention some later; but here, since I wanted a white, there was no other choice, *Bergenia stracheyi alba* being too small and 'Bressingham White' not yet on the market when I began this planting.

Ever since growing annual candytuft from seed as a child I have loved the neat formality of the little heads of flower; as its perennial cousin is happy in light shade, I set a drift of *Iberis sempervirens* at the front of the border next to the bergenia. Its almost black-green foliage emphasizes the stark white of the flowers in spring. Nearby, the variegated form of *Iris foetidissima* contributes the contrast of evergreen, sword-shaped leaves and the desired tones of cream and green in vertical striping. Although they are not evergreen, I wanted a hosta or two, not too near the iris. I chose *Hosta crispula*, which has green blades broadly margined with white; *H. undulata albo-marginata* ('Thomas Hogg'), which bears its pale lavender flowers in early summer; and *H. undulata undulata*, a smaller plant, with twisted leaves of cream edged with green.

Though it is comforting to have plenty of evergreens in a border, there is a different kind of pleasure to be had from the changing picture of herbaceous plants, from the moment the leaves first emerge. I chose *Hemerocallis lilio-asphodelus* once again, and also *H. citrina*, which opens its clear lemon, fragrant flowers towards evening, as a bonus for the commuter. Yet another is 'Corky', small-flowered and sweet-scented like the better-known 'Golden Chimes', and more suitably coloured in canary-yellow rather than the amber and mahogany of 'Golden Chimes'. Almost any of the yellow-flowered hybrids would be suitable, too, for most are fragrant; well-tried cultivars include 'Marion Vaughn', 'Whichford', 'Larksong', and the old 'Hyperion'. The huge popularity of the day lily in the United States has led to hundreds of new varieties being introduced each year, it seems; among them are some exquisite pale cultivars, testimony to the search for a white day lily, but it remains to be seen how good they are as garden plants. All too often, the modern hybrids have been bred with large, frilly flowers, from which the elegance of the species has been lost.

Later in the season come the phloxes. Although they are usually planted in conventional herbaceous borders in full sun, they do well in shade also where not overhung by branches, and are less apt to flag in the heat – for they are greedy feeders needing a soil that is not too dry. Their warm peppery fragrance epitomizes high summer. A dwarf cultivar, 'Mia Ruys', is excellent towards the border front, grouped to form plump pillows of crisp, white flower; 'Fujiyama' is a late-flowering, white form of *Phlox paniculata* with magnificent tall plumes.

Although its flowers are pale lilac, I tried also the variegated 'Norah Leigh'; but I have never found it a good doer, perhaps because the leaves are so heavily marked with ivory that there is scarcely any chlorophyll left for the plant to photosynthesize, and also I suspect because it may be infected with the bane of phloxes, eel worm. Another species, *P. maculata*, comes in white as well as mauve, and holds its smaller flowers in cylindrical spires rather than pyramids. Its season is rather earlier, and it is of manageable height at 90cm/36in. 'Omega' is a lilac-eyed white and 'Miss Lingard' a pure, declamatory white, both as fragrant as the type.

In early summer, the white form of *Thalictrum aquilegifolium* produces its sudsy froth over columbine-like leaves. Though not a plant generally recommended for shade, it does well enough where there is overhead light even if the sun does not reach it for more than part of the day. Foxgloves, by contrast, are wholly at home in shady places; the white form and the creamy-primrose are exquisite. If you fear that self-sown seedlings will gradually contaminate your pale foxgloves with the ordinary, red-purple type, then all you need do is to remove at an early stage any with purple staining on the petiole; these only will be purple flowered. Also apt to self-sow, Miss Jekyll's white columbine, *Aquilegia vulgaris* 'Nivea' ('Munstead White') with greyish foliage and pale green buds opening pure white, comes true if no other aquilegias grow nearby.

As the foxgloves and columbines go over, *Geranium clarkei* 'Kashmir White' begins its long season, its white saucers, faintly veined with purple, poised over finely cut foliage. It runs mildly, but not so as to be a nuisance, and is shorter than the closely related *G. pratense* which it somewhat resembles. Earlier to bloom is the white form of *G. sylvaticum*, a more muscular plant with bolder foliage and sheaves of clear white flower. There are white forms of the meadow cranesbill, *G. pratense*, too; a noncomittal *albiflorum*, double 'Plenum Album' and the milky white 'Galactic'. The irresistible, long- and late-flowering *G. lambertii* 'Swansdown' is an interweaver, with long stems bearing nodding, white flowers veined with crimson. It is sometimes listed as *G. candicans*, which is correctly a pale form of the cyclamen-flowered *G. yunnanense*.

The genus *Campanula* is large and polymorphic, with something for almost every situation; only fragrance is lacking. Looking for something of purer white than *C. alliariifolia*, I chose an albino of *C. persicifolia*, which has narrow leaves, fine running roots that need help in the form of regular division to find new soil lest they die out for lack of some vital trace element, and wide saucer-shaped flowers. The undoubled *alba* is simple and unsophisticated; there is a cup-and-saucer white called 'Hampstead White', a cup-in-cup named 'Alba Coronata', and doubles of varying degrees of formality from cottagey raggedness to neat symmetry, which you may find listed under such names as 'Boule de Neige', 'Fleur de Neige', or simply 'double white'. There is a white form of the tall *C. latifolia*, which has spires of many narrow bells; but it is apt to self-sow too freely for a border with pretensions to remaining well manicured. Much better behaved is the double white form of *C. trachelium*, the Coventry bells, in which the flowers are wider at the mouth; there is also a single white form.

Pale yellow is a colour all too rare among border plants; yet here I wanted nothing brighter than the clear lemon of the day lilies. Fortunately, *Phygelius aequalis* will grow in the shade of a wall or, as here, a wall-like hedge; I was fortunate to obtain, long before it reached the market, its primrose-yellow form, 'Yellow Trumpet', which flowers from midsummer until the frosts, the slender curved flowers in one-sided spires on 90cm/36in stems. 'Moonraker' is a newer hybrid of the same colouring, bearing its trumpets all around the stems.

In late summer and early autumn the Japanese anemones are as invaluable as earlier the campanulas were. The original albino, simply listed (under *Anemone* × *hybrida*) as 'Honorine Jobert', is a plant of great beauty; there is a larger white called 'Géante des Blanches' as well as the semi-double white 'Whirlwind'. Slow to settle, they flower almost as freely in open shade as in sun, the boss of golden stamens illuminating the purity of the bloom. Another good, and much less familiar, perennial which flowers in the fall is *Eupatorium rugosum*, formerly *E. ageratoides*, which accurately conjures up an image of its fuzzy flowers in structure, if not in colour: for they are a good clean white. *E. fraseri* is similar; both reach about 90cm/36in and are happy in shade.

Many more perennials would be suitable for this border than those I finally selected; but I decided to leave it at that, leavening the planting only with some narcissi: the pale, half-height trumpet 'Jenny', and 'Actaea', a garden form of the fragrant poet's narcissus. The result was a border composed of reasonably generous drifts of pale colour, from flower or leaf, set among and against a range of greens from apple and almond to the near-black of holly. Even in winter the border looked clothed, and almost always there was fragrance on the air.

Greys for Shade

It is a horticultural platitude which almost every gardener soon masters that grey-leaved plants must be grown in full sun if they are not to become straggly and turn greenish. Fortunately for those who may want to carry a given colour scheme through from sun to shade, or make matched borders facing each other, one receiving more sun than the other, there are grey-leaved plants that grow cheerfully, and not greenly, in light shade. When I said as much in an article for the Royal Horticultural Society's journal, I was gently castigated by Christopher Lloyd for talking nonsense; but I stick by what I have learned. I only ask you to remember, if you decide to try any of these for yourself in a shady spot, that I warned you not everyone agrees with me.

The list of candidates for a planting of greys in shade ought to begin with some good-sized shrubs. Several *Elaeagnus* species are silvery-grey in leaf, at least on the undersides where the scales that give them their characteristic metallic sheen are more closely concentrated. Though the deciduous species are better in sun, the evergreens grow well in shade, with a looser and more graceful habit than in full exposure. *E. macrophylla*, less often seen than *E.* × *ebbingei* and its variegated cultivars, is decidedly more silvered in young growth and on the leaf backs than the hybrid, and the individual leaf is larger and bolder, beautiful to cut for the house.

Though deciduous, several grey-leaved willows have sufficient presence to dominate the planting in which they feature. They include *Salix elaeagnos*, the rosemary-leaved willow, a big mound of needle-like foliage, grey above and white beneath, which is at its best when a breeze ruffles its feathers so the play of pewter and white is enhanced; *S. alba sericea*; and the elegant, suckering *S. exigua*, slender of habit and silvered of narrow leaf.

Several rose species do well in light shade, too. A few are markedly grey: *Rosa soulieana* and its vigorous offspring 'Wickwar', the long-flowering, suckering *R. fedtschenkoana* and arching *R. willmottiae*. A less obvious choice would be *R. glauca* which, though plum-coloured enough in full sun to have earned its former epithet of *rubrifolia*, fades to an appealing steely glaucous tone in shade. It makes an emollient companion for *Geranium psilostemon*, which flaunts black-eyed, magenta blooms on 90cm/36in stems; 'Bressingham Flare' is a slightly more subdued selection of rich lilac pink, and 'Ann Folkard' a hybrid of spreading, not upright, habit, with golden-green foliage and magenta-purple, black-eyed and veined flowers.

Among the brambles, the whitewashed *Rubus cockburnianus* is much too rampageous for polite company, but *R. thibetanus* is a very pretty shrub, with fern-like grey leaves, white beneath, and white-bloomed stems for winter effect. 'Silver Fern' is a good selection. Another year-round shrub with white stems is *Berberis dictyophylla*, a far better garden shrub than the sought-after *B. temolaica*. *B. dictyophylla* has smaller leaves, glaucous-blue until they turn to deep scarlet and crimson, very late in autumn. From midwinter, as the leaves fall, the blue-white stems stand revealed. You need to prune this berberis hard each year, to encourage the fountain-like growth of the young stems, for on the older wood the white bloom disappears.

Among smaller shrubs that will remain grey away from the sun, the willows again feature. *Salix lanata* with broad, heart-shaped leaves, *S. repens argentea* with small, oval leaves on spraying growths, and *S. helvetica* with narrow lance foliage, are all distinctly grey. As with the larger willows and the roses, the fact of their being deciduous is not necessarily a drawback. Their hardiness means that they are likely to be most used in colder areas, and in Britain at least the winter skies are most often sombre and rain-laden, the very conditions in which grey foliage looks its least appealing. The dews of early autumn, on the other hand, which enhance silvery foliage with a fine powdering of droplets, find the willows and roses still in full leaf. The effect is refreshingly cool after the dusty heat of August. Just as *Rosa glauca* turns from plum to pewter, so at a lower level *Fuchsia magellanica* 'Versicolor' is a subtle dove-grey in shade, losing much of the pink that flushes the younger growths in sun. *F. magellanica gracilis* 'Variegata', on the other hand, shows conventional cream and green variegations without the greyish tints. Either the rose or 'Versicolor' would combine subtly with *Geranium wlassovianum*, velvety of leaf and dusky violet of purple-veined flower; or with *G. pogonanthum*, which has reflexed petals of lilac-pink around crimson filaments and blue-black anthers.

Reading that halimiums are often found, in the wild, growing in open woodland, I tried the hardy *Halimium lasianthum concolor* in light shade, in rather dry soil. It quickly made a dense mound of evergreen foliage, no less grey than its fellow in the sun and just as abundantly covered in clear yellow cistus-like flowers. Certain cistuses will do in similar conditions: one of the greyest is *Cistus parviflorus*, low and spreading with dogrose-like flowers. Even lavender will do quite well in dry soil in a lightly shaded spot. And it is surprising to see, in many shaded London squares, how well and how grey *Olearia macrodonta* grows: not the bright grey called silver, but the colour of aged pewter. Many other grey-leaved shrubs recommended for full sun will grow satisfactorily enough, and remain at least reasonably grey, in light shade: in my experience these include *Brachyglottis* 'Sunshine', *Santolina chamaecyparissus* and *S. pinnata neapolitana*, and *Ballota pseudodictamnus*. However, I have no evidence that they grow naturally in shaded habitats, and without this justification I find them incongruous unless in full sun.

The choice widens when one comes to consider grey-leaved perennials. The first to come to mind is the genus *Anaphalis*, which can present a problem to the novice who plants it with his other silvers in a droughty spot, only to see it wilt miserably. In moisture-retentive soil, on the other hand, *A. triplinervis*, the taller *A. cinnamomea* (*A. yedoensis*) and narrower-leaved *A. margaritacea* will flourish in sun or shade. In drier soil, some shade, though not from overhanging branches, is essential to keep them from flopping. The grey tones of their leaves and white-felted stems are enhanced, in their late summer season, by the white everlasting flowers. A much rarer silver which dwindles fast if baked, but thrives in a retentive soil in dappled shade, is *Senecio candicans*, which has broad, slightly twisted leaves with a thick, white felting. My greatest success with this seductive thing was on a moist streambank, above water level, in the shadow of a grove of myrtles.

As pulmonarias are almost always grown in shade it is no surprise to find that the form of *Pulmonaria saccharata* known as *argentea*, in which the silver spots have merged to cover virtually the whole leaf area, is happy in a shaded border. 'Leopard' is a cleanly spotted new cultivar raised by Graham Thomas; its flowers are muted red. Another which was selected for its platinum finish is 'Margery Fish', sometime attributed to *P. saccharata* and lately to the related *P.vallarsae*. Either is greatly superior to the ordinary *P. saccharata* in leaf; the best foliage comes when you cut it down as the flowers fade and give it a thorough soak, when new, immaculately silvered leaves will emerge and stay fresh through the summer. Another spotty plant is *Hieracium praecox*, in which dark freckles are sparsely sprinkled over blue-grey leaves. Do not confuse this with *H. maculatum*, whose leaves are heavily black-blotched on a green ground. Both can become a nuisance through self-seeding, but if you remove the yellow dandelion heads promptly their invasive tendencies are effectively curbed.

The variegated *Lamium galeobdolon*, predominantly silver in leaf, is another wickedly invasive plant often recommended for ground cover in shade, yet suitable only where its insidious over- and underground activities do not matter. It is certainly not a plant for a well-bred border. The two heavily silvered forms of *L. maculatum*, however, are perfectly well behaved, preferring a fertile soil and shade. The better-known is 'Beacon Silver', with the customary magenta-pink flowers and a tendency to flush pink on the leaf in a rather unbecoming, spotty manner; far choicer than this is 'White Nancy', its albino counterpart.

Several dicentras create a greyish effect, notably 'Langtrees' and the steely-blue *Dicentra formosa* 'Stuart Boothman'; the first has palest blush lockets, the second magenta-pink. One of the greyest is a white-flowered dicentra which is tentatively ascribed to *D. formosa* ssp. *oregona*; its very glaucous foliage combines subtly with the bluer hostas such as *Hosta fortunei hyacinthina* or *H. sieboldiana elegans*, or on a smaller scale the *H.* × *tardiana* hybrids such as 'Halcyon' or 'Blue Moon', where the similar colouring points up the contrast in leaf form between the broad blades of the hostas and the ferny dicentras.

In their different ways, the pulmonarias and lamiums, dicentras and hostas are all horizontal, tapestry plants; sometimes we need a vertical accent too. *Lysimachia ephemerum* is both tall, at 90cm/36in or so, and narrow, with leathery grey leaves ascending the stems, and grey-white flowers in slim spikes in summer. It prefers a moist soil and light shade, where it slowly forms a neat clump. *Macleaya microcarpa*, on the other hand, is big, upright and enthusiastically invasive, beautiful with its large, lobed, rounded leaves, grey above and nearly white beneath, on white stems. The flowers are skin pink, brightest in the selection 'Kelway's Coral Plume'. If you cannot cope with its aggression, you should seek out the rarer *M. cordata*, which at 2m or so (7ft) is just as tall, and has similar leaves beneath white flowers. It is much less inclined to run at the root.

The suggested treatment for *Digitalis purpurea* ssp. *heywoodii* is rich soil and dappled shade. This is a very choice foxglove with velvety-grey foliage and creamy-pink flowers opening from pale lemon-green buds. I have not found it easy to keep true to form; but it is worth every effort, for it has in a high degree the quality that most distinguishes grey foliage in shade: a subtle luminosity more tender than its platinum brilliance in full sun.

Border Plantings Beneath Trees

High walls and tall enclosing hedges create one kind of shade; the shadow of a tree across a border is another. Let us suppose a single deciduous tree, open-branched, with leaves that are not too large nor too densely packed, so that some sunlight filters through even in summer. In spring, of course, the tree will be bare and will cast very little shade. This is the time to concentrate on; later, the rest of the border will be packed with summer colour and the area beneath the tree can lapse into quiet obscurity with a carpet of comely foliage.

The dominant plant, in spring, beneath a mature rowan that I know, is the pale blue Spanish bluebell, drifting through a ground-planting of *Lamium maculatum* 'Beacon Silver'. A strong, clumpy sweep of *Brunnera macrophylla* adds a deeper note of blue, and *Geranium macrorrhizum* 'Ingwersen's Variety' brings pale pink flowers and aromatic leaves to the group. A brighter note would come from 'Bevan's Variety', in potent magenta; the wildling has flowers of a pleasant purple-red, strong but not assertive. For a similar effect at half the size, the hybrid between this and little *G. dalmaticum*, known as *G.* × *cantabrigiense*, comes in two forms, 'Biokovo' with palest lilac-white flowers in deeper pink calyces, and 'Cambridge' which is soft mauve in flower and glossy in leaf. There is a good patch, too, of *Dicentra formosa* 'Bountiful' in soft plum-red. Other dicentras would do equally well here: 'Luxuriant', with fresh green, finely cut leaves and bright ruby clusters of flower; 'Adrian Bloom', greyish of leaf and rich crimson in flower; or 'Bacchanal' with deep maroon lockets. A pinker grouping still would have substituted the pink Spanish bluebell for the blue.

It would have been quite possible, too, using variants of the same species, to make this scheme entirely blue and white: *Lamium maculatum* 'White Nancy' in place of 'Beacon Silver', white (or the same pale blue) bluebells, white *Geranium macrorrhizum*, dicentras such as *Dicentra eximia alba*, *D. formosa alba* or the palest blush white, blue-leaved 'Langtrees' or 'Pearl Drops'; or the new, spring-to-autumn flowering, pure white 'Snowflakes'. The larger-flowered *D. spectabilis*, in either clear rosy-pink or white, would add a taller note but is less efficient at covering the ground than its smaller cousins. Whether in two or three colours, this grouping could be almost indefinitely extended: blue or pinky-mauve columbines, lavender or white *Geranium sylvaticum* or the assertive, violet G. × *magnificum* for a bigger, bolder component, clear blue G. 'Johnson's Blue' or the little G. *himalayense* 'Plenum' with double, reddish-violet flowers on short stems for the front of the border (the single-flowered form is nearer to true blue, deeper than 'Johnson's Blue'), the fine lavender-blue Jacob's ladder *Polemonium foliosissimum* or Margery Fish's *P. reptans* 'Lambrook Manor' which is a shade or two nearer pink, camassias in shades of blue from snowmelt to hyacinth or in ivory . . . these are just a few of the plants that spring to mind, and except for the Jacob's ladder hardly one flowers after midsummer. For colour later in the season, *Geranium wallichianum* 'Buxton's Variety' is unsurpassed, its leafy, weaving stems set for weeks, even months on end with clear blue saucers, white-eyed like *Nemophila*.

One of the smaller Japanese anemones would carry through the soft lilac-pink tendency: 'September Charm', perhaps, a selection of *Anemone hupehensis japonica* which has more and narrower petals, the semi-double, rosy 'Bressingham Glow', or rich pink 'Hadspen Abundance', all reaching 60cm/24in or so. *A.* × *lesseri* is of much the same height, with divided leaves and brighter, almost shocking-pink flowers. *Phlox* 'Harlequin', with ivory-white leaf variegations, has contrasting flowers of bright honesty-purple and needs keeping away from the tree's roots to do well; for like all phloxes it is a greedy plant. Despite its height, the fragrant *P. maculata* 'Alpha' would be welcome for its soft pink plumes on 90cm/36in stems.

A tree such as *Robinia pseudacacia* 'Frisia', much planted (some say, over-planted) for its fresh lime-yellow foliage, can be redeemed from banality if its supporting cast is chosen to emphasize its colouring. Clouds of the self-seeding *Euphorbia stricta*, a rare British native, contribute airy

candelabras of tiny, acid-yellow bracts on coral-red stems. Some say it is
too invasive, but I have found the seedlings so easy to pull, and so pretty
as they form clumpy rosettes of neat, fresh foliage through the winter,
that I cannot think of it as a weed. A spurge of more substance that would
do here, too, is *E. wallichii*, which bears its long-lasting chartreuse-
yellow bracts in wide mounds. The robust form of *E. polychroma* called
'Major' has not quite so much quality, but is a fine thing with a longer
season than *E. polychroma* itself. Mr Bowles's golden grass, *Milium
effusum aureum*, seeds itself inoffensively, its soft pale blades forming
clumps that, like the Tintern spurge, are easy to remove if they land in the
wrong place. Any bare patches of soil will be quickly covered by the
golden creeping Jenny, *Lysimachia nummularia* 'Aurea'. The cheerful
Doronicum 'Miss Mason' flowers in spring, when – at the price of a
slightly false note later from the muted tawny day lily flowers – she
would be set off by the bright emerging spears of *Hemerocallis fulva*.

A Specialist's Plants

One of the most successful shaded borders I know is given over almost
entirely to three genera: hellebores, snowdrops and peonies. A wide
expanse of rather heavy, enriched soil on the sunless side of an old house,
it is home to some remarkable hellebore seedlings and named snowdrops.
Most of the hellebores are of the Lenten rose type – hybrids of *Helleborus
orientalis*. Their colours range from pure primrose and unspeckled white
to slate-blue and plum-black. Other whites, and some of the pinks, are
heavily freckled. The shape of the bloom varies from the outfacing bowl
which is generally favoured by hellebore breeders to the more graceful,
nodding, flared-skirt form which especially becomes the darker colours;
the slate-blues in particular thus showing the wonderful smoky reverse
of the bloom. There are now very many named *H. orientalis* hybrids; and
as they are easy to divide at, or just after, flowering time, it is possible if
you have a deep pocket – for they are not quick to increase – to obtain a
range of them in the colours and shapes that most appeal to you.
Unnamed seedlings are often as good if obtained from a reliable specialist
raiser. Subspecific names, not always now botanically recognized, may
be a guide to colour: spp. *abchasicus* is deep plum-pink with a dense
powdering of maroon speckles within, ssp. *guttatus* palest greenish-blush
or white with pronounced dark freckles. *H. kochii* is a name now used
within *H. orientalis* to denote primrose-yellow forms, of which some are
scarcely more than greenish-white, others truly pale yellow; they are

usually shorter in growth and earlier to flower than the others. Creamy-rose forms, with green at their hearts but no spotting, used to be separated out as *H. antiquorum*, and unspotted whites as *H. olympicus* – now *H. orientalis* subspecies *orientalis*. The old garden plant called *H. atrorubens* (which is not the *H. atrorubens* of botanists) flowers very early, at the turn of the year; it has deep plum-maroon flowers which do not set seed, increases reasonably quickly and is perfectly amenable to being divided. Unlike the *H. orientalis* hybrids, it is deciduous.

Among all these sombre colours, the snowdrops gleam white against the dark soil. The passion for snowdrops, for collecting not only the different species but also the minutest variations between forms of the same species, is recognized as galanthomania among gardeners. The common snowdrop, *Galanthus nivalis*, is perhaps a British native; certainly it is widely naturalized, forming masses of rather glaucous foliage and slender, nodding, white blooms as early as the turn of the year. The ragged double form seems every bit as willing to increase by division (best done just as the flowers go over), and some people are perfectly content with just these two. Of the many named forms and hybrids, some are easy-going, others extremely difficult to keep alive. G. × *atkinsii* is of the first kind; it has large, long flowers appearing very early, its only fault a tendency to the odd malformed segment. No such aberrations should appear on the magnificent 'S. Arnott'. The Straffan snowdrop is another fine late-flowering, vigorous form. The large blooms of 'Magnet' are borne on long pedicels, so that it sways in the faintest breeze.

Variants in colouring are limited: sometimes the green markings at the base of the segments are bolder, rarely absent altogether (G. *nivalis poculiformis*); and sometimes there is green at the tip of the segments also, as in 'Pusey Green Tip' (a double) or 'Viridapicis'. The double 'Lady Elphinstone' is treasured for her ethereal colouring; for here the markings and even the ovary are faded to primrose-yellow. She is not especially difficult, but may often have been discarded by someone who did not realize that in the first season after transplanting her yellow markings revert to green. Some of the finest doubles are hybrids of G. *plicatus*, itself a fine thing with the leaf margins folded back, and large, solid, prominently marked flowers. Seedlings such as 'Hippolyta' and 'Desdemona' have tightly double, regular blooms.

The manner in which the leaves are arranged distinguishes one section of the genus from another; and by the gardener as well as the botanist, several different species may be recognized at a glance from the leaf. G. *elwesii* has broad, glaucous leaves, folded one inside the other; its flowers are large, and have a broad, dark green mark at the base of each inner segment. *G. caucasicus* is similar, with wide, glaucous blades and a long season of flower. It is followed by the green-leaved *G. ikariae*, which has the green markings at the tips of the segments only. This by no means exhausts the possibilities for true galanthophiles; but I will mention just one more, the autumn-flowering *G. reginae-olgae*, which is in effect *G. nivalis* at the other end of the year. It does need a little more sun than the others, and does not truly belong in the border I am describing, where the snowdrops of winter and spring appear among the slate and plum and primrose hellebores, with the first fat crimson shoots of peonies spearing through, and named forms of celandine, primrose or half-height daffodils.

Indeed, I have not described all the hellebores that grow here. A green corner is home to several species. Everyone knows the stinking hellebore, *Helleborus foetidus*; it has boldly fingered, very dark evergreen leaves topped in winter by open spires of small green bells edged with maroon. Despite its name, it does not smell foul; indeed, there is a most desirable form, usually offered as Miss Jekyll's scented form, which is deliciously endowed with a free-floating honeyed perfume. Other variants are Mr Bowles's fine Italian form, and the red-stemmed, smoky leaved 'Wester Flisk'. Also native to Britain and Europe is *H. viridis*, which is close to *H. orientalis*, with smaller, pure peridot-green flowers lasting well into summer. Then there are two fragrant, green-flowered species, the bold and beautiful *H. cyclophyllus*, and *H. multifidus* with leaves slashed into many long, narrow fingers. You may also encounter *H. dumetorum*, which is green but not fragrant. From Italy comes *H. multifidus* subspecies *bocconei*, which has good bowl-shaped green flowers over *orientalis*-type foliage. If these green species turn admirers of hellebores weak at the knees, the little Eastern European *H. purpurascens* has them grovelling. The leaves are deeply cut, the small nodding flowers maroon with a slaty-glaucous flush outside and pale green within. The almost equally desirable *H. torquatus* now seems to be recognized as a species after a long spell in taxonomic limbo.

After *H. foetidus*, no green-flowered species is so well known as *H. argutifolius* (*H. corsicus*). It forms bushy clumps of stout stems bearing three-parted, grey-green leaves with sub-prickly margins. Second-year stems are topped by upright clusters of pale jade-green, nodding cups. In another context than the border I am describing, it looks well with ferns and *Danae racemosa*, a butcher's broom relative with elegant, narrow foliage on slender stems; hostas would add another foliage contrast and summer flower, with the pale yellow shuttlecocks and maple-like leaves of *Kirengeshoma palmata* for autumn. Viridiflora tulips and the silvery-green *Ornithogalum nutans* also look well with the Corsican hellebore, with *Galtonia princeps* perhaps to follow in summer.

For some reason, I have never felt for the Christmas rose, *Helleborus niger*, the admiration that I have for the other species. I recognize all its good qualities: leathery evergreen foliage, a winter season, and large white blooms with golden stamens. But – especially in its 'improved' manifestations such as the famous 'Potter's Wheel', the selections of hellebore breeders – it stares too insolently, its flowers are too large for the stems, and the pink flush on the exterior that some find so fetching can look too much like the hectic colouring of a fevered brow. And then, to keep the flowers as near immaculate as can be, you have to cover the thing with a handlight, so that you cannot in any case see them properly.

No, give me rather its hybrid with the Corsican hellebore, *H. Nigercors*. This is just what you might expect from a cross between the two: a stout plant with good dark foliage, and green-white, open but not glaring flowers in generous clusters. Other raisers, using *H.* × *sternii* (which is *H. argutifolius* × *H. lividus* and is hardy, with the dove-pink flush of *H. lividus* about it) have given us the strain called Nigristern, which is just as good. I grew this, in one of my gardens, in a cool and shaded patch with *Ribes laurifolium*, the purple form of *Euphorbia amygdaloides*, Mr Bowles's golden grass *Milium effusum aureum*, and *Corydalis lutea*.

And what of the peonies in the big shaded border where hellebores and snowdrops grow? In winter, of course, they are sensibly below ground; by early spring, their fat, often crimson or tawny shoots are spearing through. These are not the border peonies called Chinese, nor yet the familiar old cottage plant, double crimson, or sometimes blush or white, forms of *Paeonia officinalis*. Here are grown species with often ephemeral, but always exquisitely beautiful flowers. Perhaps because of its name, so foreign-looking to English speakers, *P. mlokosewitschii* is widely known; and deservedly, for its emerging foliage is grey-green flushed with mushroom-pink, and its large, cupped flowers are of great beauty, their translucent lemony petals sheltering golden anthers. Even more fleeting are the larger, paler primrose blooms with red filaments of *P. wittmanniana*, of which the young foliage is more richly coloured; a fine companion for chilly-toned daffodils such as 'Spellbinder' or 'Binkie'. Both peonies have showy seed pods, red filled with black and scarlet seeds (sow only the black, for the red are sterile). The hybrid of *P. wittmanniana* with *P. lactiflora*, 'Mai Fleuri' with a tinge of blush to its creamy flowers, inherits the richly bronze emerging growths.

Even these are surpassed by *P. obovata alba* and the lemon-white *P. obovata willmottiae*, which have crystalline globes over softly glaucous, bronze-flushed leaves. Vivid blue seeds follow. These are shorter plants than either 'Mollie the Witch' or *P. wittmanniana*, and like them may be raised from seed. The tall *P. emodi* has fresh green foliage, and arching stems set with many pure white, fragrant flowers in late spring. None of these white or palest yellow peonies spreads much at the root, forming instead slowly widening clumps. Others, with red or pink flowers, have tuberous roots that increase fairly fast. The most vivid in colour is *P. peregrina*, with large, single blooms of intense scarlet over glossy green leaves; 'Fire King' is very bright, and a paler form of satiny vermilion sheen is called 'Sunshine'. They should be kept well away from flowers with any hint of blue in their pink or red colouring.

Close to the original species from which the old double cottage peonies arose is *P. mascula*, with pink flowers. It is eclipsed by its subspecies *arietina* and its variants. Typically, this has greyish foliage and magenta-pink flowers, deep or pale; 'Northern Glory' is very richly coloured, the creamy stamens contrasting with satiny crimson-magenta petals; and there are palest blush forms also. *P. mollis* is also of the spreading kind; the grey-lilac leaves, grey beneath, set off vivid magenta flowers. The foliage of *P. tenuifolia*, as its name suggests, is very finely cut into thin segments; the flowers are deep crimson, single or, rarely, double. Peonies with pink or cerise flowers but a stay-at-home habit can be had also. The greyish, rounded leaves of *P. mascula triternata* (*P. daurica*) set off large, bright magenta blooms; *P. veitchii* has fresh green leaves and more muted flowers with pink filaments and cream anthers. Its variant *woodwardii* has the same lush foliage below clear pale pink flowers, and there is also an ivory-white form; all have bluish seeds.

Foliage to the Fore

Some of the most exciting foliage plants we can grow in cool temperate gardens are at their best in shade. In many small, shady front gardens in London a fatsia has been allowed its head, to become a tall and imposing shrub with huge, polished, deeply fingered leaves, heightened by the pale midribs radiating out from the stalk and by the quirky lilt to the margins of each glossy lobe. Careful pruning upwards can leave you with space to plant beneath the fatsia. Add a fern – the soft and feathery *Athyrium filix-femina* 'Plumosum' perhaps , a variegated hosta, a clump of *Helleborus foetidus* with its black-green, thin-fingered leaves. . . . If you want more than one fern, keep them apart with something low that will not blur the ferns' outlines: *Rubus calycinoides*, perhaps, which makes a little mat of creeping, rooting stems set with rounded, shallow-lobed leaves, their wrinkled upper surface dark shining green, the reverse grey-felted. The mother of thousands, *Saxifraga cuscutiformis*, has ever-green rosettes of marbled maroon and green, burgundy-backed leaves; it extends its range like a strawberry, by thread-like runners bearing a plantlet at their tips. The flowers are airy sprays of white, in summer. The flowers of *Brunnera macrophylla* are like the daintiest bright blue forget-me-nots; for foliage, there are two variegated forms, 'Hadspen Cream' margined in soft yellow and 'Dawson's White' with ivory margins; 'Langtrees' is rather dull with leaves undecidedly flecked with silver. Those who like variegations also rave over *Astrantia major* 'Sunningdale Variegated'; and very striking it is at first, the jagged leaves boldly marked with primrose and cream in spring. As summer progresses it fades to green, quicker in shade than in sun.

If you want other incidents of flower – and why not – interplant snowdrops for winter, white colchicums for autumn (their leaves, broad and glossy, make their own effect in spring and are only briefly disgraceful in early summer before dying down), white martagon lilies for summer or the pale jade *Galtonia princeps*, many-headed white *Narcissus* 'Thalia' or jade and grey *Ornithogalum nutans* for spring. All these are bulbous; you could also tuck in a few white or 'Lime Green' tobaccos. *Nicotiana alata* 'Grandiflora' is the dubious name usually given to the white-flowered tobacco which closes during daylight hours so all you see are the khaki backs of the petals; but at dusk it opens, and with the awakening of the flower comes that amazing, far-carrying perfume. 'Lime Green' is fun but has no fragrance, nor does *N. langsdorfii*, though this is a charmer with its slender spires of small, tubular, green flowers, the lobes flaring around a cluster of sky-blue anthers.

When my mother was a child, the great ribbed leaves of the yellow gentian, *Gentiana lutea*, were used in the Swiss Alps for wrapping the butter made on the high summer pastures. You had to learn the difference between the gentian and the leaves of veratrums, for these made poisonous butter papers, just as they poison cows that graze upon them in the meadows. No one is likely to pick their veratrum leaves from the garden to wrap butter, for they are far too handsome to spare. The finest foliage belongs to *Veratrum nigrum*, which early in the year awakens from its winter rest, the great pleated, fresh green leaves unfurling into a knee-high mound. Flowers seem almost redundant, except that there is nothing quite like the tall, branching spikes of close-packed, mahogany-purple stars. *V. album*, on the other hand, is splendid in ivory-white, green-washed flower, the side branches standing out nearly horizontal to give a fuller, more plumy effect over leaves of scarcely less magnificence. These two are European; the North American species, on the whole, are less exciting, though *V. viride* is very fresh and sharp in green flower, and is the first to open, at midsummer. It has to be said that, like other plants with bold, entire leaves, they are not improved by the attentions of slugs, which find them irresistible. At Great Dixter Christopher Lloyd has planted the bold *Hosta ventricosa* 'Aureo-marginata' in front of his *Veratrum album*, which is a good clean, creamy-white form, and the effect is stunning in a half-shaded position near a dark wall.

You could choose instead the substantial hosta 'Francee', in deep green with a bold cream margin to the heart-shaped leaves, if you decide to emulate this grouping. This is a form of *Hosta fortunei*, and the older 'Aureo-marginata' (which used to be called 'Obscura Marginata') is a fine bold form also, and as yet cheaper to buy. If expense is no object, 'Shade Fanfare' is a striking, medium-sized hosta with leaves broadly edged in cream, while the bold, blue-green 'Wide Brim' has a very wide margin of cream and yellow to each leaf, with plenty of lavender flower spikes in summer, too. 'Ground Master' is handsome in green edged with cream, and darker violet flower spikes in late summer. But hostas and veratrums both attract slugs, so you will have to be watchful (though I have never had any trouble, myself, with slugs eating hostas, even in the damp and leafy corners where the creatures abound).

The variegated forms of *Tovara* seem less vulnerable. *T. virginiana* 'Variegata' (*Persicaria virginiana variegata*) reverses the tendency of many hostas to look best in leaf early in the season; not until high summer does it develop its full leafage of broad, pointed leaves all streaked and splashed with primrose-cream. 'Painter's Palette' is even more striking with a broad chevron of mahogany across the variegations. A different, and remarkably slug-proof, blend of leaves sets the fresh acid-yellow foliage of day lilies against the veratrums; *Hemerocallis fulva* and *H. lilio-asphodelus* for fast results, or any of the small yellow-flowered species if you want something more restrained. *H. fulva* has flowers of muted brick-pink, that show up in shady places less well than those of the lemon *H. lilio-asphodelus* which I have already extolled, and lack its delicious lily fragrance; but some people like it, and it has a double form which does not shed its flowers so fast, though the doubling spoils the elegant outline. To set divided leaves, as it might be of *Aruncus dioicus* 'Kneiffii' or ferns, by your veratrums is to be a bit obvious. But then, if the divided leaves belonged to that little elder that thinks it is a cut-leaved *Acer palmatum*, you might be excused. *Sambucus racemosa* 'Tenuifolia' is slow and dainty in leaf, and more tolerant of wind than the Japanese maples.

The Mexican orange, *Choisya ternata*, is a shrub that people seem to love or loathe. It puzzles me, always, how anyone could loathe a plant that, in a shady corner, makes a generous mound of highly polished, dark green, three-parted, evergreen leaves and bears, in late spring and often again more modestly in autumn, clusters of wide, pure white, waxy stars with a sweet fragrance. The foliage, too, is aromatic, with a pungency that perhaps explains the negative reaction to the shrub, though to my nose it is not disagreeable. 'Aztec Pearl' is a new hybrid Mexican orange with narrow leaf segments, reminding me of the wonderful *Acradenia frankliniae*, which is of course in the same citrus family.

My mother grows the more familiar old choisya in the sheltered angle formed by two walls of a barn, in the simplest of plantings with *Iris orientalis*, and *Bergenia cordifolia* 'Purpurea' spilling over the rough paving at its feet. The iris flowers as the Mexican orange is going over, while the bergenia produces its shocking-pink flowers on mahogany-red stalks earlier in spring, and all year its great leathery, rounded leaves are handsome. 'Ballawley' is a fine hybrid bergenia with flowers of purer crimson colouring on red stems over glossy, rounded leaves, that are more susceptible to frost. The only plant I have ever felt tempted to add to this simple but effective grouping is *Aster divaricatus*, which Miss Jekyll used with bergenias. A slender, shade-loving aster, it flowers in autumn, the many starry white daisies on flopping, wiry, black stems over exiguous foliage. My mother resisted my blandishments, so I used the aster and another bergenia, *Bergenia* × *schmidtii*, atop a low, drystone wall that retained a bank of cheesy clay concealed by *Prunus laurocerasus* 'Zabeliana'; thus achieving a similar play of form and texture with the glossy laurel leaf, the rounded paddles of the bergenia, and the starry aster. The pale pink flowers of *Bergenia* × *schmidtii* open earlier than many, in generous sprays on stocky stems; they are enlivened by rosy calyces.

Plants that make dense, evergreen carpets of weed-excluding foliage are to be valued, so long as they are also attractive in their own right and not merely as an alternative to the weeds. Nor do we always want bergenia-style foliage; tussock plants with grassy or sword leaves may do the job as well, and the textural result is quite different. The lilyturf of American gardeners is popular for this reason. The verb should be plural, in fact, for lilyturf is a name used not just for more than one species, but for more than one genus, albeit closely related. *Liriope muscari* has leaves rather like a dark and healthy grass, slender gleaming blades forming spreading tussocks, and shiny bead-like flowers packed into little bright violet-mauve pokers, grape hyacinth-style, in autumn. 'Monroe's White' refers to the flower colour, and 'Variegata' to the leaves, but this is a rather weakly thing. The foliage of the plain green forms is cheering in winter, and you can clip it hard back in spring so that fresh leaves, not tatty old ones, will accompany the next burst of flower. Little attentions like this make such a difference to the look of the garden. Colchicums can join the liriope in half-shaded places. *L. spicata* is shorter, but more of a spreader, with the same glossy leaves and lilac or white flowers in late summer, less striking than the vivid spikes of *L. muscari*. It is similar to the more tender *Ophiopogon japonicus*, which has indifferent white flowers in sprays, whereas *O. jaburan* corresponds in height and vigour to *Liriope muscari*, but its flowers are white, rather like a sparse lily of the valley, and are followed by bluish fruits. There is a variegated form, 'Vittatus'.

But the one that everybody enthuses over is the black-leaved *Ophiopogon planiscapus nigrescens*, the nearest thing to a truly black plant I can think of, with little wine-purple bells followed by shiny black fruits; very cute with white *Cyclamen hederifolium* in autumn, or the wide-eyed innocent white *Viola septentrionalis alba* in spring, or set about with the frail and ferny leaves, subtly coloured in apricot, grey and taupe, of *Corydalis ophiocarpa*. The green forms, once you have increased them by division, can be used in a unifying sweep at the border's margin, around trees, or among rocks. Tussocks of much finer blades belong to *Carex* 'Frosted Curls', which shares something of the tousled wig appearance of the brownish *C. comans*, but in a most subtle, sheeny-silvered green. Although it looks like a plant for sun, it has been found to put up with almost impossible conditions of dryness and shade while keeping its casual good looks.

In shade that is not too dense, shrubs with 'golden' foliage are at their best. Too much sun and they scorch; too little, and they turn to an unconvincing green. Light shade, and cool roots, is the recipe for these. *Choisya ternata* 'Sundance' is a lime-yellow form of the popular Mexican orange that shows dangerous tendencies to equal or greater popularity, so that we may come to curse the outbreak of hectic evergreenery spreading across the land. The leaves have the same polished surface as the green, and if you get the balance of light and shade right they are a fetching shade of sharp lime-green, neither too vivid a gold nor faded to washed-out green.

The same balance is needed for *Philadelphus coronarius* 'Aureus', marvellous at its fresh butter-yellow best, and endowed with the same creamy, powerfully fragrant flowers as the old fashioned mock orange of

which it is a selection. *Sambucus racemosa* 'Plumosa Aurea' has no flowers
to speak of, and should be discouraged if it gets ideas about such things,
for they will only detract from the bold sprays of deeply cut, lime-yellow
foliage, which in spring is touched with bronze. The way to treat this is
ruthlessly to cut it to a stump at the end of each winter, when it will send
up great shoots of fresh leafage. It is greatly superior to the yellow-leaved
form of the common elder, *Sambucus nigra*.

One of the toughest of 'golden' shrubs is *Physocarpus opulifolius*
'Luteus', which has the same endearing habit of looking slightly
suntanned early in the season, later fading to a uniform soft lime-yellow.
It is now less often offered than 'Dart's Gold', which is more compact but
not, I think, any brighter. The whitish flowers in summer are neither here
nor there, and you might as well cut them out to encourage new leafy
growths. There are easy and hardy yellow-leaved forms of the guelder
rose, *Viburnum opulus*, and of the dogwood, *Cornus alba*, also; respectively 'Aureum' and 'Aurea', they have additional merits in red fruits on
the viburnum, and red winter stems, though not so bright as those of
'Sibirica', on the dogwood. You will often find the suggestion that a
yellow-leaved shrub should be paired with another with coppery or
'purple' leaves. Apart from the fact that the purple fades to dingy
brownish-green in shade (whereas if you grow them both in full sun the
yellow leaves risk scorching) I think this combination, however exciting
when first conceived, is now hopelessly overdone. Far more effective, in
my view, is to contrive softer blendings, as at Kiftsgate where, in dappled
shade, the golden philadelphus grows with the great single, creamy shrub
rose 'Nevada'.

Some yellow-foliaged shrubs have pink flowers, which temporarily
makes for an uncomfortable colour scheme. Thus *Ribes sanguineum*
'Brocklebankii', quite slow-growing and very bright in leaf; you just
have to sit out the two weeks of flower, in spring. *Weigela* 'Looymansii
Aurea' disgraces itself a month or two later, when the pink trumpets open
among the yellow leaves. In fairness, some people actually profess to like
this combination, and plant catalogues tend to describe the flowers as a
bonus; though, since nurserymen are selling their wares, that is hardly
surprising.

Flower Colour in the Shady Border

I have already suggested how willingly, early in the year, the white and
lilac forms of sweet rocket, *Hesperis matronalis*, scatter their clove-scented

spires through the border; for this is a self-seeder, and may need a controlling hand. White honesty, *Lunaria annua alba*, gleams in the shade but lacks the delicious fragrance, most eloquent at dusk, of the sweet rocket. Then there are the variegated honesties, 'Haslemere' with cream and green foliage and flowers of lilac-purple, and 'Stella' with leaves more white than green, and pure white flowers. 'Munstead Purple', with plain green leaves, has the brightest purple flowers.

The honesties, of course – with the exception of *L. rediviva* – are biennial, flowers forming after a full cycle of seasons has passed. So, too, is *Cynoglossum amabile*, though if sown early under glass it should flower the same summer. The foliage of this borage relative is grey-green and soft in texture, setting off flowers of china-blue; the seed strain 'Firmament' is just the colour its name suggests, the blue of a cloudless summer sky. Forget-me-nots also do well in light shade; in the border, selected strains of deeper blue, or in shades of pink and rose or white, bring drifts of spring colour. The dainty blue woodruff, *Asperula orientalis* (*A. azurea setosa*) is that comparative rarity, a fragrant annual that also prefers a cool, part-shaded position; it is low growing, with slender, branching stems. Even ageratums will flower well in light shade; in the border the taller strains could be used instead of the dumpy edging varieties beloved of seedsmen. Their fuzzy, powderpuff flowers in lavender-blue, white or lilac-pink have great charm, until they turn brown, when rigorous deadheading is needed. I am told – though I have not tested it – that annual flax does well in part shade; the one to try would surely be *Linum grandiflorum* 'Bright Eyes', white with a conspicuous chocolate-red centre. It is a taller plant than the familiar satin-textured *L. grandiflorum rubrum* which has bright crimson flowers on 30cm/12in stems.

Some annuals are almost as muscular as perennials; thus *Impatiens glandulifera*, which grows to 90cm/36in or more, bears a long succession of helmet flowers in rose-purple and white, and seeds itself in the shady borders it prefers. *I. balfourii* is smaller and daintier, with blush, pink-lipped flowers. The flowers of the touch-me-not, *I. noli-tangere*, are ivory and primrose with orange freckles on the inside of the helmets. Both the vernacular and the botanical epithet derive from the way in which the ripe pod violently ejects its seeds when touched, ensuring that you will find seedlings in the most unexpected places. Canterbury bells, *Campanula medium*, are biennial, sturdy plants with fat bells of lilac or white, near blue, mauve, purple and lavender-pink, single, double or cup and saucer. They bring plenty of colour to the midsummer border, thrive in part shade and do not depend upon good weather, but need deadheading to remain respectable. The common evening primrose, *Oenothera biennis*, is another biennial tolerating light shade, very decorative especially in the form with red calyces to contrast with the clear yellow flowers.

The forms of *Primula sieboldii* have the look almost of a plant that belongs in the conservatory, for they manage to combine elegance and show in a way not always achieved by hardy plants, especially those that prefer cool places. Yet given a leafy soil that does not dry out, so that their shallow-rooting mats of crimpled, fresh green leaves are not left vulnerable during periods of drought, they are perfectly amenable to growing out of doors. In late spring the clusters of large flowers are borne on 15cm/6in stems; their colours range from the pure white 'Snowflake' (an improvement on plain *alba*) to the deep magenta-rose of 'Mikado' via pink 'Geisha Girl' and 'Cherubim' and the lavender-blue shades of 'Seraphim' – to name just a few of the cultivars now listed.

The flowers of the hybrid foxglove *Digitalis* × *mertonensis* are flared bells, closely packed on the stems, of a curious shade, sometimes described as crushed strawberry, but it has a little more blue in it than a strawberry should, yet is hazed with coppery-pink. At 60–75cm/24–30in, it falls between its two parents – the wild foxglove, *D. purpurea*, and the soft yellow *D. grandiflora* – in height, comes true from seed or can be divided, and has a long summer season.

XI

Walls, Courtyards and Town Gardens

GIVEN that gardens without houses are so rare as to be statistically insignificant, one can say that every garden will have at least one wall, and many will have all four house walls available for planting. This applies equally to town gardens and courtyard gardens, though the disposition of the walls may be different, inward-looking towards the heart of the garden instead of outward away from the house. Much of what I shall say in this chapter will assume not only shade but also limitations of space; we have had several expansive chapters already, and even gardeners with large acreages to plant seldom have enough wall space for everything they wish to grow. Every plant in a small area must pay rent for as long, and in as many ways, as possible. A plant with a short flowering season is not necessarily disqualified; it may have so exotic or delectable a fragrance as to be welcomed nonetheless, or it may have good foliage, autumn fruits, or a fine tracery of bare branches on the wall in winter. As for the plants that grow at the feet of your climbers or wall shrubs, they may be some of the very same that have already been described in earlier chapters; for now I want to concentrate on vertical surfaces.

Azara microphylla qualifies on all counts but that of fruits. It has tiny, polished, dark evergreen leaves disposed in ferny sprays, and half-hidden flowers, just a minute puff of yellow stamens, under the branches in winter, when their vanilla-custard fragrance is entirely unexpected. There is a variegated form with the leaves cream-marked. I am never quite sure about this; on the whole, I think that the variegation detracts from the delicate pattern of the foliage, but it is undeniably pale and pretty. With it you might plant *Itea ilicifolia*, which has leaves as dark and glossy as holly, but the marginal teeth lack holly's sharp spines. The

217

fragrant flowers are long catkins of palest green, in late summer. Most authorities tell you to grow *Bupleurum fruticosum* in the sun, but it does just as well in partial shade, and completes a green harmony, for its oblong leaves are sea-green, and its inflorescence is a dense umbel of many tiny, greenish-yellow flowers in summer. Given a wall large enough, I should want to add *Pileostegia viburnoides*. This evergreen climbing hydrangea-relative has bold, leathery, narrowly oblong leaves, and the flowers that open in late summer and autumn are massed into creamy, frothy cones that form a branching panicle. *Hydrangea serratifolia* is less common, a Chilean evergreen with similar foamy, cream flower heads in late summer.

Wherever I live, I try to find a shaded corner for *Daphne pontica*; ideally, by a door that is often used, so that nightly during its spring season I can enjoy the poignant, sweet fragrance emitted after dark by the clusters of small, yellow-green flowers. The foliage is blunt-ended and lustrous green, so that it is always comely during the months of pleasurable anticipation. If all that cream and green is simply too restrained for you, try establishing the Scottish flame flower, *Tropaeolum speciosum*. This climbing nasturtium prefers cool, moist and preferably acid soil, when its fleshy roots may agree to settle in so that, each summer, the thin trails of fresh green, five-parted leaves ascend the supporting shrubs you have thoughtfully provided. By late summer the vivid scarlet flowers are opening, bright as fresh-spilt blood.

One of the prettiest combinations I recall on a half-shaded wall (morning sun and afternoon shade) had *Akebia quinata* and *Clematis macropetala* 'Markham's Pink' flowering together, the petal-filled bells of the clematis a dusty pink that enhanced the chocolate-maroon drooping cups of the akebia. If you come close, you discover that the akebia is spicily scented; while its foliage is no disgrace with its five rounded, notched leaflets of bronzed green, setting off the clematis' silky-white, wig-like seedheads. But it has to be said that neither climber is agreeable to look upon in winter, when they present a tangled mass of stems. At least *Aconitum hemsleyanum* (*A. volubile*), a climbing monkshood that might well join this group on account of its glossy, fingered leaves and high-hooded flowers of muted lilac-purple in autumn, dies down in winter. The blue *Clematis macropetala* – 'Maidwell Hall' is a fine selection – performs just as well in shade as the pink, while 'Snowbird' and 'White Swan' are prettiest of all, their white ballet skirts bright in the shadows.

The allied *C. alpina* has flowers that are less full, simple lanterns of blue, white or sulky pink, followed by silvery-grey seedheads. 'Frances Rivis' is the largest-flowered blue, 'Pamela Jackman' is deep blue and

'Columbine' an enchanting porcelain-blue, while 'Willy' is pale and dark pink and 'Ruby' is deeper toned, not a pure pink but dusky madder. 'White Moth', 'Burford White' and 'Columbine White' describe themselves.

You will usually read that trachelospermums need a sunny, sheltered wall; but the best plants I ever knew grew in a courtyard facing away from the sun, though with full, overhead light. Both species are self-clinging evergreens, and both are deliciously fragrant in pale, propeller-shaped flower. *Trachelospermum asiaticum* is the smaller in leaf, the creamy flowers aging to Chinese yellow in late summer, while the wider flowers of *T. jasminoides* open white and age to cream. There is a most acceptable variegated *T. jasminoides* with leaves edged and painted with cream, turning to crimson-pink in winter. The form known as Wilson 776, from the collector's number of Ernest Wilson who discovered the plant in China, has leaves that vary from the normal ovate outline to narrowly lanceolate, prettily veined and often rich crimson in winter. The plant offered as *T. majus* is a vigorous, self-sticking climber with larger leaves burnished red in winter.

I fancy that it would assort well with *Parthenocissus henryana*, for which a half-shaded wall is the ideal setting; out of the sun it develops its best leaf colouring of deep velvety green, copper-flushed, with the veins picked out in silvery-white and madder-pink. The three- or five-fingered leaves turn to deep crimson in autumn. The foot of the wall shrub in this grouping must be *Skimmia japonica* 'Rubella', on account of its deep crimson winter buds that open to white cones of flower perfumed like lily of the valley.

IVIES AND CAMELLIAS IN TOWN GARDENS

Whenever I walk around the streets of London I peer into the front gardens of Chelsea and Kensington and Belgravia, and am often fascinated by what I see. A little paved garden no larger than a modest room, in one Chelsea street, is fenced and walled for privacy, and shaded by a small cherry with a leaning trunk, up which *Hedera helix* 'Goldheart' has been encouraged to grow, reaching into the lower branches. This ivy has neat, triangular leaves each with a bright gamboge flash at the centre, making a pattern of almost geometric precision in contrast to the Rackhamesque outlines of the host tree. Occasionally an all-green leaf will appear; it should be removed forthwith.

If you cannot stand variegations, a green ivy of striking leaf outline and glossy, light-reflecting surface could be no less effective. 'Sagittifolia' has rather pale green foliage, the leaves five-lobed with the centre lobe very long and the side and base lobes neatly pointed; it is a fast and dense grower. The little dark green 'Ivalace' is slower, and exceptionally pretty with upcurled margins and paler veining. The heron's foot ivy, now simply called 'Heron', has bright green, narrow five-lobed leaves with white, raised veins emphasizing the spread of the lobes. Cultivars of *Hedera helix* are legion, and could fill pages; I shall mention just a few more. Two small and compact ivies would grow well at the foot of a tree or a container, spreading forward over the surrounding paving but never outgrowing their space: 'Shamrock', with dark green, three-lobed leaves, each lobe blunt-ended and cupped; and 'Très Coupé', with tiny, narrow, five-lobed leaves like a miniature 'Sagittifolia'. If you want to bring an impression of light to a darkish corner, try one of the distinctly variegated ivies such as 'Harald' ('Chicago Variegated') in green and cream, the neat, little, silvery 'Adam' which takes on pink tones in winter, or 'Sagittifolia Variegata' which is suffused with cream, the effect so pale as to gather to itself any gleam of light.

Many shaded London gardens have a camellia or two, either in tubs or planted out, where the soil is suitable. You can grow good camellias in containers – tubs, terracotta planters, wooden *caisses de Versailles*, even those plastic garden-centre planters if you must. This is the way for gardeners with limy soil to grow them; but remember to use rain water, not tap water, except *in extremis*. With their glossy foliage and often highly formal flowers, cultivars of *Camellia japonica* are well suited to small, paved courtyards or front gardens. Town gardens are often very sheltered, so you may be able to avoid the weather damage that so often spoils full-petalled camellia blooms.

I have already described a few camellias, those that I would admit to the woodland; in a town garden, or near the house in a larger garden where there is room for a variety of planting styles, the formal doubles, the paeony form and anemone form flowers have their place. There are thousands of cultivars to choose from, and I think it a shame to fall back on 'Donation' just because it is widely available (the only camellia cultivar that is, according to *The Plant Finder*'s criterion of a listing by more than 25 nurseries). That is not to say that 'Donation' is a bad camellia. Any plant that is evergreen, easy to propagate and flowers from infancy with great freedom is bound to be popular when those flowers are pale candy pink with deeper veining and come early in the year to lift our spirits. Flanking a front door in Belgravia is a pair of 'Donation' planted in long, narrow planters, more like deep windowboxes set on the marble-paved steps, leaving room for seasonal flowers at the feet of the camellias once their own season is over. At the end of a winter which, though seldom very cold, is interminably grey, the indomitable pink blooms arouse only feelings of gratitude, not superiority.

'Donation', of course, is a *williamsii* hybrid camellia, like the paeony-flowered 'Debbie' in a colder shade of pink, and anemone-form 'Elsie Jury' in orchid-pink. The semi-double *reticulata* hybrid 'Inspiration' is rather like a brighter 'Donation' with the flowers spaced more widely on the bush. Virtually all the *williamsii* camellias have the laudable habit of dropping their fading flowers cleanly, whereas many japonicas hang on to the disgraceful brown tatters so that you have to pick them off by hand. If you have just one or two camellias, and only a tiny garden to keep tidy, that may not matter, it is true. Among the *japonica* cultivars, almost every permutation of colour and form is to be had from specialist growers: white, pink, rose and red, and the striped and stippled cultivars with two or three colours on each flower; single, semi-double and paeony-flowered, anemone-form, rose-form and formal double. Camellia buffs will know better than I what their taste runs to, so here I propose only to mention a few that, in the UK at least, are easy to obtain and easy to grow. The old 'Nobilissima', a paeony-flowered white, often opens its first blooms in early winter – before Christmas, in England. Later it is the turn of shell-pink 'Magnoliiflora' (now to be called 'Hagomoro'), each petal cupped, pointed and prick-eared so the bloom recalls a water lily rather than a magnolia. 'Adolphe Audusson' is the doyen of the reds, a big, semi-double flower of bright crimson-scarlet with golden stamens, and 'Lady Clare' (now 'Akashi-gata') is as easy in warm pink on a rather floppy, large-leaved bush. 'Elegans' is an old but still good anemone-form, peach-pink cultivar. Of several striped cultivars, 'Tricolor' is one of the best for the garden, with semi-double to single flowers, white striped with pink, or wholly red, pink or white. The slow-growing 'Donckelarii' is a good red semi-double with white marblings, and 'Contessa Lavinia Maggi' has double flowers decidedly striped in crimson, pink and white. Although they are very popular, the 'Mathotiana' cultivars in white or pink are not the best of garden camellias, as their large, perfectly formed double blooms are too easily damaged, but you may get away with them in a sheltered courtyard.

LEAVES AND FLOWERS FOR DARK COURTYARDS

Despite its potential size, *Fatsia japonica* is an excellent choice for a small, shaded garden; you can grow it in a container to restrain it, or prune it back quite hard if it gets too exuberant. There is a basement courtyard near my London flat which receives almost no direct sunshine; the overhead light is intensified by whitewashed walls. Here the strong patterns of *F. japonica* and the vertical canes of a bamboo, the slender, narrow-leaved *Sinarundinaria nitida*, both growing in tubs, cast shadows on the wall, and a mirror framed in *trompe l'oeil* trellis on which *Jasminum polyanthum* grows gives the illusion of another courtyard beyond. Sword or ladder ferns, species of *Nephrolepis*, are set out in summer, and pots of *Lilium regale* infuse the little court, and the air of the pavement above, with heady fragrance, just as the jasmine does in spring. Too tender to grow outside in most English gardens, the jasmine seems to thrive in London, helped along by a series of mild winters. The only colour in this little basement, except the rose-maroon flush on the reverse of the white lily petals, comes from a tub of pink mophead hydrangea, and another containing a fuchsia with pink petals and an ample white skirt.

Fuchsias are ideal shrubs for small, part-shaded gardens. Even among the hardy kinds the range is enormous, from the simple scarlet-crimson and purple of the original *Fuchsia magellanica* to the flaunting, full, lilac-pink skirts and pale pink sepals of 'Lena'. Everyone has their favourites; I prefer the single-flowered cultivars, and am allured by the white sepals and cherry-red skirt of 'Checkerboard', or the more subtle blush and lilac 'Chillerton Beauty'. Slightly brighter pink and lilac belongs to wide-skirted 'Display'. 'Sharpitor' is a sport of the blush-white *F. magellanica molinae*, with the same frail-seeming flowers among jade-pale leaves edged with ivory. Among brighter fuchsias, 'Phyllis' is all red, 'Madame Cornelissen' bright crimson-scarlet with a white skirt discreetly veined in red, and 'Enfant Prodigue' a flounce of crimson with semi-double, purple skirt. If kept fed and watered, they go on flowering for months, especially in the shelter of a town garden. Their colouring combines well with the cream and pink splashed leaves of *Ampelopsis brevipedunculata* 'Elegans', a vine of rather weak growth that is unlikely to outgrow its space; a sheltered position in half shade suits it well, for its purpose in life is to grow pretty leaves, not fruits.

The only thing fuchsias lack, in their summer to autumn season, is fragrance. And fragrance is especially valuable in a small, enclosed garden, where buffeting winds will not blow it away. Some roses are well endowed, and of those that thrive as well in light shade as in sun, the rugosas are particularly fragrant. *Rosa rugosa* 'Blanc Double de Coubert' has the usual bright green, crinkled leaves of the rugosas, turning to corn-gold in autumn, and paper-white, double flowers; 'Roseraie de l'Haÿ' is even more powerfully scented and its magenta flowers, like those of 'Blanc Double', keep opening for months on end. One of the most powerfully fragrant shrubs is the mock orange, *Philadelphus coronarius*. Far too big in its ordinary green-leaved manifestation for a small garden, it has two varieties that are more restrained in growth but just as swooningly scented: the lime-yellow-leaved 'Aureus', and white-variegated 'Bowles's Variety'. The first, if grown too much shaded, turns green; fleeting shade is ideal, for full sun bakes it to a crisp. Mr Bowles's mock orange is a better choice for a partly shaded, small garden; it is slow growing, and so cleanly marked with ivory that it gleams in the half-light, as though blessed with its own moonbeams. The smaller day lilies are well suited to half-shaded, enclosed gardens, where their dainty trumpets of saffron with mahogany backing are in scale as the grosser modern cultivars would not be. There are several pretty species of this style: *Hemerocallis dumortieri*, *H. middendorfii* and *H. multiflora*, which flower in that order from late spring to late summer; the last is rather tall at 1.2m/4ft, twice the height of the earlier pair. Although it is the dingiest of little flowers, I always scatter a few seeds of night-scented stock, for it grows anywhere even when shaded by taller plants, and fills the evening air with its perfume. And the old-fashioned mignonette, *Reseda odorata*, is quite content in half shade, in a cool soil.

EPHEMERALS FOR SHADY PLACES

Annuals and bedding plants such as these are often tucked into corners of little gardens. Most annuals, it is true, do better in sun, but there are those that will do well in shade, especially if you consider as annuals such bedding standbys as busy lizzies and begonias. Once you have your framework of wall plants and a shrub or two, chosen I hope for their foliage as much as their flowers, it is fun to make changes each year, jazzing up that corner with scarlet begonias one summer and with white tobaccos the next, indulging a byzantine mixture of scarlet and orange and pink impatiens or opting for restraint in white and pastels. Impatiens or busy lizzies are actually happier in shade than in sun, unless growing in cool, high-latitude gardens where the sun's rays seldom scorch. In Switzerland, we use them in the darkest corners of the courtyard and in the sunless alleys between tall houses, where their luminous colours glow against the grey stone.

Most annuals need a little more light than this; half shade rather than all-day shade. This is certainly true of *Phlox drummondii*, which also dislikes very hot weather, and goes on strike until the cooler days return. The colours of mixed strains are individually pretty, in scarlet and crimson and pink, violet, white, and a delightful soft yellow; but it is much more effective to grow just one colour. The pity is that seedsmen, especially those who sell in retail quantities, are so reluctant to supply seeds of anything in packets of individual colours, and to get them you will almost certainly have to buy by mail rather than conveniently picking up a packet or two at your local shop.

At least nobody has yet, to my knowledge, persuaded _Nemophila menziesii_ to forsake its appealing sky-blue, white-eyed flowers, which have earned it the ghastly pet name of baby blue eyes. _N. maculata_, which is just as content in cool, dappled shade, has ice-white flowers with an indigo spot at the apex of each of the five petals. Pansies come in all sorts of colours, often with cross little faces from the dark central markings; they do well in part shade, and have the advantage, for town gardeners without much space to raise seedlings, of being widely available from nurseries and street traders. However appealing the blotched and parti-coloured flowers may be individually, the plain colours, and especially the paler ones, are more restful in the garden. You can have pansies in flower at virtually any moment of the year; even in winter, from an early summer sowing.

Many plants that are normally treated as permanencies can be used once as bedding; though it helps to salve the conscience if you have a friend or relative with a larger garden, who will gladly take your rejects and give them a permanent home. My mother, one year, grew as a formal strip along a shady concrete path a regular pattern of _Viola labradorica_, which retains its purple, leaf colouring well in light shade, _Lamium maculatum_ 'White Nancy', and _Primula_ 'Wanda'. I could not help thinking how well this simple arrangement, drawn from plants grown more informally elsewhere in her country garden, would adapt to the narrow borders that might flank a paved or tiled path from gate to front door in a small town garden. Having done their stint as bedding, the violet or the lamium could be reset at the base of a tree to swirl more freely forward on to paving.

Plants as Collectors' Pieces

In an earlier chapter I promised that I would mention named primroses, both single and double, and the little double daisies, garden toys ideal for small spaces. There are two delightful, miniature polyanthuses that seem quite accommodating provided they are regularly split and replanted in enriched soil, the recommended treatment for all primroses: 'Lady Greer' and 'McWatt's Cream', both in pale primrose-cream, the first faintly pink-tinted. Little candy-pink, striped 'Kinlough Beauty' seems to need more cossetting, perhaps only because it is so small that it is easily swamped. 'Tawny Port' looks like a juliana primrose, with its very dark leaves and deep wine-red flowers; 'Buckland Wine' is similar, with bronzed foliage and velvety-red flowers. I have found them nowhere near so robust as the popular old 'Wanda', so easy that you can pop her in anywhere. These little primroses need to be under your eye, where they should be less likely to dwindle through your failure to divide and replant them, or to be smothered to death by a larger neighbour, than if you tuck them in among shrubs and perennials in a more expansive and competitive setting.

Once you get primrose fever, an affliction of gardeners not of primroses themselves (they have enough to contend with in vine weevil and primula sickness), you will start to seek out all the named kinds you can, single and double. Here I propose only to mention a few more that I have grown and loved and that are still offered commercially. Among polyanthuses, 'Barrowby Gem' is valued for its fragrance as much as for its clear sulphur colouring. 'Beamish Foam' bears heads of palest mauve-pink splashed with white. The gold-laced strains are seed-raised and always admired for their plum-dark colouring, each petal finely edged with yellow or white (sometimes called silver-laced). Also seed raised are the Cowichans, which are distinguished by colour names only, tending to rich dark tones of crimson, plum and cinnabar unmarred by the yellow eye that occurs in most primroses. In this they recall old velvety-crimson 'Bartimeus', the eyeless primrose, that seems no longer to be available, though I hope some collectors are still cherishing it. The doubles are old garden plants that have become something of a cult, but are proving increasingly difficult to grow well in Britain as, year after year, a hot dry spring precedes a dry and searing summer. Legendary names still just represented in the lists are the Bon Accords (doubles in a range of colours), 'Our Pat' (with dark bronzed leaves and deep violet, double flowers betraying its juliana blood), and 'Marie Crousse' (a double in lavender-rose splashed with white). Of other doubles, only the double white and double lilac are anything like easy, though the pale peach 'Sue Jervis', a newish double, has been in nurserymen's lists for a few years now, suggesting that it is good tempered also.

The little double daisies, forms of *Bellis perennis*, are far removed from the gross bedding varieties that add colour, white, pink, and crimson, to municipal flowerbeds in spring and early summer. First discovered as sports of the wild daisy, they were popular with cottagers in the sixteenth century, and as nurseries began to cater for gardeners in town and country alike, in the centuries that followed, more varieties were introduced. In cottage gardens they relished the cool root-run beneath a paved path; in London they were often used in window boxes. The Victorians used them as underplanting to roses, where the daisies throve on the regular applications of manure intended for the rose bushes. Though they do best with the roots cool and nourished, they need light, if not full sun, to flower well. The speckled and striped kinds are probably lost, but pink 'Dresden China', red 'Rob Roy' and the double white are still on offer. 'Alice' is a pink 'Rob Roy', and 'Stafford Pink' is also available. The hen and chickens daisy, *B. perennis* 'Prolifera', is popular after long neglect, amusing with its tiny flowers emerging from the main double white flower head. If the quaintness of double daisies and double primroses appeals, then why not also grow double violets, in white, blue or the typical violet colouring, and the nostalgic Parma violets with their cachou fragrance?

With Wall Space to Spare

The rose is everyone's favourite; in those tests when you are asked to name, without thinking, your favourite colour, number and flower, the most common responses are blue, five, and roses. Well, despite some of the names lately given to roses, there is no such thing as a blue rose, only a fetching lavender or grey-violet. And on the whole, in the British climate at least, roses need sun. But some there are that will not only grow but also flower competently in lightly shaded places, including walls that face away from the sun provided they are not also overshadowed by trees. (Mr Graham Thomas, whose trilogy on old, climbing and shrub roses is a compelling read, actually asserts that 'any hardy rose will provide a number of blooms on a shady wall, provided it is not overhung by trees.') I have already mentioned, in the context of a sunless border, the climbing rose 'Madame Alfred Carrière' in white faintly blushing with pink, and 'Golden Showers' with its delicious fragrance. To these you could add 'Paul's Lemon Pillar', a rose that combines size and elegance in its pale blooms, the colour of lemon sorbet rather than of the fruit itself, high-centred and fragrant. The shelter of a town garden suits it well, for it has tea parentage. The wonderful old Glory rose, 'Gloire de Dijon', subject of a sensuous poem by D. H. Lawrence, is even more accommodating despite its tea ancestry, giving a generous ration of warm buff, yellow and apricot flowers over a long and unbroken season. Almost as long a season belongs to 'New Dawn', a rambler with glossy leaves that has abandoned the once-flowering habit of its kin. The dainty, scrolled buds open to shell-pink, sweetly fragrant blooms.

If you have space for a sprawly, thorny climber that thinks it is a bush, 'Maigold' is a fine choice, with good glossy foliage, and semi-double, warm buff and saffron flowers full of perfume, in one huge early burst of flowers with occasional afterthoughts. The old 'Albertine' can be used in the same way and also needs space; the loose flowers are tawny-pink, as though, in Vita Sackville-West's words, 'dipped in a cup of tea'. One abundant, midsummer flowering fills the surrounding air with fragrance. The single-flowered 'Mermaid' is enduringly popular, flowering well in a lightly shaded place even in the grey climate of Britain, where the shelter of a wall is almost necessary. Even after the yellow petals have fallen the old-gold stamens are decorative. It has to be said that 'Mermaid' is only a little more willing than 'Albertine' to be disciplined. The informality of an exuberant rose, however, seems to sit quite comfortably in the formal surroundings of a walled garden, so long as practical details, such as a way to pass without being hooked on rose thorns, can be managed. In 'Albéric Barbier', a repeat-flowering rambler with polished dark leaves to set off quartered, flat-faced, ivory flowers opening from pointed, primrose buds, we have the most popular of the apple-scented ramblers, giving a generous burst of flower early in the season and more in ones and twos until autumn, perfectly content on a sunless wall and free of the mildew that besets 'Dorothy Perkins' and her kin. 'Emily Gray' belongs to the same glossy-leaved group; she grew for half a century on the north side of our English house, until finally she succumbed to senescence, and I mourned her yellow, fragrant, single blooms.

These few should disprove the assertion that only a deep red rose has the true rose fragrance. But it is true that 'Guinée', with velvety black-crimson, hybrid tea-style blooms free of any taint of purple, has a wonderful, rich perfume, everything that a red rose should have. It needs a light background: pale stone, perhaps, or white stucco. Brick, unless of pale ochre, almost Cotswold-stone colouring, kills the rose. A paler, brighter crimson belongs to 'Souvenir de Claudius Denoyel', which has flowers of the more informal, early hybrid-tea style. 'Gruss an Teplitz' is a fine repeat-flowering, fragrant, crimson rose that when trained will not much exceed 3m/10ft, making it a comfortable size where space is too restricted for the 5m/17ft 'Guinée' or 'Claudius Denoyel'.

CLIMBERS IN COMPANY

However magnificent the blooms of a rose, the framework on which they are borne is nothing to be proud of; at best we can hope for good glossy foliage. One way to compensate is to concentrate still more on gorgeous flowers, by adding to the rose a large-flowered clematis. Several grow well on shady walls; the rose stems will give added support to the clematis' stems and twining tendrils; and the colour range is complementary, for no true yellow yet exists in large-flowered clematis, but there are many near-blues. The paler colours show up best in the garden, and especially in shade where a white clematis such as the ever popular 'Marie Boisselot' is not only beautiful, but perfectly content. The broad sepals overlap to make a wide, full flower with stamens of pale ivory. Mix her with the white rose 'Madame Alfred Carrière' if you want to be very refined. 'Henryi', another white, has more starry flowers with dark stamens at the centre.

Beyond doubt the most valuable blue clematis is 'Perle d'Azur', with a long season of periwinkle-blue flowers, enchanting with the pale pink of 'New Dawn' or with any of your soft yellow roses. There are several clematis of lavender-mauve colouring, including the fine double 'Vyvyan Pennell', as full of petals as a cottage paeony in its early summer flowering (and single-flowered in autumn). The 'Nelly Moser' types of clematis are often positively better on a shaded wall, as their colouring tends to fade badly in bright sun; whether that is a disadvantage is a matter of opinion. I would not give 'Nelly Moser' or any of her cousins garden room, but some people rave over the bright carmine or magenta bar that runs like a spoke down the centre of each mauve or lavender-pink tepal. After Nelly herself, the most widely available of this type is probably 'Bees Jubilee', with 'Lincoln Star', 'Mrs N. Thompson' and the Barbaras – Dibley and Jackman – not far behind.

The brightest honeysuckles are scentless, unlike the vigorously twining woodbine and its kin, described with other inhabitants of the wild woodland. Their vivid colours seem more appropriate in the formalized setting of a walled or courtyard garden, or on the sunless wall of your house, than in informal settings. *Lonicera × tellmanniana* bears generous clusters of long, ochre trumpets flushed with copper and tangerine, opening around midsummer. Handsome though it is, it is outclassed by its parent *L. tragophylla*, a noble species from China with dark leaves, glaucous beneath, contrasting with narrow trumpets almost twice as long as those of its offspring, of rich butter-yellow, glowing in the dim shadows that suit it so well. The scarlet trumpet honeysuckle, *L. sempervirens*, needs a little more shelter and light, but where suited is very fine, with long, elegant trumpets warm yellow within and vivid scarlet on the outside; 'Superba' is a richer scarlet and 'Sulphurea' is uniformly yellow. Its hybrid offspring *L.* × *brownii* is easier to please, and scarcely less colourful with whorls of scarlet flowers among bluish foliage. 'Fuchsioides' is a selection presumably so named because of a vague resemblance to the flowers of trumpet fuchsias, while 'Dropmore Scarlet' has an exceptionally long season from midsummer through to autumn.

Despite their colours, you may feel that a scentless honeysuckle is a waste in a small garden where every plant must earn its keep. The brightest of the fragrant honeysuckles is *L.* × *heckrottii*, a half-shrubby climber with whorls of yellow flowers flushed with purple; 'Gold Flame' is a selection with orange-pink trumpets. In honeysuckles that are coloured differently within and without, such as this one, the tones flushing the exterior of the flowers are inconstant, deeper where the sun strikes and palest in shade, so that the blooms of two plants grown in different conditions can be very unlike in colour.

There is seldom a good reason for segregating climbing plants; two or more can well share a wall or even, if the sizes of host and climbers are matched, a tree. And an evergreen paired with a deciduous climber will mean that you have something more than dereliction to look at in winter. The big ivies are just the job, with their bold leafage and easy vigour. *Hedera canariensis* 'Gloire de Marengo', though a little tender, should survive even cold winters in a sheltered garden; but I find its grey and cream variegations a little chilly when the leaves are off everything else. My choice, therefore, would be one of the *H. colchica* cultivars, which have the further advantage of greater hardiness. 'Dentata Variegata' has big shield leaves boldly margined with butter-yellow, while 'Sulphur Heart', of course, has the reverse variegation, with an irregular zone of pale green where the primrose central flash melds with the dark margin.

Not every deciduous climber lends itself to a partnership with an evergreen; some are simply too vigorous, or too leafy in summer. Thus *Clematis montana*, a tough and obliging species that will grow almost anywhere. But it has terrific vigour, and if you have no ancient yew or cypress that needs cheering with a brief but generous display in spring, then it must have a wall either high or wide or both. And you will not love it in winter. You can, of course, cut your montanas hard back just after flowering, to restrain them; but that means rigorous annual discipline. If for all that you want one – and they are lovely in their short glory – then go for a good form. 'Grandiflora' is a pure white with broad sepals, making for a full-looking flower, and 'Alexander' a good creamy-white with plenty of fragrance. Pale pink 'Elizabeth', which is dependably vanilla scented (as are most montanas), fades to almost white in the shade, and the deeper 'Pink Perfection', and 'Picton's Variety' with an extra tepal or two, are of the same style in more decided pink. They derive from *C. montana rubens*, which has noticeably dark-flushed foliage.

The deciduous climbing hydrangeas, *Hydrangea petiolaris*, *Schizophragma hydrangeoides* and *S. integrifolium*, flower best in sun but perform very adequately in shade, where their white, lacecap flowers in summer reflect what light there is. The hydrangea is the most familiar to most gardeners, usually seen on a wall but sometimes on a tall tree trunk, or simply left to form a wide-mounded shrub. It is rather a slow starter, but tall and vigorous once established, quite able to cover a high sunless wall with fresh greenery spangled at midsummer with lacy flowers. The winter stems are a cosy fox-brown. The sterile bracts that form the showy part of the flower are bolder in the schizophragmas, especially in *S. integrifolium*, which is the colour of clotted cream. In its native China it grows in cool, moist valleys, covering the rocky cliffs.

Both Virginia creeper and Boston ivy are used in Switzerland to cover the stark concrete walls alongside newly constructed roads, and both do equally well in sun or shade, even beneath overpasses. The main reason for growing them is their brilliant autumn colour, which may be dimmed if the plants are grown in too much shade. Both are vigorous, self-sticking climbers, and both, after excursions into *Vitis* and *Ampelopsis*, are currently residing in the genus *Parthenocissus*. These frequent name changes have not helped the confusion between the two vernacular names. It should be easy enough to remember that the creeper beginning with V has five leaflets, V being the Roman notation for five, and simply to ignore past botanical epithets. Virginia creeper, then, is *P. quinquefolia*, distinguished by its five leaflets from the Boston ivy, *P. tricuspidata*, with three-lobed leaves. The original introduction of this species, with purple-tinted young leaves, is known às 'Veitchii'. By contrast with these divided leaves, those of *Vitis coignetiae* are as large and round as dinner plates, and even in a partly shaded position this vine will usually colour acceptably, in shades from plum to scarlet, in autumn. It has great vigour, and will fill a middling-sized tree, but also looks very well against masonry, as in one garden I know where it has been encouraged to twine along the lichened, grey-stone balustrade of a terrace.

WALL SHRUBS AND CLIMBERS COMBINED

Many climbers can be planted among wall shrubs of substance that will act as support, disguise their bare legs in the growing season, and – if you sensibly choose an evergreen – draw the eye from the bare tangle of stems in winter. *Choisya ternata* is a good choice, smelling sharply aromatic when you crush a leaf, and smart all year unless distressed by an exceptionally severe winter. The pyracanthas are all good shady-wall shrubs, with two good seasons of effect – creamy flowers in fuzzy hawthorn-like heads in early summer, bright fruits in autumn – and foliage which, though in itself of no particular merit, is evergreen and clothes naked walls becomingly. Both *Pyracantha coccinea* and, especially, *P. atalantioides* are big shrubs needing a high wall, but there are newer hybrids that are more suited to a smallish space, with a range of berry colour from butter-yellow and amber to scarlet. 'Soleil d'Or' is, naturally, yellow, and so is 'Golden Charmer'. The spreading, dense 'Shawnee' is a shade nearer to orange, and 'Orange Glow' is brighter still. 'Mohave' is a good orange-red. There are several more, including the egregious 'Harlequin' with leaves measled in white and pink. It has to be said that pyracanthas fruit more freely in the sun, but they will put up a fair display in shade also.

Although they are not evergreen, the Japanese quinces are valued for the beautiful colouring of their flowers, and for their willingness to grow in part shade, as it might be on a sunless wall with open sky above. They flower in early spring, when their pure scarlet or soft orange-reds blend with the yellow of *Forsythia suspensa* (itself no mean performer on a shaded wall, the pale lemon of its flowers set off by near-black stems in var. *atrocaulis* and 'Nymans') or with any white flower, but quarrel with the pink of almond or peach blossom. Several of the *Chaenomeles* also live up to their vernacular name by producing large, yellow fruits with a generous spicy aroma, suitable for jelly or simply for leaving in a bowl indoors, in winter. *C. japonica* is suitable for small spaces, reaching little more than 1.2m/4ft, with spreading branches set in early spring with soft orange-scarlet blossom; it is, however, a touch less easy than the cultivars of *C. speciosa* or the hybrids, needing sun for more than half of the day and shelter from cold winds. 'Knap Hill Scarlet' is a famous hybrid quince, taller than *C. japonica*, its pale scarlet flowers enlivened by golden stamens. 'Crimson and Gold' is bolder in colour, and a terrific grower apt to elbow out neighbouring plants, fine if you have space to fill but less than ideal in a small garden. Here 'Rowallane' would be a better choice, or 'Pink Lady' if you do not want a red. One of the most appealing is 'Yaegaki', a low shrub with large, double rosettes of pale coral, while 'Coral Sea' has single flowers one tone darker of the same shade. Cultivars of *C. speciosa* vary from the white of 'Nivalis' and apple-blossom pink 'Moerloosei' to the oxblood-red of 'Simonii', a low and spreading shrub.

The classic shrub for a wall that faces away from the sun is the winter jasmine, *Jasminum nudiflorum*. A sprawler rather than a climber, it can be trained to the wall, its long growths pruned back after flowering. Indeed, whenever this is the recommended procedure, the pruning may as well take place while the flowers are still on the branch, so you can enjoy them indoors. Whether indoors or out, there is something enormously cheering about those vivid yellow stars on their green twigs, opening all through the winter in defiance of the sinking clouds that lower our spirits. By contrast, I always find the drooping, grey catkins of *Garrya elliptica* rather depressing, as also the comment that tends to accompany the description in catalogues: 'useful for furnishing sunless walls'. I want my plants to be beautiful, bold or dainty, brash or elegant; but am seldom enthused by mere usefulness. The leathery leaves are evergreen, so that the 'furnishing' is year-round; and in the best male forms, such as 'James Roof', the catkins are undeniably striking despite their muted colouring. Female plants bear long clusters of mahogany-purple fruits; but though I have more than once seen a female garrya, I have never succeeded in obtaining one. Either of these shrubs could be enlivened, in summer, by allowing a clematis to filter through them; perhaps one of the *viticella* hybrids such as 'Alba Luxurians', which is sometimes all white and more often, very fetchingly, green-flushed at the tepal tips. *Clematis viticella* itself is immensely elegant, with wide, nodding, violet-purple bells on long stalks; *C. campaniflora* is of the same style with smaller, skim-milk blue flowers. Half shade seems to suit them perfectly well, though the deeper colours of 'Kermesina' in rich burgundy-purple or deepest velvety-purple 'Royal Velours', and even the brighter 'Abundance', disappear into the shadows until the sun reaches them. 'Minuet', 'Venosa Violacea' and the paler 'Little Nell', in white, margined and veined with mauve-purple, show up better.

XII

Meadow Gardening

IN many older gardens, apples and pears and plums were planted orchard fashion, grafted on more vigorous rootstocks than we commonly use today so that they formed proper trees to which you had to take a ladder to harvest the crop. If two or three orchard trees are gathered together in grass, you have the makings of a meadow garden, where wild flowers from many lands can be grown in the grass beneath the filtered shade of the apple trees: bulbs and orchids and perennials that will flower before you make the first cut of the grass, in summer.

Like Christopher Lloyd, who is the chief publicist in Britain for this type of gardening both in his books and articles and, of course, in his garden, I grew up in a garden where narcissi and fritillaries and primroses grew beneath apple trees and were duly mown down with the grass some time after midsummer. In the other garden of my childhood, the Swiss one, the grass was always coarser, even where regularly mown, for that climate is not kind to the fine swards of England; but for all that, little plants that could duck beneath the blades grew at least as well as the grass beneath the Fellenberg plum, the little wild peaches from the vineyards and the black cherry: bugle, self heal, and daisies, of course.

Perhaps it was partly on account of these wild flowers that in both gardens there were always plenty of butterflies: the little, dancing orange tips, deckle-edged commas and showy peacocks, red admirals and tortoiseshells and the graceful painted lady and silver-washed fritillary. Today more and more people are leaving a corner of their garden untamed, as a gesture towards conservation, remembering the vanished buttercup or cowslip meadows of their childhood. Sometimes the result is not merely untamed but unkempt; but it need not be so, unless for the

233

brief period when the grass is yellowing and untidy but you are waiting for the last of the fritillary seeds to fall.

You can, of course, start from scratch to create a planted meadow; but as this is a book about gardening in the shade, I am assuming that the apple trees and the grass exist already and that you want merely to add to the tapestry of flowering plants and grasses growing there. That means that I can almost take as given a community of grasses of comparatively sparse growth, for the trees will, no doubt, have taken much of the nutrients from the soil during their years of flowering and fruiting. You will still need to mow two or three times a year, and to remove the clippings, so that in rotting down their goodness can go elsewhere in your garden via the compost heap, not back into the orchard to make the grasses lush and encourage docks and nettles.

If, over the years, the clippings have been left uncollected, and the grass is rather coarse as a result, you can take the extreme action of spraying the whole thing, in spring, with a translocated contact herbicide (the kind that kills by being absorbed, via the leaves which you have sprayed, into the roots) such as glyphosate. If you do this when the grass is in its surge of vigorous spring growth, soon it will turn orange then brown. Areas free of tree roots can be rotavated, but nearer the trees you will have to just scrape away the dead topgrowth. You can then sow with a more suitable mixture of grasses, avoiding rye grass: species of grass that are recommended for a flowering meadow include creeping red fescue, brown bent, crested dog's tail, sweet vernal grass and meadow foxtail. Velvet bent (*Agrostis canina*) is especially good for shaded areas. Of course, this technique will be no good if your grass, even though too coarse, already contains some of the very flowering plants you are trying to establish – unless you laboriously lift them, to replace them after the killing and reseeding treatment. On the whole, it is probably easier to be patient, mowing and carting away the clippings scrupulously in future, and eschewing any fertilizer even if you think your trees need it; in time, the coarser stuff will give way to the fine grasses as semi-starvation sets in.

If, on the other hand, you have been close-mowing the grass beneath your apple and pear trees for years, like a lawn, then the soil is likely already to be somewhat impoverished, and if you start to introduce the flowers you want, at the same time allowing the grass to grow longer and following the regime of cutting twice or thrice a year, you have a good chance of establishing a Primavera meadow with relative ease. Even in short turf, however, it is much more effective to take a little extra trouble with the plants to be introduced, raising them in pans, flats or boxes, pricking them out, potting them on and generally treating them like any other plant you want to make into a good specimen, which you will then set in the turf from which you will have removed an appropriately sized plug to make room for the newcomer. Sowing the seed of flowering plants with your grasses sounds like a simple way of ending up with a flowery mead, but it seldom works, though once the plants are established, they will quite cheerfully seed themselves, such is the perversity of nature.

BULBS IN GRASS

Many people make the mistake of planting big, gaudy, trumpet daffodils in grass, or the mongrel mixtures sold by the sack 'for naturalizing' by bulb merchants. If you are lucky enough to have avoided these, you can start with just one or two kinds, avoiding the grosser manifestations to choose those that look right among the trees. The lent lily, *Narcissus pseudonarcissus*, and the late-flowering pheasant's eye, *N. poeticus recurvus*, both have the right look to them, informal and small-flowered in their different ways. 'Actaea' is an old and popular *poeticus* with fuller flowers, opening a little earlier than the old pheasant's eye; good though 'Actaea' may be, *N. poeticus recurvus* has an even more wonderful fragrance to add to the elegant looks of its white, swept-back perianth around a tiny, yellow cup fringed with tangerine, and flowers even after the snake's head fritillary. In the wild, *Fritillaria meleagris* produces a fairly constant proportion, around one in ten, of albinos among the sombre murrey and madder, chequered bells of the type. I have found, though, that like *Cyclamen hederifolium*, in the garden the proportions are almost reversed; more than half, certainly, come white from seed that I sow, which I do in pans, planting the seedlings in the grass once they have fattened a little. They are all beautiful.

Primroses, aconites (*Eranthis hyemalis*), the dog's tooth violets (*Erythronium dens-canis*) and snowdrops prefer thinner turf, and are happy close up against trees. In the garden of my childhood the orchard came to an end near the house where a venerable medlar spread half-weeping branches; in late winter the ground beneath was carpeted with aconites and snowdrops, for the ample leafage of the medlar had shaded out the grass long before I was born. Primroses were concentrated at the other end of the orchard, near the path which separated it from the kitchen garden; all but the wild, pale yellow type and its albino seedlings were suppressed, for we all disliked the muddy pinks that resulted from illicit unions with the polyanthus in the formal spring garden. A clump of

doronicums – I cannot tell, at this distance in time, which one – flowered
year after year at the foot of a big Bramley apple. The soft blue *Anemone
apennina* and vivid ultramarine *Scilla siberica* and *Chionodoxa sardensis* all
held their own, with grape hyacinths to follow, and so no doubt, if we
had allowed them in in the first place, would bluebells, *Hyacinthoides non-
scripta*. *Scilla messenaica* is pale blue, with heads of smaller flowers fuzzy
with blue anthers; it is a busy colonizer soon spreading a sheet of sky
beneath the trees. The little white star of Bethlehem, *Ornithogalum
umbellatum*, can safely be left to itself in grass, though it spreads like mad
in the border. No less territorial is *Crocus tomasinianus*, which is scarcely
visible when its slender, buff-backed petals are closed, awakening when
they part to reveal the inner, pale lilac or deeper purple and violet shades.
C. aureus is the bright orange crocus that brings so much colour to the
grim days of late winter; *C. sieberi* is even earlier to flower, with lilac
petals around an orange stigma. These species, with their small flowers,
are far more beautiful in an informal setting than the fat Dutch hybrids,
even though these come in a range of pretty colours and stripings. The
easier forms of *C. chrysanthus* do well in thin turf also, as consolation to
those who must have stripes and featherings on their crocuses: 'Cream
Beauty' and 'Snow Bunting', which both have an expensive-smelling
perfume quite out of character with their modest stature, 'Blue Bird' and
'Blue Pearl', violet-striped 'Ladykiller' and mahogany-on-saffron 'Gipsy
Girl' or 'Zwanenburg Bronze' are cheap to experiment with.

The yellow *Tulipa sylvestris*, which spreads by stolons, is perfectly
happy in grass, and its flowers are fragrant. I should be more hesitant
about trying the late-flowering, pale scarlet *T. sprengeri*, for it seems to
need a little more cossetting in cool, leafy soil in light shade in most
gardens; but having seen how freely it seeded itself in a garden I once
visited, not only among the lime-yellow hostas and ferns with which it
was originally planted, but also into a bed packed with plants where even
groundsel seemed unable to get a foothold, I wonder if it would not do
equally well in the thin grass beneath orchard trees. The camassias which
flower at the same early summer season are well able to take care of
themselves in grass and even to survive years of neglect, and their spikes
of starry, pale or deeper blue flowers are held well clear of the grass at that
time of the year. There are three species worth trying, *Camassia quamash*
with pale flowers, *C. cusickii* and the best of them all, *C. leichtlinii*, which
has a pretty form, *alba*, of green-washed ivory, as well as pale and dark
blue – *caerulea* and *atroviolacea*. I like to see these gentle tones near the
bright magenta of *Gladiolus communis* ssp. *byzantinus*. In one of the
gardens I cared for, a strain of pale pink columbines seeded itself about on

a shaded, grassy slope, the colour just right among the soft blue and magenta. Blue columbines of the 'Hensol Harebell' type would do the same. The mountain knapweed, *Centaurea montana*, prefers sun but flowers obligingly enough in light shade, where its deep blue cornflowers open above narrow, greyish leaves.

WILD OR INTRODUCED

Dandelions, buttercups, hawk's beards and celandines, plantains and clovers are likely to come of their own accord, with lady's smock or cuckoo flower in damp soils. The greater stitchwort, *Stellaria holostea*, is a plant of shady hedgerows, where its starry, milk-white flowers gleam in the shadows in late spring. It is more modest than the moon daisies, which some call ox eye daisies. In acid soils creeping sorrel – a fearful nuisance among shrubs – can be left to wave its little, tawny-red plumes among the grasses. But cowslips are almost rarities these days, worth raising from seed in pans, to be planted in a plug of encouraging compost among the grasses. If they like you they will increase by seeding.

You may have to introduce *Geranium pratense* using the same technique as for everything else that you want to get started in your orchard grass, of planting out pot-grown seedlings; for though the meadow cranesbill grows wild on British roadside verges, locally abundant, you cannot assume that scattering some seed will automatically give you the same results. Once established, of course, it and much else probably will self-seed. Its wide, violet-blue flowers appear in summer over divided leaves; there is a pearly-white form with lavender striations, 'Striatum', which seeds itself as freely as the type. The plant usually labelled 'Mrs Kendall Clarke' is lavender with paler grey veining; but the true form should be grey flushed with rose. Whatever the imposter, it is an obliging plant of pretty colouring which should do as well in grass as in the border. The doubles, of course, have no place here but belong in the flower border.

The tufted vetch, *Vicia cracca*, is the only leguminous plant I should actually encourage, and in any case bird's foot trefoil and the vetchlings prefer sunny, open meadows. But the tufted vetch is beautiful, its deep violet-blue spikes lasting well into summer, after the moon daisies are over. If you like the freshness of blue and white, you can contrive to introduce it near the ivory froth of *Filipendula ulmaria*, the meadowsweet. In the thinnest turf beneath the trees, you may succeed with *Campanula patula*, which bears flowers like large, starry harebells of purple-blue on thin stems; it is a biennial but will seed itself if happy. The true harebell, *Campanula rotundifolia*, is adorable, but is more suited to open, sunny meadows. The grasses themselves, of course, are flowering by now, the pale clouds of common bent as pretty in the mass as any petalled flower. Very soon it will be time to cut everything to the ground.

This means that your autumn-flowering crocuses and colchicums will have as their setting a flattering short sward. The easiest crocuses to start with are *Crocus longiflorus*, in lilac, sometimes feathered, with yellow throat, and a sweet fragrance; and the bluer *C. speciosus*, its colouring enhanced by a large, bright orange stigma. It tends to flop after a day or two, which makes it look untidy in a bed or border but hardly matters in grass, where it can be left to increase by seed and bulbils as much as it wants. *C. nudiflorus* is happy enough in grass to have naturalized itself in grassland here and there in Britain, spreading by stolons; the large flowers are deep purple, almost like a colchicum. *Colchicum autumnale* is, of course, wrongly called the autumn crocus; the two genera are not even in the same family. Then, too, colchicums are much pinker than most crocuses, though there is still some mauve in their colouring. As well as *C. autumnale*, you could try *C. speciosum*, which is larger and more splendid in mauve-pink or, gloriously, in white; the leaves that follow in spring are large and glossy green. Having extolled the white form, I admit that nothing would induce me to plant it in grass unless I already had a good stock of it growing in the same garden.

Orchids in Grass

Several orchids can be induced to grow quite happily in light shade in grass, where the soil is cool and moist. First to open in spring is the early purple orchis, *Orchis mascula*. The early marsh orchid is *Dactylorhiza incarnata*, with mauve or lilac flowers. A month or more later comes *D. fuchsii*, the spotted orchid, with pale mauve flowers spotted and scribbled with purple, or white scrawled with pink, over dark-spotted leaves. *D. maculata* is closely related, a fine, tall orchid with long spikes of flower varying from blush-lilac to purple. Other European orchids that are easy garden plants where suited include the military orchis, *Orchis militaris*, with purple flowers, spotted on the lip – a plant of shady meadows and hedgerows; and *O. purpurea*, in purple with white, densely freckled lip. *O. morio* is the deliciously fragrant green-winged orchis, of quieter colouring than some, though not all green as the vernacular name might suggest. It is a plant of damp meadows.

If your garden is on chalk soil, you might succeed with the pyramidal orchid, *Anacamptis pyramidalis*, and with *Gymnadenia conopsea*, the fragrant orchid, which bears up to 200 sweetly scented, pink flowers on each stem. The late-flowering lady's tresses, *Spiranthes spiralis*, will come to your garden if it wants, not if you try to entice it, and if it appears one year may vanish again the next, or the year after that; it is small and slender, with white flowers in a one-sided spike.

If you want to move an orchis (as it might be from a friend's garden to your own; never, I beg, from the wild, unless the bulldozers are already there) you can normally lift them at any time when you can see them, using a trowel and taking a good clod of soil with them; the tubers are unlikely to be as much as a trowel's length deep. Tuck them straight into their new quarters, water them well, and they should settle down quite happily. Never, on any account, pick the flowering stems. Most orchids rely on seed to perpetuate themselves, and some actually die after flowering, such as the bee orchis, *Ophrys apifera*; the accommodating *Dactylorhiza elata* is unusual in the readiness with which it increases its fingered tubers. And that being so, you must also be sure not to cut the grass too early where your orchids grow. The early purples may be able to set and shed seed with the other spring flowers that accompany it, but the summer-flowering spotted orchis should be left undisturbed until early autumn to allow it to scatter its dust-fine seed where it will. And if it likes you, it certainly will, far and wide, so that seedlings may appear in odd and unexpected corners of your garden.

Border Plants in Grass

A surprising number of border plants will grow quite happily in grass, though many of the most satisfactory – oriental poppies, *Crambe cordifolia*, the perennial pea, the original blue *Lupinus polyphyllus*, the common red hot poker and others – are better in full sun. That still leaves a fair choice if you have a shady garden and want some bigger, bolder plants. In spring there are all the larger, brighter daffodils, if these are to your taste: some of the older cultivars are offered quite cheaply 'as dug', for naturalizing. Then, too, brightly coloured polyanthus last well in heavier, retentive soils; if the original plants die out, seedlings will usually appear nearby, of polyanthus or primrose form, and all you may need to do is dig out the muddier colours if they offend your eye.

The bigger doronicums, which might seem coarse in the border, follow the early yellow daffodils and are every bit as cheerful. The great leopard's bane, *Doronicum pardalianches*, has roots that are too invasive for polite company, but in grass that hardly matters, and it is an advantage, here, that its yellow daisies on branching stems are not too large. The slighter, shorter *D. austriacum* flowers earlier but has the same spreading, tuberous roots. The best of the leopard's banes is *D. plantagineum* 'Excelsum' ('Harpur Crewe'), with large, yet not coarse, daisies. In summer come the wide, many-rayed, rich yellow daisies of *Telekia speciosa* (*Buphthalmum speciosum*), a massive plant with big, aromatic leaves and flowering stems as much as 1.5m/5ft tall; it is even more ambitious than the doronicums, but likes moisture, though it will not flop as badly as *Senecio tanguticus* (described in Chapter III but also suited to growing in grass) without it. The two inulas described in Chapter III will also cope happily with the competition from turf so long as the soil is moist. There is a limit, though, to one's tolerance of rumbustious yellow daisies; let them grow in one place or the other, the damp garden or the flowery meadow, but hardly in both.

In spring, Spanish bluebells will do just as well in turf as their slighter, more northerly cousins; and *Hyacinthoides hispanica*, which seems to be the name they are currently to be known by, comes in white or soft mauve-pink as well as china-blue. Their colours are soft enough not to quarrel, and the same is true of old-fashioned columbines in blue, pink and plum. Darwin tulips and Dutch irises have a wider, and often brighter range of colours; if you accumulate a surplus you can plant them in grass, where the flowers will diminish in size and look, in consequence, more appropriate than in their grosser, open-border mode.

The old cottage paeony, *Paeonia officinalis*, with its full-petalled flowers of deep crimson, pink or white, will grow for years, it sometimes seems for centuries, in grass if the soil is not impoverished and you give it a headstart by keeping it clear of competition for the first year or two; the crimson, 'Rubra Plena', is especially forgiving. If you prefer single paeonies, try *P. mascula*, with paler magenta-pink flowers. The foliage of all these is dark green and luxuriant, and the plants seem to bear no grudge if they come under the mower in late summer, but you should skirt round them when you make the first summer cut. The tall, freely seeding *Campanula latifolia* follows the paeonies, its clear or rich lilac, white or pale twilight bells forming spires that quickly run to seed and scatter their potential progeny far and wide. The great generous plumes of *C. lactiflora* are at their best in early summer; the typical milky blue-lilac may deepen to violet, or blush to mauve-pink, while there is a white form of great beauty. The bell flowers look at you and heavenwards rather than nodding, as those of *C. latifolia* often do. Even the wickedly invasive *C. rapunculoides*, the rampion, is safe enough in grass, and very lovely with 90cm/36in stems set with starry, blue-purple bells. What a dearth of words there is to describe the colours between blue and purple, especially in the deeper tones!

The powerfully fragrant turk's caps of *Lilium pyrenaicum*, yellow or rusty-red, open early in the lily season over the leafy clumps, very willing to grow in grass beneath the shade of trees. So, too, is *Fritillaria pyrenaica*, of the mahogany, gold-lined bells. Later, it is the turn of the common montbretia, *Crocosmia* × *crocosmiiflora*, which will grow in sun or shade, flowering freely unless in the darkest corners or when the corms have so increased as to crowd themselves into a vegetative state. If that is the problem, it can be simply cured by lifting some of the clumps and splitting them, filling the holes with nourishing compost; they will flower again next season. In subalpine meadows, the great yellow gentian, *Gentiana lutea*, and veratrums both grow, to flower in summer; but both are so fine as border plants that it is a shame to waste them in grass. Should you ever – an unlikely prospect – have more than you need, then by all means try them among your orchard trees. Here, too, you can plant the surplus from your more robust hostas; spare divisions of *Aruncus dioicus*; and, where the soil is damp, the great pink meadow-sweets and *Eupatorium purpureum*. But this is all getting rather far from the Primavera effect that is so enchanting in spring, and that to me is the apotheosis of meadow gardening.

Bibliography

BAILEY, L. H. & E. Z & STAFF OF L. H. BAILEY HORTORIUM, CORNELL UNIVERSITY: *Hortus Third* Macmillan, 1976

BEAN, W. J.: *Trees & Shrubs Hardy in the British Isles* 4 vols, 8th (revised) ed. John Murray, 1976–80

BEAN, W.J.: Supplement to 8th ed. John Murray, 1988

BROWN, GEORGE E: *Shade Plants for Garden and Woodland* Faber & Faber, 1980

CHITTENDEN, F. J. (ed): *The Royal Horticultural Society Dictionary of Gardening* Oxford University Press, 1965

CROWE, SYLVIA: *Garden Design* Thomas Gibson, 1981

CULLEN, J. & CHAMBERLAIN, C. F.: *Revision of Rhododendron. Notes from the Royal Botanic Garden Edinburgh* Vol.39, 1 & 2 1980 and 1982

CURTIS'S *Botanical Magazine* (now *The Kew Magazine*) 1787 et seq.

EVANS, ALFRED: *The Peat Garden and its Plants* Dent, 1974

FARRER, R.: *The English Rock Garden* T. C. & E. C. Jack, 1918

FISH, MARGERY: *Gardening in the Shade* Collingridge, 1964

HAWORTH BOOTH, M.: *Effective Flowering Shrubs* 2nd ed. Collins, 1970

Hillier's Manual of Trees & Shrubs David & Charles, 1977

Ingwersen's Manual of Alpine Plants Ingwersen & Dunnsprint Ltd, 1978

JEKYLL, G.: *Colour Schemes for the Flower Garden* Country Life, 1936
   Wood and Garden Longman Green, 1899

KRÜSSMANN, GERD: *Manual of Cultivated Broad-leaved Trees & Shrubs* 3 vols. Eng. ed. trs. Michael Epp, Batsford, 1984–6
   Manual of Cultivated Conifers Eng. ed. trs. Michael Epp, Batsford, 1985

LEWIS, PETER & LYNCH, MARGARET: *Campanulas* Christopher Helm, 1990

LLOYD, C.: *Clematis* Collins, 1977
   Foliage Plants Collins, 1972
   The Adventurous Gardener Allen Lane, 1983
   The Well Chosen Garden Elm Tree Books, 1984
   The Well Tempered Garden Collins, 1970

MORSE, H. K.: *Gardening in the Shade* Charles Scribner's Sons, 1939

PAGE, R.: *The Education of a Gardener* Collins, 1962

PATERSON, ALLEN: *Plants for Shade* Dent, 1981

PHILIP, C. & LORD, TONY: *The Plant Finder* Headman Ltd for The Hardy Plant Society, 1990

The Plantsman RHS London

RIX, MARTYN & PHILLIPS, ROGER: *The Bulb Book* Pan, 1981

ROBINSON, W.: *The English Flower Garden* 8th ed. John Murray, 1900, and revised Amaryllis Press USA, 1984

THE ROYAL HORTICULTURAL SOCIETY: *The Rhododendron Handbook – Rhododendron Species in Cultivation* RHS, 1980

THE ROYAL HORTICULTURAL SOCIETY's *Journal* (now *The Garden*)

SALLEY, H. E. & GREER, H. E.: *Rhododendron Hybrids: A Guide to their Origins* Batsford, 1986

SCHENK, GEORGE: *The Complete Shade Gardener* Houghton Mifflin, 1984

TAYLOR, J.: *Collecting Garden Plants* Dent, 1988

  Kew Gardening Guides: *Climbing Plants* Collingridge, 1987

  The Milder Garden Dent, 1990

THOMAS, G. S.: *The Art of Planting* Dent, 1984

  Climbing Roses Old & New rev. ed. Dent, 1978

  Perennial Garden Plants 2nd ed. Dent 1982

  Plants for Ground Cover Dent, 1970

  Shrubs Roses of Today Dent, 1962

  The Rock Garden and its Plants Dent, 1989

TREHANE, PIERS: *Index Hortensis* Vol I: Perennials. Quarterjack Publishing, 1989

TRESEDER, NEIL G.: *Magnolias* Faber & Faber, 1978

WALTERS, S. M. (ed) et al: *The European Garden Flora* Vols I & II Cambridge University Press, 1984 & 1986

WRIGHT, TOM: *Large Gardens and Parks* Granada, 1982

YEO, DR P.: *Hardy Geraniums* Croome Helm, 1985

Index